ST JOHN CHRYSOSTOM

The Cult of the Saints

ST VLADIMIR'S SEMINARY PRESS
Popular Patristics Series
Number 31

The Popular Patristics Series published by St Vladimir's Seminary Press provides readable and accurate translations of a wide range of early Christian literature to a wide audience—students of Christian history to lay Christians reading for spiritual benefit. Recognized scholars in their fields provide short but comprehensive and clear introductions to the material. The texts include classics of Christian literature, thematic volumes, collections of homilies, letters on spiritual counsel, and poetical works from a variety of geographical contexts and historical backgrounds. The mission of the series is to mine the riches of the early Church and to make these treasures available to all.

Series Editor
BOGDAN BUCUR

Associate Editor
IGNATIUS GREEN

* * *

Series Editor
1999–2020
JOHN BEHR

ST JOHN CHRYSOSTOM

The Cult
of the Saints

Select homilies and letters introduced,
translated, and annotated by

WENDY MAYER

with BRONWEN NEIL

ST VLADIMIR'S SEMINARY PRESS
CRESTWOOD, NEW YORK
2006

Library of Congress Cataloging-in-Publication Data

John Chrysostom, Saint, d. 407.
  [Homilies. English. Selections]
  The cult of the saints : select homilies and letters / St. John Chrysostom ;
introduced, translated, and annotated by Wendy Mayer with Bronwen Neil.
      p.   cm. — (St. Vladimir's Seminary Press "popular patristics" series)
      Includes bibliographical references.
      ISBN–13: 978–0–88141–302–1 (alk. paper)
      ISBN–10: 0–88141–302–X (alk. paper)
      1. Christian saints—Sermons.   2. Orthodox Eastern Church—Sermons.
    3. Sermons, Greek—Translations into English.   I. Mayer, Wendy, 1960–.
    II. Neil, Bronwen.   III. Title.   IV. Series.

BR65.C43E5 2006
270.1092'2—dc22

2005036299

COPYRIGHT © 2006
ST VLADIMIR'S SEMINARY PRESS
575 Scarsdale Rd, Crestwood, NY 10707
1-800-204-2665
www.svspress.com

ISBN 0–88141–302–X
ISBN 978–0–88141–302–1

Preface

This book grew out of two other translation projects concerning John Chrysostom in which I have been involved in the last four years. Of the two books which have appeared as a result,[1] the first focuses on homilies of John Chrysostom that illustrate his remarkable skill as a preacher and carer of souls; the second focuses more specifically on the martyr homily as a genre, in which four of John's more powerful sermons on the martyrs are offered, alongside homilies by Basil of Caesarea, Gregory of Nyssa, Asterius of Amasea, and Hesychius of Jerusalem. In those two volumes translations of John's homilies on Saints Philogonius, Pelagia, Julian, and Babylas, on all saints, on the day after the feast of the Maccabees, and on the occasion of the translation of relics at Constantinople are published.

The cult of the saints is a phenomenon that expanded rapidly in the fourth century. John's witness to its growth as seen through the eyes of his homilies is an important one. Yet, the majority of John's homilies on the saints and martyrs have been ignored in the English translations of his homilies previously available, most notably in the volumes dedicated to Chrysostom in the *Nicene and Post-Nicene Fathers*. While working with Johan Leemans on his book on the martyr homily, it became clear that, when gathered together, those of John's homilies on saints and martyrs left untranslated after completion of the above two volumes would make up a nicely sized volume on their own. Rounding out the picture are two letters: the first is written by John from exile and concerns the use of martyr relics in a

[1]W. Mayer-P. Allen, *John Chrysostom*, The Early Church Fathers, (London: Routledge 2000); and J. Leemans, W. Mayer, P. Allen and B. Dehandschutter, *"Let Us Die that We May Live": Greek Homilies on Christian Martyrs from Asia Minor, Palestine and Syria (c. 350–c. 450 AD)* (London: Routledge, 2003).

mission context; the second, in Latin, is written by Vigilius, bishop of Tridentum (Trent), who makes the offer of fresh Italian relics to John. Aside from this, Gus George Christo's recent book on John's theology of martyrdom[2] has on its own been crying out for a companion volume of the martyr homilies in translation. Several other circumstances added to my interest in creating this volume. Over the past seven years, I have been slowly investigating the liturgical, topographical, and pastoral aspects of the martyr cult at Antioch and Constantinople in John's time. Producing a volume focused on the cult of the saints provided an opportunity to draw together in the introduction in abbreviated form much of my yet unpublished research in this area. Finally, the cult of the saints is still very much alive in Roman Catholic and Eastern Christian piety. There are still parts of the world where the cult is observed in ways that differ little from those that were established at its very beginning. In this respect, the homilies that John Chrysostom preached on the feast days of his local saints and martyrs remain fresh and alive for us today.

The book was originally planned as another joint venture with Pauline Allen, who then became too busy with her own books on Severus of Antioch and Maximus the Confessor to be able to continue. I am deeply grateful to my colleague, Bronwen Neil, who stepped in at the last minute to translate the letter sent by Vigilius of Tridentum to John. Her expertise with difficult late antique Latin is at present far superior to mine. Thank you, Bronwen. The rest of the translations, and any errors, are my own.

Wendy Mayer
Australian Catholic University, Brisbane
January 2004

[2]G. G. Christo, *Martyrdom According to John Chrysostom: "To Live is Christ, To Die is Gain"* (Lewiston: Mellen University Press, 1997).

Table of Contents

Abbreviations

AnBoll	Analecta Bollandiana
BHG	*Bibliotheca hagiographica Graece*, Subsidia hagiographica, 8a, F. Halkin, 3rd ed. (Société des Bollandistes: Brussels, 1957)
CPG	*Clavis patrum graecorum*, ed. M. Geerard, 5 vols (Turnhout: Brepols, 1974–1987)
CTh	*Codex Theodosianus*
HE	*Historia ecclesiastica*
HR	*Historia religiosa*
Leemans et al.	J. Leemans, W. Mayer, P. Allen, and B. Dehandschutter, *"Let Us Die that We May Live": Greek Homilies on Christian Martyrs from Asia Minor, Palestine and Syria (c. 350–c. 450 AD)* (London: Routledge, 2003)
Mayer-Allen	W. Mayer and P. Allen, "John Chrysostom," *The Early Church Fathers* (London: Routledge 2000)
OrChrAn	Orientalia christiana analecta
OCP	*Orientalia christiana periodica*
PG	Patrologia cursus completus: Series graeca, ed. J.-P. Migne (Paris, 1857–1886)
PGL	*Patristic Greek Lexicon*, ed. G.W.H. Lampe (Oxford University Press: Oxford, 1961)
PL	Patrologia cursus completus: Series latina, ed. J.-P. Migne (Paris, 1844–1864)
PO	Patrologia orientalis, ed. F. Graffin (Paris, 1903–)
Wright	W. Wright, "An Ancient Syrian martyrology," *Journal of Sacred Literature* 8 (1866): 45–55, 423–33.

Introduction

The rise of the cult of the saints

Numerous books and articles have been written about the origins and rise of the cult of the saints in the Mediterranean world,[1] a phenomenon that came to prominence in the fourth century CE. Prior to this, important elements of the cult can be traced through the first three centuries. For instance, some of the followers of Jesus died violent deaths for their faith and were accorded a special status in the memory of other followers,[2] and the practices of seeking burial next to a martyr (*depositio ad sanctos*) and of celebrating a Eucharistic meal at the grave of a martyr on their anniversary can be documented from at least the third century.[3] It is in the fourth, after the

[1] H. Delehaye, *Les origines du culte des martyrs*, Subsidia Hagiographica 20 (Bruxelles: Société des Bollandistes, 1933[2]), and W. H. C. Frend, *Martyrdom and Persecution in the Early Church: A Study of a Conflict from the Maccabees to Donatus* (Garden City, NY: Doubleday, 1967), remain classics, although much of their discussion about the cult's development has been superseded. Influential among recent writings on the topic are P. Brown, *The Cult of the Saints. Its Rise and Function in Latin Christianity* (Chicago: University of Chicago Press, 1981); P. Maraval, *Lieux saints et pèlerinages d'orient. Histoire et géographie des origines à la conquête arabe* (Paris: Les éditions du CERF, 1985); G. Bowersock, *Martyrdom and Rome* (Cambridge: Cambridge University Press, 1995); D. Boyarin, *Dying for God: Martyrdom and the Making of Christianity and Judaism* (Stanford: Stanford University Press, 1999); and U. Volp, *Tod und Ritual in den christlichen Gemeinden der Antike*, Supplements to *Vigiliae christianae* 65 (Leiden: Brill, 2002). Their notes and bibliographies provide easy reference to much of the other literature written in this field. See also the introduction to J. Leemans et al., *"Let Us Die that We May Live"* (London, 2003), where a useful overview of the development of the cult, its location, and the liturgical and devotional practices associated with it is provided.

[2] Acts 7 records the death of Stephen, who is styled as the first Christian martyr.

[3] For a third-century example both of *depositio ad sanctos* and a Eucharistic graveside meal see *Life of Polycarp* 20, 24–9 (ed. Stewart-Sykes 2002). On the recent re-dating of the *Life* which Stewart-Sykes assigns to the second half of the third century, see

flood of fresh martyrs slows to a trickle, however, that the first burials of martyr remains inside urban boundaries are recorded and it is
in this period that we observe the cult of the saints developing into
a mature and distinct phenomenon. By the fifth and sixth centuries
it had become well established throughout the Mediterranean, with
the broad rippling of the cult of local saints outward to other cen-
ters, and rapid growth in Christian hagio-tourism or pilgrimage. By
this stage, a rich and varied literature had grown up around the individual saints and the notion that their relics channeled supernatural
powers had become firmly established. The periods during which
John Chrysostom lived at Antioch in Syria (c. 349–397 CE), in Constantinople (late 397–404), and in exile in Armenia (mid 404–407)
span a crucial phase in these developments.

    The story of the rise of the cult of the saints and its development
into an identifiably Christian phenomenon is one of the adoption
and transformation of a number of related concepts and practices
that already existed in the ancient Mediterranean world. That is, few
of the elements of the cult are unique to Christianity. Many, in fact,
were already present in the society out of which Christianity grew
and were familiar to people of all religious backgrounds. Chief
among those which were already prevalent are the concept of martyrdom; the practice of traveling to sites associated with divine power
for the purpose of celebrating festivals, consulting oracles or receiving healing at such sites; the role accorded the dead within a world
fully engaged with the supernatural; and the beliefs and practices
associated with death. In their beginnings, all of the constituent
elements of the cult looked and felt little different from the same
features in their non-Christian settings. For instance, the idea that

A. Stewart-Sykes, *The Life of Polycarp. An Anonymous* vita *from third-century Smyrna*,
Early Christian Studies 4 (Strathfield: St Pauls Publications, 2002), 4–22. On the early
history of Eucharistic, funeral and *agape* meals at the grave of a saint see ibid., 74–84.
Stewart-Sykes, 150 n. 61, also argues that the location of Thraseas' remains in the cemetery at Smyrna at the time of Boukolos' burial must mean that they had been translated there at an earlier date from their natural burial site. If so, this is an early case of
the relocation and reburial of a saint's remains (a phenomenon known as translation).

martyrdom was not just a preference for violent death over compliance with an official decree, but had attached to it recognition of the individual after their death and a notion that the individual would receive some reward, could already be found in Jewish literature in the account of the death of the Maccabees.[4] Annual visits to the tomb of a dead family member on the anniversary of their birth, and festive meals at the tomb on prescribed days were a regular part of the rituals associated with mourning in both Greek and Roman culture.[5] Group and individual travel to a particular temple or healing shrine for the celebration of a festival or to consult an oracle or seek healing (perhaps by incubation)[6] was, if not widespread, at least a recognized feature of ancient Greek society.[7] Addressing the souls of the dead with prayers and supplications in the name of a particular god or gods is a facet of some pre-Christian Greek and Roman funerary inscriptions and papyri.[8] The addition of saints' feast days to the local calendar, too, was neither new nor strange in a world where the civic calendar had long been dominated by Greco-Roman religious festivals. Even the recorded lives of the saints, which became such an important feature of their commemoration and were material in the geographic spread of the reputation of a particular saint, find their origins in the Greco-Roman biographies of philosophers,[9] while the vivid descriptions of the martyr's sufferings in homilies and in saints' lives descend directly from the detailed descriptions of torture found in secular Greek and Roman rhetoric.[10]

[4]Boyarin, *Dying for God*, 94–5, argues that it is "perhaps the oldest, most clearly pre-Christian element of martyrology."

[5]Volp, *Tod und Ritual*, 60–61 and 77–80.

[6]The practice of sleeping overnight in a healing shrine. This was usually accompanied by a dream vision of the god (e.g., Asclepius) as a consequence of which the petitioner woke up healed. In response, votive offerings in the shape of the healed body part were left at the shrine.

[7]See M. Dillon, *Pilgrims and Pilgrimage in Ancient Greece* (London: Routledge, 1997).

[8]Delehaye, *Les origines*, 100–102.

[9]Stewart-Sykes, *Life of Polycarp*, 26–36, provides a useful discussion.

[10]See H. Maguire, *Art and Eloquence in Byzantium* (Princeton, NJ: Princeton University Press, 1994), 34–5.

Whereas many of the constituent elements of the cult already existed in the pre-Christian Mediterranean world, what brought them together and led the cult of the saints to develop in the way that it did were a number of fundamental conceptual shifts that took place within the second to fourth centuries. The cult's original point of focus was the Christian martyrs—those followers of the Jesus-movement who died in confession of their faith either at the hands of other Jews or at the hands of the Roman administration. While on the one hand martyrdom itself was not new, on the other it was transformed into something novel due to a shift in the discourse of martyrdom among rabbinic Jews, other Jews, and Christians. This shift, then, was not exclusively Christian. As Daniel Boyarin describes it: ". . . in the past, martyrs refused to violate a negative commandment—to worship idols. Now, we find martyrs fulfilling through their deaths a positive one—to love God."[11] In Christian texts this aspect is central to the experience of imitating Christ, in rabbinic texts it is a fulfillment of the command to "love the Lord with all one's soul."[12] In the process, within the martyr literature death as a love-act became powerfully eroticized and mysticized and was accompanied, on the part of the victim, by a conscious "sense of the ecstatic privilege that [the martyr's] death conferred."[13] Another distinctive feature in this conceptual shift was the location at the center of the action in the martyr story of a "ritualized and performative speech act associated with a statement of pure essence"—in Christian texts, a declaration of the essence of self ("I am a Christian"); in rabbinic texts, the declaration of the oneness of God ("Hear O Israel").[14] All of these conceptual elements, we see realized to varying degrees in the martyr homilies preached by John Chrysostom.

[11]Boyarin, *Dying for God*, 114. It is precisely in "dying for God" as a human being that the notion of intimacy with God on the part of the saint developed, leading to the notion that the Christian martyr was able to intercede for and protect fellow human beings. See Brown, *Cult of the Saints*, 6.

[12]Boyarin, *Dying for God*, 95.

[13]Boyarin, *Dying for God*, 120 and 122.

[14]Boyarin, *Dying for God*, 95.

A second shift, this time one distinctive of the Christian conceptual world and only fully emergent in the second half of the fourth century, was equally fundamental. In this instance, Volp's recent study of death and ritual in late antiquity is instructive. Under both Greco-Roman and Jewish law, death was associated with ritual impurity. Corpses, in particular, were thought to pollute their surroundings.[15] Under Roman law, for instance, the burial of a human body inside the boundaries of a city was forbidden,[16] and as late as the emperor Julian (362), it was thought that the presence of the bodies of Babylas and other martyrs in the vicinity of the temple of Apollo in Daphne (the pleasure suburb of Antioch) was the cause of that oracle's recent loss of powers.[17] In the world within which Christianity emerged, notions of impurity and purity in relation to corpses, graves, worship, and sacred space were all interconnected. Partly because of the extensive Jewish rules regarding (im)purity, Christians from the beginning began to develop a discourse counter to them. A shift in the understanding of the different levels of impurity developed, in which, while the language of (im)purity was not abandoned, its importance was diminished by "employing concepts inherited from the Graeco-Roman literary traditions (such as stressing the . . . [virtue] of the deceased . . .)."[18] In association a "distinct

[15]See, however, *CTh* 9.17, which preserves a series of laws dating from the 340s to the 380s proscribing the robbing of tombs for their building materials, indicating that by the mid fourth century people appear to have had few reservations about the monuments built to house the dead.

[16]*CTh* 9.17.6, promulgated by the emperors of both East and West on July 30, 381, reiterates that bodies should lie outside the city. See also John Chrysostom, *In Matth. hom.* 73/74 (PG 58.676 ll.18–21) where he states that no tomb is prepared in a city and that doing this "is forbidden here," confirming that this law was adhered to in his own day.

[17]The bodies had been located there not long before by the Caesar Gallus. On the notion that the proximity of "Christian" worship sites to human bodies made them impure, and regarding Julian's responses see Volp, *Tod und Ritual*, 255–6. Volp (p.253) also points out that it was not only non-Christians who believed this. In the early fifth century there were still numerous Christians who thought that the presence of corpses within the worship space endangered the sacraments and made the altar impure.

[18]Volp, *Tod und Ritual*, 262 and 270.

theology of relics and the resurrection" arose, which held that relics neither made a place impure nor had a neutral impact, but in fact purified the place where they resided, a reversal of traditional beliefs which paved the way for the placement of relics initially inside places of worship and ultimately within churches located inside city precincts.[19] These developments were accompanied from the beginning by debate among Church leaders about the validity for gentile Christians (and later for Christians as a whole) of the Jewish purity laws and the laws regarding death and burial. Side by side with this conceptual shift, the appropriation and application of the discourse of exorcism to the bones of martyrs enabled the promotion of the relics' capacity to expel impure daemons[20] as a guarantee of the purification of the place where they resided, as well as of their own ritual purity.[21]

A third, associated shift, which underwrote the rise of the cult of the saints, was one in which the rituals surrounding death, which had essentially been a private, family observance, became public.[22] Among Christians the notion of family expanded to embrace all Christians (the full body of Christ) so that it was not just the martyr's blood family, but also their spiritual family who came annually to their tomb to celebrate their "birthday." At the same time, within

[19]Volp, *Tod und Ritual*, 260–2. See also L.V. Rutgers, "The importance of Scripture in the conflict between Jews and Christians: The example of Antioch," in L.V. Rutgers et al. (eds.), *The Use of Sacred Books in the Ancient World* (Leuven: Peeters, 1998), 287–303, at 301, who localizes this argument to the situation at Antioch in regard to the Christian cult of the Maccabees.

[20]The term "demon" is part of a Christianizing discourse, which places a negative value on such supernatural entities. Within Greco-Roman and Jewish culture at this period there was no consistent codification of daemons in terms of moral value. The current practice of using the term *daemon* (a transliteration of the Greek) is intended to reflect this ambiguous status. See D. Kalleres, *Exorcising the Devil to Silence Christ's Enemies: Ritualized Speech Practices in Late Antique Christianity* (Ph.D. dissertation, Brown University, Providence, RI 2002), 2 n. 5.

[21]For these ideas see Volp, *Tod und Ritual*, 249, 259, 262–3, and 269–70.

[22]Volp, *Tod und Ritual*, 242–7. See, however, Brown, *Cult of the Saints*, 32–4, who talks at the same time of a "privatization," an appropriation of a dead martyr by prominent local families.

the Christian conceptual world the birthday commemoration became a death-day celebration, as the idea of death as not an end but a birth into eternal life developed. Such transformations of long-held norms within the Greco-Roman and Jewish worlds are a fundamental part of the discourse that developed side by side with the physical cult of the saints. By the late fourth century, unlike other burials the martyr's relics were not a grim reminder of death (a *memento mori*) but rather a triumphal expression of death's suppression. Whereas the fetid smell of death hung around ordinary bones, those of the martyr exhaled the sweet smell of sanctity.[23] At the translation of relics the social order became inverted, with the emperor and/or empress stripped of all outward show and, along with the rest of the city, humbly obedient to the martyr, indicating the subservience of earthly power to the divine power present in the ash and bones.[24]

One further conceptual shift of significance, this time one as much brought about by the emergent cult of the saints, as significant to its development, concerns the idea of "holy places." As Robert Markus observes: "In its first centuries Christianity was a religion highly inhospitable to the idea of 'holy places'; by the end of the fourth century it had become highly receptive."[25] In this instance, the resistance of the Christians to a theology that embraced this idea initially made them distinctive from the Jewish and Greco-Roman thought-worlds within which they functioned. Their eventual enthusiasm for the idea saw them meld once again with those conceptual worlds in a way which again brought about a transformation. This

[23]Brown, *Cult of the Saints*, 75–6. Regarding the conceptual shift that occurred in the fourth century in relation to the religious role of sense perception see S. Ashbrook Harvey, "On Holy Stench. When the Odor of Sanctity Sickens," *Studia Patristica* 35 (2001): 90–101.

[24]See Brown, *Cult of the Saints*, 98–100, who also talks of the unifying and reintegrating effect upon the city of the absorption of the *adventus* ceremony (observed at the arrival of the emperor in a city) and all its associations into the cult of the saints.

[25]R. Markus, "How on Earth could Places become Holy? Origins of the Christian Idea of Holy Places," *Journal of Early Christian Studies* 2 (1994): 259.

development, too, helps to show how the conceptual shifts associated
with the rising cult of the saints could be greeted even in the late
fourth century with mixed feelings. The shift was less a change in
Christian views about places (which were ambivalent and remained
more hostile for a longer period of time), than in their attitude to history, which came about as a result of "new feelings associated with . . .
holy places, notably, the burials of martyrs."[26] As Markus observes,
the newly advantageous conditions under which Christianity oper-
ated in the mid-fourth century, after Constantine's official endorse-
ment of it as a religion, required a major adjustment of its adherents.
"They needed to be able to see themselves as the true descendants of
the persecuted Church and the rightful heirs of the martyrs."[27] In the
cult of the martyrs, particularly in the rituals that came to be associated with it, they found a way to bridge the gap between present and
past, and in reclaiming the past, the gulf that had loomed between the
two was abolished. As a natural consequence of this privileging of
historical time, place also took on a great sense of importance. Since
it originated within a specific Christian community or family, the cult
of a martyr was in essence always a local, private celebration. That celebration commemorated a particular person in a particular local
event, a martyr who died in that place, and at whose tomb past and
present were conflated. As the cult expanded to include the veneration of relics and as it became integrated into the regular worship life
of urban communities, this new sanctification of places became
enhanced and extended. The relics, like the tomb, linked the commemoration of the martyr to a local holy place, and as relic and tomb
became dissociated, the way was paved for shifting the commemoration away from the annual walk to the martyr's tomb into the urban
churches and the regular cycle of their liturgy.[28] It was this conceptual
shift in particular that informed the rapid expansion of the network

[26]Markus, "How on Earth," 262.

[27]Markus, "How on Earth," 268. See also Markus, *The End of Ancient Christianity* (Cambridge: Cambridge University Press, 1990), 90–95.

[28]Markus, "How on Earth," 268–70.

of holy places and sites of pilgrimage that occurred in the second half of the fourth century.

The homilies and correspondence of John Chrysostom offer a unique window onto a dynamic and vital period in the development of the cult of the saints. Through them, we can observe in action many of the conceptual shifts that took place and the way of talking about martyrdom that accompanied them. At the same time a diverse array of the ritual elements of the cult—for example, the annual commemoration, processions to the tomb, the translation of relics, private devotion, invocation of the saints, and meals at the tomb—and associated practices—such as the dividing up and acquisition of relics, *depositio ad sanctos,* and the exorcistic and healing powers of relics—offer themselves for our perusal. Rich as this picture is, it is further enhanced by the different circumstances of the two cities within which John preached his sermons. One, Antioch, displays for us a cult that had developed naturally over a long period of time and in which the historic link between past and present was concrete and immediate. It is a city that provides the earliest record of some of the fourth-century cultic developments and in which the tombs of martyrs are still confined to the exterior of the city limits. The other, Constantinople, takes us into a cult that has a shallow past and few historic links between past and present. It is a city in which relics have been deliberately imported into the urban churches and in which the peculiar topography and its imperial status have led to the appropriation of imperial ritual. The cult in each place has a quite distinct flavor. At the same time, both manifestations of it display a variety of common elements. The capacity to observe the similarities and differences not just between two major cities in the East, but over a neat two-decade time span (386–406 CE) contributes further to the value of this small body of literature.

The cult of the saints at Antioch and at Constantinople[29]

A variety of factors created a climate in which the cult of the saints developed deep roots in Antioch and the surrounding countryside. The city had been evangelized by Jesus' apostles at an early date, with Paul and Peter, among others, spending considerable periods of time there. In association, at an early stage in Christianity the city became a base for missionary activities to Asia Minor.[30] As a result of the age, stability, and size of the Christian community embedded in that city, it was only natural in the centuries that followed that, at times when the followers of Jesus were persecuted by the Roman administration, citizens of Antioch were often among the martyrs. Ignatius, one of the first bishops of the city, died at Rome in the first decades of the second century under the emperor Trajan. His remains were later brought back from Rome to Antioch. In the mid-third century, another Antiochene bishop, Babylas, was martyred during the Decian persecutions. In the opening years of the fourth century, as a result of persecutions carried out under Diocletian, Antioch became associated with a number of martyrs. Romanus, a member of the clergy of Caesarea died for his faith while temporarily resident in the city. The remains of a mother, Domnina, and her two daughters, who fled Antioch for Edessa at that time, were brought back and interred locally. It is possible that the young female martyr, Pelagia, also fell to her death in Antioch during this period. Lucian, who numbered among the clergy of Antioch, was killed not long afterwards under Maximinus Daia. Even as late as the emperor Julian (in the early 360s), two soldiers who served under him, Juventinus and Maximinus, were imprisoned and died at Antioch because of their resistance to Julian's revival and promotion of Greco-Roman religions. Because of their close association with the city, and in many instances their actual death there, in the majority of these cases the remains were

[29]For an introduction to worship at Antioch and Constantinople in John's time in general, including some comment about the cult of the saints, see Mayer-Allen, *John Chrysostom*, Intro. § 2.

[30]Acts 11.19–30, 13.1–3, 14.26–8, 18.18–23; Gal 2.11–14.

buried in the local cemetery which lay within easy walking distance outside the gate to the south-west, beside the road leading to Daphne. This natural development ensured that the confessors remained alive in local memory, as well as providing a convenient locus for any cult that might develop. In addition to these indigenous Christian martyrs, it is probable that the bones of the mother of the Maccabees, if not also her seven sons, were located near the city in the suburb of Daphne.[31] The development of a shrine over the "grave" and of a cult associated with healing was already of some antiquity among the Antiochene Jews, and by the fourth century, regardless of their religious affiliation, when they sought healing, many of the local inhabitants were in the habit of sleeping at the shrine which contained the relics (the Cave of Matrona).[32] Thus by the time of John Chrysostom at Antioch a number of the ingredients essential to the natural development of a cult around any or all of these "saints" had been in place for some time.

At Constantinople the situation was quite otherwise. Dedicated under its new name as the site of the Eastern imperial capital only in 324, prior to that time it had spent its life as Byzantium, an unimportant town on the coast of Thrace with what seems to have been only a small Christian presence. For much of the middle decades of the fourth century the Eastern emperors based their courts in the city only occasionally, preferring to shift around in response to military needs and other factors. It was only in the late 370s that the city became the permanent seat of the emperor. The emperors worked

[31]M. Vinson, "Gregory Nazianzen's Homily 15 and the Genesis of the Christian Cult of the Maccabean Martyrs," *Byzantion* 64 (1994): 183–4.

[32]The place of the Cave of Matrona and the nature of its link to the Maccabees in Jewish thought at Antioch are difficult to assess. Rutger's dismissal of Vinson's argument regarding the shrine, however, remains unconvincing and ignores the subtlety of her argument, although both Vinson and Rutger make a valid point when claiming that Jewish thought on the question of bodies and impurity made it impossible that relics of the Maccabees could have been buried anywhere near either of their synagogues (that is, the synagogue in Daphne and the one in Antioch itself in the district called Kerateion). See L.V. Rutgers, "The importance of Scripture in the conflict between Jews and Christians: The example of Antioch" (n. 19).

hard, however, to make up for the city's humble beginnings. The city was substantially rebuilt by Constantine and his successors in programs that included the construction of new public spaces and churches,[33] and the importation and translation into those churches of foreign relics. Only a few local martyrs can be identified. A former Nicene bishop of the city, Paul, who had been deposed c. 350 by the emperor Constantius in favor of installing a semi-Arian bishop, and who had been sent into exile in Armenia and strangled to death (presumably on order) by his guards, is honored as a saint in the time of Theodosius I and his remains recovered in 381 and interred in a church inside the city walls. By the time that John arrived, in late 397, it was known locally as "St Paul's." On the other hand, the Church of St Acacius, which is mentioned in the title to several of the homilies preached by John at Constantinople,[34] and which was situated outside the city walls, is unlikely to have contained the remains of the Nicomedian military martyr Acacius, as once thought. It now appears more likely that the name of the church refers instead to a rich local senator who paid for its construction.[35] The saint Mokios to whom a church that *is* situated in an old cemetery beyond the walls is dedicated, however, represents one of the few other cases where a church at Constantinople indicates by its name the burial of a local saint. Mokios was thought to have been martyred in the old city under Diocletian. The fact that one of the Tall Brothers (monks from Egypt who spent some two years at Constantinople seeking redress against their bishop) upon his death in 402 was buried there[36] rather than in a cemetery, suggests that the status of the church as the focus of a local cult was by that time well established.

[33]See G. Dagron, *Naissance d'une capitale. Constantinople et ses institutions de 330 à 45*, Bibliothèque Byzantine, 7 (Paris: Presses Universitaires de France, 1974), 29–47, 388–409; and R. Krautheimer, *Three Christian Capitals. Topography and Politics* (Berkeley: University of California Press, 1983), 42–6.

[34]*Novae homiliae* 14–15 (*CPG* 4441.14–15), both unedited.

[35]The *comes* Acacius, Constantine's most senior Christian official. See D. Woods, "The Church of 'St.' Acacius at Constantinople," *Vigiliae Christianae* 55 (2001): 201–7.

[36]Sozomen, *HE* 8.17.

More common by far at Constantinople was the importation of foreign relics to make up for this deficiency. Significantly, from the very beginning of this practice the long-standing taboo on locating human remains within the city precinct was set aside, superseded by the notion that the relics' derived purity and divine power made their location within the major churches of the city desirable. Thus, in 336 Constantine procured the relics of the apostles Andrew and Luke and had them placed in a purpose-built building inside the city walls, which was also intended as his mausoleum. When Constantius brought the remains of Timothy to the city in 356, they were deposited in a new cruciform church attached to the mausoleum, and the relics of Andrew and Luke were transferred there also.[37] The emperor Theodosius sponsored the retrieval of a head of John the Baptist, which was brought to Hebdomon, just outside the city walls, and deposited in a church there. During the time that he was bishop of Constantinople, John himself presided over at least two separate translations of new relics,[38] and was offered yet others by the bishop of Tridentum in Italy.[39] It was not only the emperor and the bishop who arranged the importation of martyr remains. In the 390s, the praetorian prefect Rufinus brought to Constantinople relics of Sts Peter and Paul, which he deposited in a chapel on his estate across the Bosphorus near Chalcedon. According to the *Life* of the monk Isaac, another high-ranking official, Aurelian, paid for the construction of a martyrium to St Stephen in the early 400s, with the intention of procuring the appropriate relics for it (*Vita s. Isaacii* 4.18).

[37]For new discussion on the date of these translations see R. Burgess, "The *Passio s. Artemii*, Philostorgius, and the Dates of the Invention and Translations of the Relics of Sts Andrew and Luke," AnBoll 121 (2003): 5–36.

[38]See *On St Phocas*, and *Hom. delivered after the remains of martyrs etc* (Mayer-Allen, *John Chrysostom*, 85–92).

[39]See *Letter of Vigilius to John* below. There is some argument that the martyrs offered by Vigilius and those translated on the occasion of *After the remains of martyrs* are one and the same (see J. Vanderspoel, "Claudian, Christ and the Cult of the Saints," *Classical Quarterly* 36 [1986]: 244–255), but there is no evidence beyond the circumstantial to support this conclusion.

The topography of each city further contributed to distinctive developments in the cult at each location. Antioch lay on a plain some miles inland from the eastern Mediterranean coast, bounded by mountains on one side and the river Orontes on the other; Constantinople was a coastal city, surrounded by water on three sides. The city life of Antioch was intimately connected with that of its elevated suburb, Daphne; the city of Constantinople proper formed a conurbation with the city of Chalcedon, on the opposite shore of the Bosphorus, and the suburbs of Galata and Sykae to the north of the waters of the Golden Horn. Because of its history, at Antioch chapels naturally sprang up over the tombs of martyrs in the cemetery beyond the city walls and in the surrounding countryside. At this early period, the only exception known to us is the Church of St Babylas, which was built across the Orontes from the city by Bishop Meletius in the late 370s to house the translated remains of that saint.[40] At Constantinople, remains were frequently brought to the city across the waters of the Bosphorus and were conveyed in procession to the Great Church before being laid to rest in locations both inside and outside the city. As a result, the waters that surrounded Constantinople often played an important role in the ceremonial,[41] as we see in the homily *On St Phocas*. Moreover, whereas at Antioch in the main the martyria appear to have been reserved for liturgical celebrations on the saints' anniversaries and to have been visited privately for devotion in the interim, at Constantinople churches which contained saints' remains and which were inside the city walls appear to have been in regular use. In John's time the Church of St Paul, for instance, was home to a congregation of Nicene Christian Goths, who worshipped in it in their own language. The Church of the Holy Apostles, too, which was adjacent to the imperial mausoleum and contained the relics of Andrew,

---

[40]For a brief outline of Babylas' triple translation at Antioch see Leemans et al., "*Let Us Die that We May Live*," 140–8.

[41]See W. Mayer, "The Sea Made Holy. The Liturgical Function of the Waters surrounding Constantinople," *Ephemerides Liturgicae* 112 (1998): 459–468.

Timothy, and Luke, was used on more than just special occasions.[42] At Antioch we find only a trace of this practice in regard to the Church of St Babylas, at which the festival homily *On Sts Juventinus and Maximinus* was also delivered and at which John says, on the occasion of the festival of Babylas,[43] that he was wanting to continue the theme he had preached on in that church recently but was obliged to preach on Babylas instead.

At the same time, many of the elements of the cult followed the same basic pattern in both cities. The feast day was usually observed by holding a worship service in the martyrium that contained the tomb of the martyr. In order to reach the martyrium in the first instance, the participants gathered at a predesignated point in the city and moved solemnly in procession through the streets to the martyrium. There is some evidence that, at Antioch at least, the relics of the martyr were carried through the streets to the martyrium at the head of the procession (*On St Drosis* § 4).[44] Also in the lead were the bishop (or his delegate) and, at times, the most senior representative of secular authority available (in general, the provincial governor or emperor). Such processions were usually on foot and were often accompanied by the singing of the appropriate verses of a psalm. The crowds that attended these festivals tended to be drawn from all strata of society and there was a noticeable increase in attendance on such occasions. The homilies *On St Meletius, On St Phocas,* and *Delivered after the remains of martyrs etc* provide a clear illustration of these aspects. At the martyrium itself, the service included at least one, sometimes several homilies,[45] in which the death and acts of the martyr were usually detailed. In John's own

[42]See W. Mayer, "Cathedral Church or Cathedral Churches? The Situation at Constantinople (c.360–404 AD)," *OCP* 66 (2000): 49–68.

[43]See *On St Babylas* § 1 (Leemans et al., *"Let Us Die that We May Live,"* 142–3).

[44]At Constantinople the same phenomenon can be seen when the procession accompanies translated remains. See, e.g., *Hom. delivered after the remains of martyrs etc* (Mayer-Allen, *John Chrysostom,* 85–92).

[45]See *On St Babylas* and *Concerning blessed Philogonius* (Mayer-Allen, *John Chrysostom,* 184–95).

hands, however, the martyr's story was rarely an end in itself, but rather an opportunity for moral instruction.[46] In addition to the procession and homily, scripture readings, a nightlong vigil, and celebration of the Eucharist could all be incorporated,[47] and, on occasion, it seems that the celebration extended to two days (*On the Maccabees hom. 2*, *On Julian*). On the days of the year other than that of the martyr's commemoration, private devotion was an important feature of the cult. Christians were urged to walk to the martyrium, to visit the tomb, to weep over the coffin, to anoint themselves with oil that had touched the holy remains, and to pray, using the martyr as their advocate.[48] Such prayers included those of a wife for the safe return of her husband, and those of the emperor for success in battle and of thanks for the martyr's help on his triumphant return (*On all the martyrs* § 9). People from a range of social strata, it seems, would come privately to the martyrs' tombs.

Other less immediate, and sometimes less spiritually beneficial, practices were by this time associated with martyr festivals. Where there was such a large gathering of people, particularly when people from the surrounding countryside flooded into the city on such occasions,[49] there were also commercial opportunities. As a result, the feast days of martyrs gradually became associated with markets, to which producers from the surrounding countryside would bring their wares, as we see suggested in the homily *Concerning blessed Philogonius.*[50] In a world where travel was difficult for those situated in outlying areas, convenience dictated too that, at Antioch at least, the bishop take the opportunity martyr festivals afforded for local

[46]See *A homily on martyrs* (Mayer-Allen, *John Chrysostom*, 93–7), where John quickly moves onto advice to the audience not to divert into taverns and get drunk on the way home from the festival; and *On St Phocas*, where he spends much of the homily addressing theological misconceptions.

[47]See *A homily on martyrs* (Mayer-Allen, *John Chrysostom*, 95–6).

[48]See, e.g., *On St Ignatius* § 18, *On Sts Bernike, Prosdoke and Domnina* § 24, and *A homily on martyrs* (Mayer-Allen, *John Chrysostom*, 96).

[49]See *On the holy martyrs* § 1 (Leemans et al., "*Let Us Die that We May Live,*" 115–26).

[50]Mayer-Allen, *John Chrysostom*, 184–95.

synods with his rural clergy.[51] We also see John complain about the habit of those in attendance of celebrating the vigils and processing to the martyrium in an orderly fashion, but disappearing into pubs, where they drank heavily and played dice, on the way home.[52] Festivals, too, could clash on the calendar with other long-standing celebrations with their roots in less restrained Greco-Roman religions. Thus towards the end of *On Julian* we see John work hard to persuade his audience that they should come back for the second day of the celebrations, rather than join everyone else in Daphne for a raucous festival associated with banqueting. If they must enjoy the hospitality of a meal outdoors together, he argues, they can stay behind after the gathering at the martyr's tomb and have a picnic under the shady vines, with the martyr watching over their behavior.[53]

Of the practices and conceptual shifts that grew up around the cult of the saints in general, we see evidence of a wide variety at both locations. At not just Constantinople, but also Antioch, we observe the translation of a saint's remains in the case of both Babylas and Meletius. Meletius, who had been bishop of Antioch in John's youth and who had died at Constantinople while presiding over the ecumenical council of 381, was initially buried in Constantinople in the Church of the Holy Apostles and his remains subsequently brought back to Antioch by land, where he was buried next to Babylas in a purpose-built double sarcophagus. This event offers an example of not just the procession of remains during (in this case a very extended) translation,[54] but also demonstrates the desire to have

[51]See Frans van de Paverd, *St. John Chrysostom, The Homilies on the Statues: An Introduction* (OrChrAn 239: Rome, 1991), 290–1, who argues that *Cat.* 8 and *On the statues hom.* 19 were delivered shortly after a martyr festival that brought Syriac-speaking clergy to the city.

[52]See n. 46 and *On Pelagia* § 3 (Leemans et al., *"Let Us Die that We May Live,"* 148–57).

[53]*On Julian* § 4 (Leemans et al., *"Let Us Die that We May Live,"* 126–40).

[54]Sozomen, *HE* 7.10, records that on their way from Constantinople to Antioch, by the emperor's command Meletius' relics were received within the walls of each city along the way with the antiphonal singing of psalms.

one's body buried next to a saint (*depositio ad sanctos*). This is significant when we consider that Meletius himself almost immediately attained the same status and rapidly developed his own cult following (see *On St Meletius*). A similar example occurs at Constantinople, where the monk Isaac is buried in the church built by his patron, the Martyrium of St Stephen, on the opposite side of the altar from the holy martyr.[55] Isaac himself takes on the status of a saint shortly after. In the case of both Babylas (at Antioch) and Phocas (at Constantinople) we see examples of the way in which the imperial *adventus* ceremony was being appropriated for the reception of translated holy relics.[56] When Babylas' remains were removed from the martyrium at Daphne and brought back to the city, the people flooded out to meet them.[57] In the same way, the relics of Phocas are honored by an official delegation, this time headed by the emperor and empress (*On St Phocas* § 1–3). We also find clear evidence in homilies from both cities of the belief that the relics of the saints have the power to cast out demons (*On all the martyrs* § 10, *On St Drosis* § 6, *On St Barlaam* § 10). In both cities, too, we find the relics of saints buried within places where worship occurs more regularly than at martyr shrines, indicating an advanced acceptance of the idea that the saint's body is pure rather than impure, even if at Antioch the conceptual shift is incomplete and such churches are not yet located inside the city walls. Finally, in the *Letter of John to Rufinus* we catch a hint of the status of relics in the early fifth century in Armenia and in a mission territory of Antioch. Their capacity to repel demons and to protect the territory where they are located, as

[55] *Vita s. Isaacii* 4.18.

[56] The convergence of the nuances between the religious aspects of the ceremony and the theology of martyrdom provided fertile ground. The *adventus* already had religious overtones, with the emperor seen in some sense as an all-victorious god as well as a savior, benefactor, and lord (see S. MacCormick, "Change and Continuity in Late Antiquity: The ceremony of *adventus*," *Historia* 21 [1972]: 721–2). The triumphal martyr, who stood at the throne of God and had direct access to his ear, came to be seen as an equally powerful benefactor of the city.

[57] See *On St Babylas* (Leemans et al., "*Let Us Die that We May Live*," 147).

well as their provision of an attractive and not unfamiliar alternative cult for non-Christians, may well be some of the underlying reasons for their deployment in that context.

The saint and martyr in John's thought

When we examine how John frames the stories of the martyrs in his homilies, the shape that he gives them conforms to several of the conceptual shifts discussed by Daniel Boyarin, at times with some subtle differences. Death for the martyr is indeed a powerful love act framed in ecstatic language, just as in Lucian's martyrdom, the classic declaration "I am a Christian" is located at the center of events. The martyr can scarcely wait to die out of love for God and embraces both the tortures and death with great enthusiasm (*On Sts Juventinus and Maximinus* § 1, *On the holy martyrs* § 2, *On St Drosis* § 8). In the case of Romanus, however, the love that is expressed in his martyr act moves beyond love for God; he dies as much out of love for his fellow human beings. Martyrdom without love, John declares in this homily, is empty (*On St Romanus* § 3). The female martyr, too, is for the most part presented no longer as a "virulized" virago but as a docile virgin.[58] When it is a mother who is the subject of attention, she is both presented as female, in her display of maternal feeling, and as moving beyond the limits of her gender in her display of courage (*On Sts Bernike, Prosdoke and Domnina* § 19–22, *On the Maccabees hom.* 1 § 5–10, and *hom.* 2 § 5–6). For John, women martyrs are the ultimate expression of love for God, since the obstacles they must overcome are far greater than those faced by their male counterparts (*On St Drosis* § 7).

Another element that lies at the center of many of these homilies is the martyr's voice. Paradoxically, stripped naked and physically defenseless the martyr has nonetheless as their unassailable

---

[58]On this shift see Boyarin, *Dying for God*, 67–92. For examples of the docile virgin see *On St Drosis, On Sts Bernike, Prosdoke and Domnina,* and *On Pelagia* (Leemans et al., *"Let Us Die that We May Live,"* 148–57).

defense their tongue and voice (*On St Barlaam* § 1–12). Even when their tongue is removed or their head cut off, they speak with a spiritual voice more powerful than anything their body ever generated (*On St Romanus* § 8, *On Sts Juventinus and Maximinus* § 9). In one memorable passage, Julian utters a single sound at the point of death, which pierces the heavens and flies, escorted by cherubim and powers, straight to the throne of God (*On Julian* § 4), while the skin of Drosis as it peels off and falls into the flames makes a strident noise which repels the evil powers attacking her (*On St Drosis* § 9). Ignatius' sole declaration on his death ("Bless the wild animals!": *On St Ignatius* § 16), too, is framed in the context of the contrast between the mildness of his spoken blessing, the relative mildness of the lions' mouths, and the savagery of the mouths of his torturers. In *On the holy martyrs*, the martyrs in their silent tombs speak loudly through their deeds.[59] In these homilies the declaration mouthed by Lucian (the "I am a Christian" of the martyr) becomes just one of many images of the power that resonates in the confessing mouth, voice, tongue, or sound. Even the demons are complicit in this confession; their flight from the martyr's relics is a vocal witness to the relics' power (*On St Drosis* § 6).

While for John it is clearly understood that it is Christ who has conquered death, that it is he for whom the martyrs shed their blood and without whose sacrifice the martyr act is meaningless, and that, moreover, in dying the martyr-soul gains the prize of being close to God and being able to speak freely with him in heaven, emphasis is also placed by him on the essential humanity of the martyrs. For him this is a key component in his pastoral message. Because they are human and because their bodies remain unresurrected on earth, they provide a powerful example for us to imitate (*On Julian* § 4), as well as being a source for us of reassurance. God takes their souls to himself immediately, but their bodies remain on earth as a reminder that after suffering in this brief life, unimaginable rewards await us

[59]§1–2 (Leemans et al., *"Let Us Die that We May Live,"* 115–26).

in heaven. At the same time, the silent witness born by the martyrs' deeds (which come to mind when we visit their tombs) is a spur to us to imitate them in our daily struggle against the desires and passions that "torture" us, counseling us to have patience and bringing us comfort and consolation.[60] It is precisely because of their human nature and because they were framed in human bodies that their physical remains are still present here, and that we can relate to them and their sufferings in an intimate and meaningful way. Being able to clasp the martyr's coffin, to see one's tears splash upon it, and to anoint oneself with oil that has caressed the martyr's bones is a powerful reality—a fact of which John constantly reminds his audience in the closing and opening remarks of his homilies. For John, the two messages: "if they were human and could overcome such tortures, so can we" and "see them, touch them, know that this is true" are a constant refrain in his preaching.

All of these themes are an essential part of presenting the martyr or saint as an exemplar of virtue. Within the context of hagiography (the life of the saint), the intention is never to present the historical life of the individual but to shape them for the audience as a holy man or woman who is worthy as a spiritual model.[61] As a result, in John's homilies we rarely receive the full picture of the saint's life, but are instead presented either with the moments of torture and death or, in the case of Babylas, with an incident that happened decades later, but which emphasizes the martyr's continuing power and virtue.[62] Vigilius' letter to John, in which he extols the virtues of the three Anaunian martyrs as part of his agenda to persuade John of their importance, is an example of how this genre could be expressed in a number of literary forms. This basic emphasis on the holiness of the

---

[60]*On the holy martyrs* § 2 (Leemans et al., *"Let Us Die that We May Live,"* loc. cit.).

[61]On the role of the martyr homily within hagiography see the introduction by J. Leemans in Leemans et al., *"Let us Die that we might Live."*

[62]*On the martyr Babylas* (Leemans et al., *"Let Us Die that We May Live,"* 140–8). John takes up the episode of the lightning strike on the temple of Apollo following the forced removal of Babylas' body from its proximity, an event which occurred in the time of the emperor Julian.

subject of the homily, letter or story made it simple for models other than martyrs to be added to the picture. We see this in the homilies on Meletius and Eustathius, both former bishops of Antioch who died relatively natural deaths, the one while presiding over a synod in Constantinople, the other in exile in Thrace. In each instance, these heroes of the Nicene Church at Antioch are styled as saints and their lives framed and described in language similar to that used for the martyrs. It is interesting to note that at this point in the development of hagiography John feels it necessary to emphasize the continuity between these new saints and the martyrs. In Meletius' case, he is said to be as good as a martyr by virtue of his practice of asceticism.[63] In the case of Eustathius, he too is said to be a martyr, if not in deed, then in will (*On St Eustathius* § 5). At this stage in the development of the cult, it is likely that for the audience, at least, saint and martyr were still synonymous, and it was important to frame new saints in these terms.

The connection that John explicitly draws between asceticism and martyrdom in the case of Meletius leads us to another theme that is implicit within his homilies on the saints and martyrs. This is the notion of martyrdom as the ultimate denial of the flesh, or rather of asceticism as a transmuted martyrdom, which comes to the fore in society after the time of Constantine, when martyrdom, the ultimate act of denial of self and flesh, is a rare option. In the final paragraph of *On the Maccabees hom.* 2 we find the clearest expression of this, when John exhorts everyone to imitate the mother of the Maccabees, including those who practice the harshest forms of asceticism, since she outstripped even them in her philosophy. Throughout these homilies, moreover, we find frequent mention of the philosophy of the martyr or of the martyr's encouragement of the audience to live a philosophic life. In John's writings this term often refers implicitly to the ascetic life[64] and, if we consider the

---

[63]This is stated explicitly not in the homily *On St Meletius* itself, but in *On Babylas* (Leemans et al., *"Let Us Die that We May Live,"* 147–8).

[64]See G. J. M. Bartelink, " 'Philosophie' et 'philosophe' dans quelques oeuvres de

moral program that he promotes in these particular homilies, with his exhortations to imitate the martyr by overcoming the "tortures" of this life and to exercise oneself in constant prayer and vigils, there is a hint that an agenda of promoting the ascetic (i.e., "martyr") life to the laity in a palatable and achievable form is part of John's pastoral strategy. This same agenda has recently been identified elsewhere in John's preaching.[65]

Of the other themes that enrich John's theology of martyrdom, several deserve particular mention. One is the notion of martyrdom as baptism, an early theological development in martyr literature. We see it here both in the more common notion of martyrdom as baptism by blood (*On St Lucian* § 5) and also in another form in the homily *On Sts Bernike, Prosdoke, and Domnina*. There martyrdom literally becomes a baptism as the mother drowns herself and her daughters in the flowing waters of a river to preserve their virginity. In that homily, too, we find the less common idea of martyrdom as ordination, in which the mother in baptizing her daughters becomes herself a priest. The idea of suicide as a licit means of martyrdom for virgin women is promoted in this same homily, where John emphasizes the willingness of the daughters, a theme that is more explicitly developed in the homily *On Pelagia*. Another theme of importance is the prefiguring of martyrdom in the Old Testament. Here we see particular reference to Abraham's sacrifice of Isaac (*On St Eustathius* § 5, *On the Maccabees hom.* 1 § 6), as well as to the episode of the three boys in the furnace recorded in Daniel (*On St Drosis* § 8, *On Sts Juventinus and Maximinus* § 1, *Letter of Vigilius to John* § 11). The mother of the Maccabees, her seven sons and the priest Eleazar, on the other hand, represent a special case. In the homily *On Eleazar and the seven boys*, considerable space is devoted to the argument

Jean Chrysostome," *Revue d'ascétique et de mystique* 36 (1960): 486–92, esp. 489–90; and J. L. Quantin, "A propos de la traduction de philosophia dans l'*Adversus oppugnatores vitae monasticae* de saint Jean Chrysostome," *Revue des Sciences Religieuses* 56 (1987): 187–97.

[65]See A. Hartney, *John Chrysostom and the Transformation of the City* (Duckworth: London, 2004).

that they are Christian martyrs in the fullest sense, despite their martyrdom before the coming of Christ. The framing of the mother and her sons as Christian martyrs is continued in the two homilies *On the Maccabees.*

Translation notes

In regard to the claim that, together with the two earlier volumes mentioned in the Preface, this book completes the project of translating into English all of John's homilies on the martyrs and saints, for the sake of completeness it should be mentioned that the homily *In quatriduanum Lazarum* (*CPG* 4356), which refers in moderate detail to the feast day of Bernike, Prosdoke and Domnina is not included. Doubt is cast on its authenticity by Sever Voicu,[66] and on looking at it carefully, the vocabulary and on occasion the syntax arouse sufficient concern about its status to warrant its exclusion. The homilies *Dicta praesente imperatore* (*CPG* 4441.2) and *In illud: Vidi dominum hom. 3* (*CPG* 4417) are also not included. While both were delivered on the day of martyrs' festivals, mention of the festival or of the martyrs is exceedingly brief and the bulk of each homily is taken up by other topics. Neither has anything meaningful to contribute to our understanding of the cult of the saints in John's time.

Several of the terms used by John have a variety of nuances in his writings. *Pistoi* (lit. "the believers," "the faithful") is often used by him to differentiate the baptized from the unbaptized within an audience, but in some contexts it is used by him to differentiate those who adhere to the Christian faith and those who do not. In the latter instances, the term and its opposite (*apistoi*) are translated as "Christians" and "non-Christians." Similarly, *eusebeia*, which is usually translated as "piety," can carry overtones also of "true religion," even "orthodoxy," as opposed to "false religion" (*asebeia*). In instances where piety is simply being discussed or opposed to impiety, the

---

[66]"Pseudo-Giovanni Crisostomo: I confini del corpus," *Jahrbuch für Antike und Christentum* 39 (1996): 105–15.

terms are translated in that fashion. On a few occasions, however, the opposition is clearly that of true with false religion, in which cases that translation is adopted. In general, the once commonly used terms "barbarian" (Gr. *barbaros*) and "pagan" are avoided in favor of the more neutral terms "foreigner" and "Greek." In the latter case, the term carries the nuance of a person imbued thoroughly in Greek culture and in the old Greco-Roman religions. An attempt has been made to use inclusive language wherever possible. In the preaching of this time, masculine terminology is the default in all discussions of martyrs, often obscuring the fact that when martyrs are being spoken of as a group, women may be included. In regard to the biblical citations, all of those that derive from the Old Testament are cited according to the Septuagint titles and numbering (LXX). This is the biblical text that was used by the preachers of the Greek-speaking world in John's time and it often differs significantly from the Hebrew in books such as Psalms, Proverbs, and Ecclesiastes. Finally, the division of each homily into short paragraphs is an attempt to make the progress of the argument stand out for the reader. For the most part, it bears little relationship to the paragraph or section divisions in the editions or manuscripts on which the translations are based. While almost all of the homilies in this book are offered here in English translation for the first time, two have been unavailable to scholars even in a reliable Greek text. As explained in the introductions to *On Eleazar and the seven boys* and *On all the martyrs*, in the first instance the only available text has a major lacuna, is missing the ending and contains a passage interpolated by accident from another homily. In the second case, the homily is unedited and survives in only one manuscript. The publication of translations of complete texts of both homilies makes the contribution of this volume especially valuable.

Homilies on the
Saints and Martyrs

On Saint Meletius

This homily was delivered at Antioch in 386 CE, since John clearly says both that five years have passed since Meletius died in Thrace († 381) and that Thrace and the city where John is currently preaching are quite distant from one another. He further confirms the location by saying that the saint is buried locally.

Appointed bishop of Antioch in 360 by the then dominant Arian Christian faction, Meletius turned out to have Nicene leanings and became instead bishop of the dominant Nicene faction at Antioch for some two decades (360–381 CE).[1] During that time, he presided over the teenage John's baptism and, according to Palladius (*Dial.* 5), from the moment of John's baptism on took a close personal interest in him.[2] After Meletius' death, John became closely attached to his successor, Flavian. Because of his Nicene stance, Meletius was exiled three times (in 360/1, 365 and 371), the first occurring only a short time after his appointment, when Meletius' Nicene leanings became obvious. He spent most of his various exiles in his homeland in Armenia. Despite not being acknowledged as the legitimate Nicene bishop of Antioch by Egypt and the West (the leader of the smaller faction, Paulinus, was recognized by these Churches), Meletius presided over the Second Ecumenical Council in Constantinople, where he died unexpectedly in 381. It is likely that his body was temporarily placed in the Church of the Apostles in the imperial capital, since Gregory of Nyssa in his funeral oration for

---

[1]For a brief discussion in English of some of the politics of the Antiochene schism see W. Mayer, "Antioch and the West in Late Antiquity," *Byzantinoslavica* 61 (2003) 23–7.

[2]See J. N. D. Kelly, *Golden Mouth: The Story of John Chrysostom—Ascetic, Preacher, Bishop* (London, 1995), 16–18.

Meletius stresses the cohabitation of the latter with the apostles.[3] His body was subsequently conveyed back with ceremony to Antioch, where it was placed next to that of Babylas in the church dedicated to that martyr. Meletius had personally initiated and supervised the construction of the Church of St Babylas in the late 370s. John recalls this part of Meletius' history towards the end of the homily that he preached on the festival of St Babylas.[4] Upon its completion, the remains of Babylas were translated from the main cemetery at Antioch to a purpose-built double sarcophagus in the centre of this cruciform church, suggesting that Meletius had all along intended to be buried next to him.

John's homily in praise of St Meletius is of great interest for its witness to the speed with which an annual commemoration of Meletius became established within the local liturgical calendar and for the information it supplies regarding the strength of the personal following of Meletius and regarding the location of the present festival (presumably the Church of St Babylas, since the audience is said to be flocking around his coffin). It is of even greater interest when we reflect that the smaller Nicene faction at Antioch, which had been led for a long time by the bishop Paulinus (362–388), is unlikely to have had the same veneration for Meletius. This raises the possibility that the festival was specific to the non-Paulinian Nicene community and that there may have been at least two variant liturgical calendars in operation in Antioch at this time. It is noteworthy that although Meletius was not a martyr in the strict sense, in the conclusion to the homily *On Babylas* John says that in his asceticism Meletius imitated the martyrs' acts.[5] In this way, John is able to present him as a virtual martyr himself, as well as martyr enthusiast. Since John began his preaching career only on ordination to the rank

[3]Gregory of Nyssa, *Oratio funebris in Meletium episcopum*; Jaeger-Langerbeck eds., GNO IX, 441 1–10. See W. Mayer, "Cathedral Church or Cathedral Churches?," *OCP* 66 (2000): 63 n. 56.

[4]*On Babylas* (Leemans et al., *"Let Us Die that We May Live,"* 147).

[5]Leemans et al., *"Let Us Die that We May Live,"* 148.

of presbyter in February 386, this is one of the earliest surviving sermons which he preached on a saint's festival.

Contents:

1–3. John praises the love of the audience for Meletius, which they exhibit now in the size of the crowd in attendance, and exhibited from the beginning by naming their children after him. Such is the mania surrounding Meletius that people had his image carved on rings, seals, and cups and painted on their bedroom walls.

4–6. Meletius' first exile further demonstrates the virtues of the man and the love people held towards him.

7–8. God ordained that Meletius die in Constantinople at a major synod both to spare the Antiochenes greater grief and to publicize Meletius' virtues more widely and ensure that the blessings that radiated from him were more broadly distributed.

9. God softened the grief of the Antiochenes by sending them a bishop of equal virtue in his place. Although he is dead, Meletius is by no means forgotten. With the passage of time enthusiasm and love for him grows, rather than fades.

10. John urges the audience to pray with Meletius' assistance.

Translated from PG 50.515–520.

Homily of praise on our father among the saints
Meletius, archbishop of Antioch the Great, and on the
enthusiasm of the assembled

1   As I cast my eyes all around this holy flock and see the whole city in attendance, I can't decide whom to call blessed first—the holy Meletius, because he enjoys such great honor, even after death, or your love, because you demonstrate such good will concerning your shepherds, even after they are dead and gone. For while he is blessed, because he had the power to release such love[6] in all of you, you too

[6]Gr. *philtron*, employed throughout this homily in addition to John's usual term for love (*agapē*), has nuances that are difficult to capture in English. The term is used

are blessed because after you received the deposit of his love, you persisted in preserving it intact for the depositor up to the present. For we have already raced past the fifth year since he departed for Jesus whom he longed for and, just as if you'd seen him yesterday or the day before, you have come to meet him with fervent love today. He is to be envied because he fathered such [daughters and] sons. To be envied are you, too, because you were allotted such a father. Noble is the root and wonderful, but the fruit, too, are worthy of this root. For truly, just as a wonderful root is concealed by the folds of the earth and isn't seen itself, yet through the fruit the strength of its special quality is revealed, so indeed, too, blessed Meletius, hidden in this coffin, is not evident to us with our physical eyes, yet through you, the fruit, the strength of his special grace is revealed. Even if we were silent, the festival alone and the fervor of your enthusiasm are sufficient to proclaim louder than a trumpet the love of the holy Meletius for his children. For he has so inflamed your mind towards passion for him that you are heated through at just his name and are excited at the very mention of it.

2   It's for this reason that at present I, too, am continually weaving his name into my sermon, not at random but intentionally and from respect. Indeed, just as someone who weaves a gold wreath and next sets pearls in it renders the diadem more brilliant with the density of the gems, so in fact I, too, in today weaving a crown of praises for his blessed head densely weave into the sermon the constancy of mentioning his name like some pearls, hoping by this to render him more desired and brilliant. For this is the custom of lovers and such is their habit, to embrace even just the names of their loved ones and to get heated up at their very mention, which is what you, too, have experienced in the case of this blessed man. For from the beginning, you welcomed him when he arrived in the city, and you each named your own child after him, each thinking that through employing the

of a love-spell or charm. John implies here that Meletius has cast a spell over the city. People can't help but love him.

name you were introducing the saint into your own house and, bypassing fathers and grandfathers and ancestors, mothers gave the name of blessed Meletius to the children they gave birth to. For the love of piety overcame nature and, from that time on, the offspring were more desirable to their parents, not just as a result of natural love, but also from the affection for that name. For they thought that the name itself was an adornment to relationship, security for the household, a safety measure for those so-named, and a comfort for love. And, just as when people are sitting in the dark, they light up many lamps from a single lamp that's been lit, and each person introduces it into their own house, so, too, when that name burst into the city like a light, each person, as if lighting up a lamp, at the time introduced the name of that blessed man into their own house, as if, through assigning the name, they were embracing a warehouse of innumerable blessings.

3   And what happened was an education in piety. For, since they were perpetually compelled to have that name in mind and to have that holy man in their heart, they had the name as a repellent for every irrational feeling and thought. And it became so frequent that this name echoed around from every direction everywhere both in side streets and in the marketplace and in fields and on highways. But you didn't experience so much just at the name, but even at the depiction of his body. At least, what you did with names, this you practiced, too, in the case of that man's image. For truly, many carved that holy image on finger rings and on seals and on cups and on bedroom walls and all over the place so that one didn't just hear that holy name, but also saw the depiction of his body all over the place and had a double consolation for his loss.

4   As it was, the moment he entered he was expelled from the city, since the enemies of truth drove him out. And God yielded, wanting to show at the same time both that man's virtue and your courage. For when he arrived like Moses in Egypt, and freed the city from heretical error and, by cutting off from the rest of the body the limbs

that were festering and in an incurable state, brought back uncont-
aminated health to the majority of the Church, the enemies of truth
couldn't endure the correction, and stirring up the emperor of the
time, expelled him from the city, hoping by this to subvert the truth
and overturn the correction of events. But the opposite of what was
expected took place, and your enthusiasm was demonstrated all the
more and the proof of that man's pedagogical expertise shone forth.
On the one hand, [this was so] in that he was able to so ground you
in the enthusiasm for faith in thirty days or not even that, that, when
countless winds were attacking afterwards, that instruction
remained unshakeable. On the other hand, your fervor was demonstrated in that in thirty days or not even that you so precisely took
in the seeds that were thrown down by him that you sent their roots
down to the depths of your mind and from that moment gave in to
none of the temptations that were brought forward.

5   It is worth not passing over either what happened in association
with his expulsion. For when the urban prefect, driving his chariot,
exited through the middle of the marketplace with the holy man
seated next to him, showers of stones were hurled at the prefect's
head from all directions. [This was] because the city couldn't bear
the separation, but chose even to quit the present life rather than to
see that holy man cast out. So, what did that blessed man do then?
When he saw the hurling of the stones, he wrapped the prefect's head
up and hid it in his own clothing, in the one stroke shaming the enemies with the excess of his fairness and teaching his students how
much forbearance one should display towards those who do wrong,
and how it wasn't just appropriate for them to do nothing terrible,
but that even if danger attacked them from other sources, they
should fend it off with complete dedication. Who didn't tremble
then and wasn't struck with amazement, when they saw the city's
manic love and the teacher's high-reaching philosophy and his fairness and gentleness? For what happened at that time was truly
incredible. The shepherd was driven away and the sheep weren't

scattered; the helmsman was thrown out and the vessel didn't sink. The farmer was chased off and the vine abundantly bore fruit. For since you were bound to each other by the bond of love, not the introduction of trials, nor an increase in dangers, nor the length of the road, nor the abundance of time, nor anything else was able to distance you from being in the company of the blessed shepherd. Instead, although he was expelled, and as a result was at a long distance from his children, the opposite took place. For you were all the more constrained by the bonds of love. And he took the entire city with him when he went off to Armenia. For, although his body was fixed in his homeland, his intellect and mind, elevated by the Spirit's grace as if by some wings and hovering around you the entire time, carried this entire populace around in his heart, which was indeed your own experience. For, although you were situated here and circumscribed by the city, by love's spirit you were lifted up to Armenia day after day and saw his holy face and heard his most pleasurable and blessed voice, and so came back again.

6   It's for this reason that God allowed him to be driven from the city straight away, so that, as I started out saying, he might demonstrate the strength of your faith to the enemies attacking you and [Meletius'] skill at teaching. And it is clear from the following. For after his first exile, on his return he spent here not just thirty days, but even months or a year or one or two or more. For since you gave adequate demonstration of your firmness in regard to the faith, [God] granted you to luxuriate again in your father without fear. For it was indeed the greatest luxury to enjoy that holy face. For not just his teaching or speaking, but even his simply being looked at was enough to introduce every teaching on virtue into the viewers' soul. At any rate, when he rode in to meet you and the entire city sailed out to the road, some got close and touched his feet and kissed his hands and heard his voice. Others, prevented by the sheer numbers and only seeing him from afar, as if they had received sufficient blessing from seeing him and had obtained no less than those who

were near him, in this way went away with complete conviction. And what happened in the case of the apostles, happened also in his. For just as in the case of the apostles, when their shadow extended and touched from a distance all those who couldn't approach and be near, they drew to themselves the same grace and left likewise made well. So, too, now all those who couldn't get near went away filled with every blessing from just seeing him, as if they had felt a certain spiritual glory be sent forth from that holy head and pass through to those who were furthest away.

7   And when it seemed good to the common God of all to summon him at that point from the present life and to enlist him in the chorus of angels, not even this took place in a random way; instead, although an imperial edict summoned him, it was God who stirred the emperor. He summoned him not anywhere close or nearby but to Thrace itself, so that Galatians and Bithynians and Cilicians and Cappadocians and all those who inhabit Thrace might learn of our blessings. So that bishops all over the world, by looking at his holiness as if at an archetypal image and receiving from him a clear example of the service associated with this office, might have a secure and absolutely clear standard by which they ought to administer and govern the Churches. Indeed, because of the magnitude of the city and because of the close involvement of the emperor, many bishops from many places in the world flowed together there at that time. And the bishops of the Churches were all summoned by imperial letters, on the basis that they had received those Churches that, after a lengthy battle and storm, had restored the beginning of peace and calm. And so, at that time, he, too, was present there. And, just as in the case of the three boys, when they were about to be heralded and crowned, they extinguished the fire's force, trampled on the tyrant's pride, put on trial every form of impiety, and had the entire world watching them as spectators (for although the satraps from all over the world and consuls and prefects had been summoned for another reason, they became spectators of those athletes), this is how

it turned out, too, on that occasion, with the result that the theater became magnificent for that blessed man. Summoned for another reason, the bishops who administer the Churches all over the world were in attendance and watched that holy man. And when they watched, and got to know every detail of his discretion, his wisdom, his enthusiasm for the faith, that every virtue appropriate to a priest was perfected in him, it was then that God summoned him to himself.

8   This happened, too, in order to spare our city. For if he had quit his life here, the weight of the disaster would have been unbearable. For who would have endured seeing that blessed man breathing out his last breaths? Who would have endured seeing those lids closing over his eyes and his mouth shutting after uttering its last words? Who, on seeing these things, wouldn't have been distraught at the magnitude of the disaster? So that this might not occur, then, God arranged that he quit his life in another country, so that, having in the meantime worked through the disaster beforehand, when we saw the corpse entering [the city], we wouldn't be stricken to our soul , since we had become accustomed to the grief in our mind. Which is what in fact took place. For when the city received that holy body, it did indeed mourn so and set up a great howl. But the grief swiftly dissolved, both for the aforementioned reason, and because of what I am about to relate.

9   For God who loves humankind had compassion on our grieving and quickly showed us another shepherd, who with great accuracy adhered to the characteristics of [Meletius] and kept alive the image of every virtue. Indeed, when he mounted the throne he immediately stripped us of the dress of mourning and extinguished our grief, and instead refreshed the memory of the blessed man. And while our pain faded, our love flared up more fervently, and our despondency completely disappeared. And yet this is not the way it usually happens at the loss of one's nearest and dearest. Rather, when a person loses a much-loved son, or a wife a respected husband, for

as long as he or she faithfully keeps his memory fresh, the grief, too, wallows excessively in their soul. But when time moves along and the grief softens, the flourishing of the memory, too, is extinguished together with the severity of the pain. But in the case of this blessed man, the opposite took place. Although the despondency was completely expelled, the memory didn't disappear with the grief, but grew intensively. And you, who after so long a time are flitting around the body of blessed Meletius like bees around honeycomb, are witnesses. But the love for him did not arise from nature, but from reason associated with correct judgment. For this reason it was not extinguished by death, nor did it fade with time, but it grew and advanced dramatically. And it was not just that of those of you who saw him, but even of those who didn't see. For this is the most amazing thing, that everyone who is younger than when he was alive, they themselves too are inflamed towards the same level of love. And so, while you the older generation can claim an advantage over those who didn't see him in that you actually spent time with him and enjoyed his holy company, those who haven't seen him can claim an advantage over you in that, although they didn't see the man, they demonstrate no less a love for him than you who saw him.

10   Let us all pray together, governors and governed, women and men, old and young, slaves and free, taking blessed Meletius himself as a shareholder in this prayer (for truly he has greater boldness now and a more fervent love towards you), that this love be increased in us and that, just as we are here near this coffer, there too we may all be considered worthy of being able in the same way to be near his eternal dwelling and to attain the blessings stored up [for us]. May we all attain them through the grace and loving kindness of our Lord Jesus Christ, through whom and with whom be glory and power to the Father, together with the Holy Spirit, forever and ever. Amen.

On Saint Eustathius

The Eustathius celebrated in this homily was a native of Side in Pamphilia, who was bishop first of Beroea in Syria, and then in 324 of Antioch. It is probable that his immediate predecessor as bishop of Antioch was Philogonius, about whom John also preached a festival homily.[1] An opponent of the Arians, Eustathius was exiled to Trajanopolis in Thrace on disciplinary, rather than theological grounds, following the Council of Antioch in 327. As John indicates here, Eustathius did not undergo martyrdom in the strict sense. Rather, John styles him as a martyr by virtue of Eustathius' suffering for his confession of Nicene Christianity in the face of Arianism, which he associates with his exile. This claim is similar to the one that John makes in the homily on St Meletius, where he asserts that Meletius' ascetic lifestyle made him a virtual martyr.

That John is preaching on this occasion in Antioch is made clear not just by the connection between Eustathius and that city, but also through the mention of Eustathius' place of burial, Thrace, which is said to be a great distance away, and through John's comment that Eustathius was formerly "in command of the Church in our community." It is likely that his festival was celebrated not long before 18 November, since in another homily John says that he recently preached on the topic of the dispute at Antioch between Peter and Paul, then on the next day he delivered a homily of praise on Eustathius and after him on Romanus.[2] The Syrian martyrology locates the festival of Romanus on 18 November.

The homily is significant for the way in which Eustathius is portrayed as a keystone in the foundation of Nicene Christianity at

[1] Mayer-Allen, *John Chrysostom*, 184–95.
[2] *In illud: Domine, non est in homine*, PG 55.154 ll.6–16.

Antioch, making him a saint of the Nicene community, and for the way in which John glosses over the complex history of the Antiochene schism, which has its origins in the rise of Arianism at Antioch and the episcopate of Eustathius. He conveniently ignores the fact that Meletius was in fact ordained by the Arians and therefore suspect to a large number of Nicene Christians. Of particular interest is the claim in the conclusion to the homily that Flavian, the present bishop of Antioch, shepherded the Nicene Christians of that city in the intervening period between the expulsion of Eustathius and Meletius' ordination as bishop.[3] This claim appears in no other surviving source, although in his *Church History*, Theodoret says that Flavian and one or two others held the Nicene community together during the possession of the churches by the Arians during Meletius' exiles (*HE* 4.22, 24; *HR* 8.6–7) and that as laymen Diodore and Flavian led protest vigils in the martyria of Antioch at the time of Bishop Leontius' ordination of the radical Arian Aetius to the diaconate (c. 355) (*HE* 2.24.8–11). Again, the question arises as to whether both Nicene communities in Antioch held Eustathius in equal honor and celebrated his festival on the same day.

Contents:

1–2. It is acceptable to call Eustathius blessed, since he is already dead and has passed beyond the mutability of life and its empty luxuries.

3–4. Eustathius died in a foreign land, since his enemies wanted to suppress his influence. The opposite has been the outcome. Instead, he is famous and every person present today is his living memorial.

5. Despite dying a normal death, Eustathius can be called a martyr in disposition.

[3]If Flavian was a young man at the time of Eustathius' exile, that would put him in his early 80s at the time of the Antiochene riot in 387 CE, which is not impossible. Since a considerable length of time elapsed between Eustathius' exile and Meletius' ordination it is more likely, however, that John is being loose with chronology here and that Flavian ministered to the Nicene community for only the latter part of those decades, which would take away the necessity for Flavian to have been old enough to engage in active ministry immediately upon Eustathius' expulsion.

6–7. The circumstances of Eustathius's "martyrdom": exile to a foreign country at the beginning of the Arian heresy.

8–9. Eustathius is expelled from Antioch in order to show how strong the faith is and to reveal God's power. He makes sure that the Church is ready to defend itself.

10. Flavian takes up the defense of the Antiochene Church and protects its members until Meletius becomes bishop.

Translated from PG 50.597–606.

Sermon of praise on our father among the saints Eustathius, archbishop of Antioch the Great

1   A certain wise man, knowledgeable in philosophy, who had thoroughly and accurately learnt the nature of human affairs, and recognized their feebleness, and how they contain nothing trustworthy or secure, advises all people alike not to consider anything blessed before death (cf. Sir 11.28). For this reason, since blessed Eustathius is dead, we can at this point sing his praises with complete security. I mean, if one shouldn't consider anyone blessed before death, bestowing blessing on those who deserve it after their death would be innocent of blame. For certainly he has gone past the strait of worldly affairs, he has been freed from the turmoil of the waves, he has sailed toward the calm and tranquil harbor, he is not subject to uncertainty about the future, and is not liable to fall; instead, as if he is now standing on some rock or elevated crag, he scorns all the waves. For this reason blessing [him] is safe, praising [him] blameless. For he has no fear of reversal, is not suspicious of change. My point is that we who are still alive, like people tossing in the middle of the sea, are subject to many reversals. And, just as the latter are at one moment lifted up high, when the waves are at their peak, at another carried down to the very depths, yet neither is being up high

safe, nor being down low stable—for both these things result from water flowing and not staying still—so, too, in the case of human affairs nothing is secure and fixed, but reversals come thick and fast one after the other. While one person is carried up on high by happy circumstances, another is dragged down to a great depth by bad luck. But let neither the first get swellheaded, nor the second discouraged. For with utter swiftness each will receive reversal. But not [Eustathius], who has been translated to heaven, who has gone away to the Jesus whom he desires, who has gone to a place free of confusion, where grief and pain and groaning have run away. There is no semblance of reversal there, there is no shadow cast by change; rather, everything is fixed and immovable, everything is secure and firmly set, everything is imperishable and immortal, everything is untouched and endures eternally. It's for this reason [scripture] says: "Call no one blessed before their death" (Sir 11.28). On what basis? The future is unclear and nature weak. The will is lazy, sin is hovering, and the snares are many. "Know," it says, "that you walk in the midst of snares" (Sir 9.13). Temptations come one after another, the crowd of affairs is large, and the war [waged] by demons unceasing, and the rebellion of the passions unrelenting. It's for these reasons scripture says: "Call no one blessed before their death." That's why it's safe to bless the deserving person after death. Rather, not simply after death, but a death of this kind: when a person has lost their life with a crown, when [they have lost it] with confession and unfeigned faith. For if a certain person called those who have simply died blessed, how much more those who died in this fashion?

2   "And who called those who have simply died blessed?," you ask. Solomon, Solomon that utterly wise man. Don't simply pass over the man, but consider who he was and how he lived and with how much freedom from anxiety and indulgence he lived the soft and painless life. For he conceived of every type of luxury and came up with all sorts of paths of spiritual guidance and discovered diverse and versatile kinds of pleasures, and detailing these he said: "I have built

myself houses, planted myself vineyards, made myself orchards and gardens, made myself pools of water; I have acquired male slaves and young female slaves, and have slaves born at home; I have acquired herds and flocks; I have gathered silver and gold the equivalent of sand; I have created for myself male and female singers, male and female wine-pourers" (Eccl 2.4–8). What then did this self-same man [say] after such great wealth of money, of possessions, of luxury, of indulgence? He said: "I have called the dead blessed as opposed to the living, and the person who does not yet exist good as opposed to them" (cf. Eccl 4.2–3). This man, who cast such a vote against luxury, is a truly trustworthy critic of it. For if one of those who had lived in poverty and on the skids had produced this vote against luxury, it would have appeared that he wasn't condemning these things in truth, but through lack of experience. But when this man who had traveled it and traversed every path of it dishonored it, his condemnation was immediately beyond suspicion. Perhaps you think that our sermon has fallen off the current topic. But if we just pay attention, we'll find that what I've said keeps to it in particular. For on martyrs' commemorations it is essential and logical to discuss philosophy too. Indeed, we say these things not in condemnation of the present life—heaven forbid!—but from casting a slur on luxury. For it is not to live that is bad, but to live in a pointless and random fashion.

3   Thus if a person were to live the present life with a view to good works and in expectation of the blessings to come, they would be able to say like Paul: "It is far better to live in the flesh. For [my] work is fruitful" (Phil 1.22). Just so, then, was it the case too with blessed Eustathius, who conducted himself properly in both life and death. For he endured [death] for Christ's sake not in his own land, but in a foreign place. This was the achievement of his enemies. For while they drove him out of his home territory with the intent of dishonoring [him], he instead became more brilliant and famous through his migration into exile, as the outcome of events indeed showed. For

his fame became so great that, although his body is buried in Thrace, his memory flowers among us day after day and, while his tomb is in that barbarian region, after so long a time the desire [for him] among us, who are separated from him by so great a distance, grows day after day. Rather, if one must tell the truth, even his tomb is among us, not just in Thrace. For saints' memorials are not urns or coffins or columns or inscriptions, but good works and a zeal for faith and a healthy conscience towards God. My point is that truly this church[4] has risen up more brilliant than any column over the martyr, carrying inscriptions that are not voiceless but that through events themselves cry out his memory and brilliance louder than a trumpet, and each of you who are present is that saint's tomb, a tomb that has life and soul. For, if I were to open up the conscience of each of you who are present, I would find this saint dwelling inside your mind.

4   Do you see how his enemies made no further gain? How they didn't extinguish his glory, but raised it higher and made it more brilliant, creating so many tombs instead of one—tombs with life, tombs that give voice, tombs prepared for the same enthusiasm? For this reason I call the saints' bodies springs and roots and spiritual perfumes. On what basis? That each of the items mentioned doesn't just keep its own virtue to itself, but also transmits it all over the place to a considerable distance. For instance, springs bubble up lots of water; even so, they don't keep this contained within their own basins. Rather, by giving birth to lengthy rivers, they mingle with the sea, and, as if by stretching out a hand, through their length reach the ocean's waters. Again, the root of plants is hidden in the bowels of the earth, but doesn't keep all its virtue contained below, and this is the nature of tree-climbing vines in particular. For when they extend their branches to the high up twigs, they advance their shoots to a considerable distance by creeping through those stalks, creating

[4]It is not clear here whether John is referring to the building in which the present celebration is being held, or metaphorically to the local Christian community in Antioch.

a broad canopy with the density of their leaves. Such too is the nature of perfumes. For while often they are stored in a little house, their sweet smell tumbles out through the windows into streets and alleyways and marketplaces and teaches those walking outside the virtue of the spices stored inside. If a spring or a root or a plant's or spices' nature has so much strength, much more so do the saints' bodies. And that what I've said isn't false, you are witnesses. For although the martyr's body lies in Thrace, you're not spending time in Thrace; instead, far removed from that region, you share his sweet smell at so great a distance and have come together because of it—the length of the road hasn't put you off, nor has the abundance of time extinguished [your enthusiasm]. The nature of spiritual achievements is like that. They aren't cut off by any physical impediment, but flower and grow day after day, and neither does the abundance of time wither them, nor a road's length wall them off.

5   Don't be astonished if, when I began the sermon and praises, I called the saint a martyr. For in fact, his life came to a natural end. How, then, is he a martyr? In response to your love, I've often said that it's not just the death that creates a martyr, but also the disposition. For often the martyr's crown is woven not just from the way out, but also from the will. Indeed, it's not I, but Paul who gives this definition of martyrdom when he speaks in this way: "I die every day" (1 Cor 15.31). How do you die every day? How can a single mortal body possibly undergo countless deaths? "Through one's disposition," he says, "and through being prepared for death." This too is the way God revealed. For truly Abraham didn't bloody the knife, didn't redden the altar, didn't sacrifice Isaac, yet completed the sacrifice nonetheless. Who says this? The very one who received the sacrifice. "Because of me," he said, "you didn't spare your beloved son" (Gen 22.12). And yet, he (sc. Abraham) took him alive and brought him back healthy. How, then, didn't he spare [him]? "In that I judge such sacrifices not from the outcome of events, but from the disposition of those making the choice," says [God]. "His hand didn't kill,

but his will did. He didn't bathe his sword in his child's neck, he didn't slit his throat, yet even without blood it's a sacrifice." The initiated know what I'm saying. On this basis, that sacrifice also took place without blood, since it was destined to be a type of this one. Do you see its image outlined in advance in the Old Testament? Don't doubt the truth!

6   Now, this martyr (for the argument has shown us that he is a martyr), prepared himself for countless deaths and endured them all with his will and eagerness. He endured many of the dangers that attacked him too by way of actual experience. For in fact they drove him out of his country and translocated him into exile, and at that time set in motion many other [assaults] against that blessed man, although they had no legal grounds on which to prosecute, on the basis that, when he heard Paul say: "They worshipped and served the creation rather than the creator" (Rom 1.25), he fled the sacrilege and was alarmed at the lawlessness. But this [action] deserved crowns, not condemnation. Consider, if you please, the Devil's wickedness. For when the pagan war[5] had newly ended, and all the Churches had just recovered from the cruel and successive persecutions, and it wasn't much time since every temple[6] had been locked up, altars extinguished, and all the raging of the demons quelled, and these things grieved the wicked demon and he couldn't mildly bear the Church's peace, what then did he do? He introduced a second cruel war. For while the first had an external origin, this was factional. Such wars are rather difficult to guard against, and readily overpower those involved.

[5]Lit. "Greek war," i.e., the war waged by a follower of Greco-Roman religion, alluding probably to the emperor Diocletian.

[6]The Greek text of Montfaucon reads *laoi* (peoples), but what was clearly read by the Latin translator (*naoi* = temples) is preferable. This may simply be a typographic error in the Migne publication of Montfaucon's text. John seems to be referring here to Constantine's conversion to Christianity (c. 319 CE) and subsequent support for that religion. The last great persecution occurred under the emperor Diocletian in 303–5.

7   Now, at that time this blessed man had command of the Church in our community, and although the sickness arose like some cruel plague from the Egyptian regions, then next traveled through the cities in between in a hurry to attack our city,[7] he, being alert and sober and foreseeing everything that would happen from afar, beat off the approaching war. Indeed, before the sickness attacked our city, from his base here he prepared medications like a wise doctor and steered this holy ship with a great deal of safety, running around everywhere, training the sailors, the marines, all those sailing [on her], preparing [them] to be sober, to be alert, on the basis that pirates were attacking and attempting to steal away the treasure of faith. But he didn't employ this forethought just here, but also sent throughout all regions people who instructed, encouraged, discoursed, who blocked the enemies' attack in advance. Truly he was well trained by the Spirit's grace that a church's leader should not just be concerned for the church entrusted to him by the Spirit, but also for the entire Church situated throughout the world. Indeed, he learnt this from the holy prayers. "For if one is obliged to offer prayers," he said, "for the universal Church from one end of the world to the other, one should show far more forethought, too, for it all, and similarly be concerned for them all and care for all of them." Indeed, what happened in the case of Stephen eventuated in his case too. For just as the Jews, powerless to resist Stephen's wisdom, stoned that saint, so too these men, powerless to resist his wisdom and seeing the fortresses secured, at that point expelled the herald from the city. But his voice was not silent. Rather, while the person was expelled, the word of his teaching was not expelled. After all, Paul was bound, yet the word of God was not bound (cf. 2 Tim

[7] As Joseph Kelly, *The World of the Early Christians* (Collegeville, MN: The Liturgical Press, 1997), 196, succinctly summarizes: "In 318 an Egyptian priest named Arius taught that the son of God was inferior to the Father ... [and] went on to say that the Son was a created being who once did not exist. When Alexander, bishop of Alexandria (313–328) , condemned Arius' teaching, the priest fled to Palestine where his views commanded support. Soon the Eastern bishops were lining up on either side ..." The Council of Nicaea in 325 was convoked in direct response to these events.

2.9). And this man was in another country and yet his teaching was among us. So then, after expelling [him] they attacked in a tight pack, just like a forceful torrent. But they neither carried away the plants, nor buried the seeds, nor damaged the cultivation. So well and skillfully were they rooted, since they had been cultivated by his wisdom. But, it is appropriate that I mention the reason why God allowed him to be driven away from here. The Church was only just recovering. It had as no ordinary comfort that man's command. He blockaded it on all sides and beat off the assaults of its enemies.

8   For what reason, then, was he expelled, and did God agree to their leading him away? For what reason? Whatever you do, don't think that what I say is the solution to just this question. Rather, whether you happen to argue about such matters with Greeks or other heretics, what I am about to say is enough to solve every question. Whereas God agrees to his true and apostolic faith being warred against in many ways, he allows the heresies and Greco-Roman religions[8] to enjoy indemnity. What on earth for? So that, on the one hand, you might learn the latter's feebleness, since without being harassed they fold of their own accord; while, on the other, you may recognize the faith's strength, in that despite being embattled it grows even by means of the people blocking it. And that this is not a conjecture of mine, but a divine oracle sent from above, let's hear what Paul says about these things. For truly whatever he too suffered was human. For if Paul actually existed, then he shared our nature. What did he suffer? He was driven out, embattled, whipped, plotted against in countless ways, externally, internally, by those who appeared to be of his own party, by outsiders. And what can one say about the many afflictions he endured? Well, when he was worn out and no longer coping with the assaults of his enemies, who were always cutting off his teaching and opposing his argument, he fell down before the Master and entreated him, and said: "Satan's angel

[8]Lit. "Hellenism." While this term has traditionally been translated as "pagan-ism," it is now recognized that the label covers a diverse range of beliefs and practices.

was given to me as a thorn in the flesh, in order to discipline me. On this subject I have entreated the Lord three times and he said to me: 'My grace is sufficient for you. For my power is made perfect in weakness.'" (2 Cor 12.7–9). And while I know that some think that it was a physical weakness, this is not the case, not at all. On the contrary, Satan's angel is what he (sc. Paul) calls the people who opposed him. For "Satan" is a Hebrew word. An adversary is labeled "Satan." And so he calls the Devil's instruments and those people who serve him his "angels." "Why, then," you ask, "did it apply to the flesh?" Because while the flesh was whipped, the soul was lightened, lifted up by the hope of things to come. For he (sc. the Devil) didn't get hold of the soul, nor trip up the thoughts within; instead his machinations and war stopped at the flesh, unable to enter within. Since, then, it was the flesh that was cut, the flesh that was whipped, the flesh that was bound (for it's impossible to bind the soul), it's for this reason that he said: "Satan's angel was given to me as a thorn in the flesh, in order to discipline me," hinting at the trials, the afflictions, the persecutions. Then what? "On this subject I have entreated the Lord three times." That is, he says, "I often asked to be given a little respite from my trials." You remember the reason I mentioned: that God allowed his servants to be whipped, driven away, to suffer countless tortures, so that he might show his own power. Well, look, here truly is a person who asked to be distanced from his countless tortures and adversaries, but who didn't attain what he asked for. Who, then, is responsible? After all, nothing prevents us from recalling it again: "My grace," he says, "is sufficient for you. For my power is made perfect in weakness."

9   Do you see that it's for this reason that God allowed Satan's angels to keep up their assault on his servants and to provide countless opportunities, so that his power might be obvious? For truly, whether we dispute with Greeks or with the miserable Jews, this suffices for us as a proof of the divine power, that, once introduced, the faith prevailed through countless wars, and although the whole world

was doing the opposite and everyone was quite vehemently rejecting those twelve men (I mean, the apostles), people who were being whipped, driven away, suffering countless tortures were in a short period able to prevail to an incredible extent over those who were doing these things. It's for these reasons that God allowed blessed Eustathius too to be escorted off into exile, so that he might show us in a major way both the power of truth and the heretics' feebleness. So then, when he was about to depart for the journey abroad, he let go of the city, but he didn't let go of his love for you. Nor, when he was expelled from the Church, did he think that he was alienated either from the leadership or from caring for you; rather, it was then that he expressed care and concern in a major way. Indeed, he summoned everyone and entreated them not to yield, nor to give in to the wolves, nor to betray the flock to them, but to remain inside curbing them and disputing, while securing the less corrupted of the brothers and sisters. And that he gave good orders, the outcome proved. For if you hadn't remained in the Church then, the majority of the city would have been corrupted, while the wolves ate the sheep in a deserted place. But his word prevented them from displaying their own wickedness with impunity. It's not just the outcome that proved it, but also Paul's comments. For in fact he (sc. Eustathius) gave this advice based on instruction from him. What, then, did Paul say? Once when he was about to be led off to Rome on his final journey, after which he wouldn't see the disciples again, he said: "I won't see you again" (cf. Acts 20.25). He said this not out of a desire to cause grief but to provide security. And so, when he was about to journey away from there, he more or less secured them in this way, saying: "I know that after I leave, savage wolves will enter among you, and men from right among you will rise up and say distorted things" (Acts 20.29, 30). The war was threefold: the nature of the wild animals; the severity of the war; that those doing the warring were not foreign but actually his own people. For this reason it was more severe. With reason. For if someone from outside was to assault me and war against me, I would be able to subvert that person easily. But if the ulcer arises from the body internally, the evil is difficult to cure. This is in fact what happened then. Which is why he gave advice, saying: "Pay attention to yourselves and to the whole flock" (Acts 20.28). He did not say: "Abandon the sheep and flee outside."

10   It was on the basis, too, of this training that blessed Eustathius gave advice to his own disciples. So, when this wise and noble teacher[9] heard this advice, he brought the theory to fruition in practice. At any rate, when they invaded, he didn't abandon the sheep, even though he hadn't ascended to the throne of office.[10] But this was nothing for that noble and philosophical soul. My point is, while he gave up the honors officials enjoy to others, he himself undertook the officials' duties, circulating inside among the wolves. For the wild animal's teeth didn't harm him at all, so much stronger was the faith he possessed than their bites. And so, by circulating inside and occupying them all with the war being conducted against him, he prepared considerable security for the sheep. He didn't just do this by blocking up their mouths, stopping short their blasphemies, but he also went around the lambs themselves and got to know whether anyone had taken a hit, whether anyone had received a severe wound, and immediately applied the medication. Truly, by doing these things he fermented everyone into the true faith, and he didn't give up until God provided blessed Meletius to come and take the whole dough. The former sowed the seed, the latter came and harvested it. So too did it happen in the case of Moses and Aaron. For truly they too, by circulating like a yeast in the midst of the Egyptians, made many people enthusiasts of their own piety. And Moses is a witness to this when he says that a very mixed group of people went up in the company of the Israelites (cf. Ex 12.38). Copying Moses, this man too performed the tasks attached to the office

[9]I.e., Flavian, the current bishop of Antioch, who is apparently within the audience. John is probably pointing to him at this moment.

[10]I.e., the office of bishop. John tends in his homilies to use the throne on which the bishop sat in the church and which symbolized his authority, as a periphrasis for the episcopal office.

before [he possessed] the office. For truly he (sc. Moses), though not yet entrusted with the leadership of the people, punished the wrong-doers very vigorously and nobly, defended those wronged, and abandoning a royal table and honors and high status, ran off to the mud and brick-making, in the belief that caring for his own people was of greater honor than any luxury and leisure and honor. With his eyes on [Moses] he (sc. Flavian) too at that time reproved all officials with his care for the people and before leisure put hard work and constantly being driven out of every place, while attracting hostility day after day. But for him everything was easy to bear. For the pretext for the events provided him with sufficient comfort for what occurred. Let's give thanks to God for all these blessings and become enthusiasts of the virtues of these saints, so that we too may share their crowns with them, through the grace and loving kindness of our Lord, Jesus Christ, through whom and with whom to the Father, together with the Holy Spirit, be glory, honor, and power forever and ever. Amen.

On Saint Lucian

Delivered on 7 January, since in the course of the homily John says that the Feast of Epiphany was celebrated yesterday, it is probable also that this homily was preached at Antioch. Although there are no certain grounds for asserting this,[1] Lucian is closely associated with Antioch historically and the cult was by John's time presumably well established in the local festival calendar. It is also possible that the "mother" referred to in the opening paragraph is to be identified with the Old Church (the *Palaia*) at Antioch, since the same language is used of this church in *On the beginning of Acts hom. 2*.[2] If this is the case, then the particular celebration of Epiphany at which John preached in the year in question was celebrated in the Old Church, rather than the Great Church at Antioch. It is unclear, on the other hand, in precisely which church or martyrium the present festival of St Lucian is being celebrated.

John's account of Lucian's martyrdom is one of the earliest that survives. In stating that Lucian died of starvation, after insistently

[1] For the argument that the opening of the homily recalls John's opening remarks in his only surviving Epiphany sermon (*De baptismo Christi*, CPG 4355, delivered in Antioch probably on 6 January 387), to the effect that he grieves because he knows that tomorrow the majority of the crowd present today will stay away again until the next major festival, see the summary of Montfaucon in W. Mayer, *The Homilies of St John Chrysostom–Provenance. Reshaping the Foundations*, OrChrAn 273 (Rome, 2005), 80. The connection is by no means as secure as scholars assume, since John may have made the same complaint every year, while only the one Epiphany sermon survives. The vocabulary used when he recalls his complaint of the previous day does reflect that used in the Epiphany homily, but the recollection is far too brief and the vocabulary too common to allow the drawing of any firm conclusion.

[2] "After a long interval, we have returned again to our mother . . . to the mother of ourselves and of all the churches (sc. in Antioch). I mean that [she is] 'mother,' not because she is older in time, but because she was founded by the hands of the apostles." (PG 51.77 ll.1–6).

uttering the confession "I am a Christian," it matches the fifth-century account of Philostorgius, an Arian church historian. Philostorgius is in turn followed closely by Symeon Metaphrastes (*BHG* 997), who provides a report of Lucian's life that is, however, much expanded, particularly in regard to events after Lucian's death. There also exists an unedited version of his life (*BHG* 996z), which apparently varies from that offered by Philostorgius and Symeon, in that Lucian is not arrested in Antioch before being imprisoned in Nicomedia, but leaves Antioch voluntarily to spread Christianity in Asia Minor.[3] The sources generally agree that Lucian was originally a citizen of Samosata in Syria, who dedicated himself to the ascetic life, was later ordained a presbyter in Antioch, and died in Nicomedia probably in 312 under the emperor Maximinus Daia. His death is said to have occurred on the day after Epiphany.[4]

What is of particular interest here is the adoption of Lucian as a saint in the calendar of this faction of the Nicene community. In his wholehearted embrace of Lucian as a martyr, John ignores the fact that Lucian taught at Antioch a radical subordinationism that anticipated Arius. This is especially noteworthy, when we consider that in several of his other martyr homilies John is at pains to address the heresy of subordinationism and makes pointed reference to the teachings of Arius. It may be this difficulty that causes John, who may simply have inherited the commemoration of the saint within the local calendar, to emphasize so firmly in this instance the central performative and ritual speech act of the martyr: "I am a Christian."[5] The repetition of this definitive confession here has the effect of bringing Lucian's status as a martyr to the fore and takes attention away from (and perhaps even nullifies) any other consideration.

---

[3]Jacques Noret, "S. Lucien, disciple de s. Lucien d'Antioche. A propos d'une inscription de Kirsehir (Turquie)," AnBoll 91 (1973): 370–6, who surveys the hagiographical literature on Lucian, believes that this latter account could date to as early as the fourth or fifth century.

[4]See also Eusebius, *HE* 9.6.3.

[5]See Boyarin, *Dying for God*, 95.

Contents:

1–4. John's fears of yesterday have been realized today. Attendance is much smaller. He concentrates on persuading the audience of the benefits of attending church. Today particular blessings attach to attending church, because of the martyr.

5–6. Yesterday was the day of Jesus' baptism; today is a martyr's day. In the case of this martyr none of the usual tortures worked, so the Devil aimed at a torture that was both lengthy and excruciating—starvation.

7–8. Starvation had no effect, so the Devil added to the torture by tempting the martyr with food that had been sacrificed to pagan gods. When this had no effect the martyr was taken back to court and interrogated. To each question he replied only: "I am a Christian." Having at the same time answered the questions and confessed his faith in this way, he died.

9. John exhorts the audience to train themselves, even though it is not a time of persecution, and to imitate the martyr through control of the stomach and through confessing the faith in front of Greeks.

Translated from PG 50.519–526.

Homily of praise on the holy martyr Lucian

1   That which I feared yesterday has happened and now come to pass. When the festival finished,[6] in a mass the crowd left us and our gathering became smaller. Even though I knew with certainty that this would happen, that doesn't mean that because of it I kept away from giving advice. For even if not everyone in the audience yesterday was persuaded, yet not everyone was unconvinced. This is no small reason for comfort for us. For that reason neither shall I keep away from this advice today. After all, even if they don't hear it via us, they'll certainly, at least, hear what we've said via you. I mean,

---

[6]I.e., Epiphany, a festival of longer standing and at this time greater importance than Christmas.

who could put up with their great laziness in silence, or concede them pardon or defense when, on seeing their mother after so long a time and enjoying the fine things inside her, they kept away and couldn't bear turning up again for a second time? They mimicked not Noah's dove, but the crow (Gen 8.6–12), and this when the choppy waves and that storm still lingered and the surging waves were intensifying with each successive day, and this holy ark was in front of everyone's eyes and calling everyone and drawing them to herself, and providing considerable safety to those in flight. She beats off not attacks of waters or waves but the constant assaults of utterly irrational passions and removes envy and suppresses arrogance. For here, when they hear from the divine scriptures that "All flesh is grass and all human glory like a grass' flower" (Is 40.6), neither will the rich person be able to ignore the poor person, nor will the poor person, when they too hear another prophet say: "Don't be afraid when a person is rich or when the glory of their house abounds, for when they die they won't take everything nor will their glory accommodate them" (Ps 49. 16–17), be captive to jealousy when they see another person enjoying wealth. For such is the nature of this wealth. It doesn't exchange places along with its possessors, it doesn't depart with those who have it, nor does it assist people there when they're being judged and have to render their accounts, but is instead completely cut off by death. And it has abandoned many even before death. Its use is unreliable, its enjoyment insecure, its possession dangerous.

2   But the elements of virtue and of charity are not like this. Instead, this warehouse is robber-proof. On what basis is this clear? The person who speculated about this wealth and said: "Their glory will not accommodate them after them" (Ps 49.17) educated us too about the warehouses of charity that last forever and are never robbed, when he expressed it this way: "He distributed, he gave to the poor. His righteousness endures for ever" (Ps 111.9). What is more incredible than this? What is gathered perishes, and what is

distributed lasts, and rightly so. For the latter God receives and no one can snatch it from God's hand, while the former is put away in human warehouses, where it is subject to numerous plots, where there is a great deal of envy and jealousy. Don't, then, be careless, beloved, about spending time here. For if some despondency is troubling [you], here it is chased away; if business concerns, they run away; if irrational passions, they are extinguished. We go home from the marketplace and the theater and the other gatherings in the outside world trailing a great number of worries and despondencies and sicknesses of the soul. If you constantly spend time here, you will completely discard those evils which you received out in the world. But if you turn away and flee, you will completely destroy even those blessings you acquired from the divine scriptures, while your wealth is gradually sucked down the drain by the gatherings and conversations in the outside world. And that these assertions are true, when you go home from here make an effort to catch sight of those who stayed away today and you will see how substantial the divide is between your cheerfulness and their despondency.

3   A bride seated in the bridal chamber is not as beautiful and pleasing as a soul that appears in church, giving off spiritual perfumes, is wonderful and glorious. For the person who attends here with faith and dedication goes away taking countless treasures. If they just open their mouth, immediately they fill those in their company with every sweet smell and spiritual wealth. If countless disasters attack, they endure everything easily, having taken away from the divine scriptures here enough of a starting-point for patience and philosophy. And, just as the person who constantly stands on the rock mocks the waves, so the person who enjoys constant worship and is watered by the divine words, seeing that they have stood themselves on the correct assessment of matters as if on a rock, is captured by not a single human matter, in that they have situated themselves above the incursion of day-to-day affairs. They leave, taking countless blessings home, after reaping much benefit and

spiritual guidance not just from admonishment, but also from prayer and from the father's blessing and from a shared assembly and from the love of fellow Christians,[7] and from any number of other things.

4   See, then, what great blessing you will enjoy today, but what great penalty they will be subject to. For while you will go away, having received a reward from martyrs, they, in addition to being stripped of this bonus, will also be subject to another penalty as they trail a lot of litter of worries arising from their pointless pursuits. "Just as the person who welcomes a prophet in a prophet's name, will receive a prophet's reward, the person who welcomes a righteous person in a righteous person's name, will also receive a righteous person's reward" (Mt 10.41). So the person who welcomes a martyr in a martyr's name, will receive a martyr's reward. The welcoming of a martyr is to come together in his memory, to share the story of his contests, to marvel at what happened, to strive to imitate his virtue, to convey to others his brave deeds. These are the host's gifts for the martyrs. In this way one welcomes these saints, just as you too have thus done today.

5   Now then, while yesterday our Master was baptized with water, today his servant is baptized with blood. Yesterday heaven's gates were opened, today Hades' gates were trampled flat. Indeed, don't be astonished if I called his martyrdom a baptism. For in fact here too the Spirit flits around with abundant generosity, and obliteration of sins takes place and a certain wonderful and incredible purification of [the] soul. And, just as those who are being baptized wash in water, so those being martyred wash in their own blood, which is precisely what happened in the case of this man. But before [speaking of] his slaughter it is essential to mention the Devil's cunning. For when he realized that [the martyr] mocked every form of torture and punishment and that he couldn't subvert the saint's philosophy either by

[7] Lit. "brothers [and sisters]."

igniting a furnace or digging a pit or preparing a wheel or leading him up to a stake or hurling him over cliffs or throwing him into the jaws of wild animals, he conceived of another more cruel means and went around seeking to find a torture that would at one and the same time be the most intensely painful and the most drawn out possible. For since, when it comes to punishments, the unbearable ones furnish an extremely quick release, while the more drawn out ones temper the pain, he worked hard to find a punishment that provided both simultaneously—namely, duration and a viciously cruel excess of pain—so that through both the severity and abundance of time he might defeat his (sc. the martyr's) firmness of mind.

6   What did he do? He exposed this saint to starvation. When you hear 'starvation,' don't simply pass over what I've said. For of all deaths this is the cruelest. And those who've had experience are witnesses. No, heaven forbid that we should gain experience! We have been taught well to pray that we not enter into temptation (cf. Mt 26.41). For like an executioner it (sc. starvation) sits inside in the guts and scourges all the limbs, consuming the body all over more fiercely than any fire or wild animal, producing an unrelenting and unspeakable pain. Indeed, that you may learn what starvation is like, often even mothers have made a meal of their children, unable to endure the pressure of this evil. And the prophet spoke of this disaster in tragic tones: "The hands of compassionate women boiled their own children" (Lam 4.10). Mothers ate the ones they gave birth to and the belly that gave birth[8] became the tomb of the children borne, and starvation triumphed over nature. Rather not just nature, but also intent. But it did not triumph over the nobility of this saint. Who wouldn't be amazed at hearing this? And yet what is more powerful than nature? What more finely balanced than intent? But so that you may learn that nothing is stronger than the fear of

[8]Gr. *gastēr*, can mean either womb or stomach, which causes difficulty if one thinks in strictly anatomical terms, since it was the stomach that became the tomb, not the womb. "Belly" allows the play on words while generally preserving the sense of the sentence.

God, intent was seen to be better tuned than nature and, while it (sc. starvation) put mothers on trial and caused them to forget the pain of giving birth, it could not trip up this saint—neither did the punishment subvert his philosophy nor the torture triumph over his courage. Instead, he remained stronger than any adamant, luxuriating in good hope and taking pleasure in the pretext for the competitions, with the starting-point for the contests as sufficient comfort. In particular, day after day he heard Paul saying: "In starvation and thirst, in freezing cold and nakedness" (2 Cor 11.27), and again: "Up to the present hour we are hungry and thirsty and without clothes and being beaten up" (1 Cor 4.11). For he knew, he knew clearly that: "A person shall not live on bread alone, but on every word that issues from God's mouth" (Mt 4.4).

7   When the foul demon saw that he (sc. the martyr) wasn't yielding to the sheer necessity of events, he made the torture yet more cruel. What he did was to take food that had been sacrificed to idols, fill the table with it and have it placed in front of his (sc. the martyr's) eyes, so that the convenience of having it on hand might relax the firmness of his will. After all, when it's not obvious that things are set as bait, we aren't caught in the way that we are when they're lying in front of our eyes. My point is, one would more easily overcome the desire for women, if one wasn't looking at a gorgeous woman or constantly gazing at her. But even so, the just [martyr] triumphed over this ambush too, and what the Devil thought would relax his courage anointed him more than anything for the contests. For not only did he not experience anything at the sight of the food that had been sacrificed to idols, but, even more, he shunned and hated it. And that which we experience in regard to our enemies— the more we look at them, the more, on the contrary, we hate and shun them—this he too experienced at that time in regard to that foul sacrifice. For, on seeing it, he was, on the contrary, disgusted and turned away, and the constant sight inclined him instead towards hatred and avoidance of what lay in front of him. And, even though

starvation was shouting loudly at him from within and urging him
to touch what was lying in front of him, the fear of God stayed his
hands and made him forget nature itself. And when he was looking
at a table foul and polluted, he was reminded of another table, awe-
inspiring and filled with the Spirit, and was so fired up as to prefer
to endure and suffer anything rather than make a meal of those foul
bits of food. He recalled too the table of the three boys who, captured
at an early age and bereft of any supervision, displayed such great
philosophy in an alien land and foreign region that their courage is
sung of up to the present day (cf. Dan 3). And, while the Jews, even
when they were in possession of their own land, were impious and,
though spending time in the temple, worshipped idols, those
youths, though taken away into a foreign land, where there were
idols and grounds for every kind of impiety, worshipped by preserving the culture of their homeland. "So then, if those who were
captives and slaves and young displayed such great philosophy
before [the time of God's] grace," he asked, "what kind of pardon
would we deserve, if we weren't even able to achieve the same virtue
as them?"

8   With these thoughts in mind he mocked the Devil's wickedness,
despised his evildoing, and gave in to not one thing that he saw. So,
when that foul [demon] saw nothing further happening to him, he
escorted him back into court and tortured him and applied incessant questions. But to each question he replied only: "I am a Christian."[9] And when the executioner said: "What country are you
from?," said: "I am a Christian." "What's your occupation?" "I am a
Christian." "Who are your parents?" To everything he said: "I am a
Christian." With this single unadorned statement he struck the
Devil's head and constantly and unremittingly inflicted wounds on
him. Even though he had taken part in the education [offered] in the
outside world, he knew clearly that there was no need for rhetorical

[9]This is the classic confession of the martyr, a declaration at the center of martyr stories in both Latin and Greek tradition (Boyarin, *Dying for God*, 95).

skill in such contests as these, but faith. Not for cleverness of argument, but a God-loving soul. "One statement is sufficient," he said,
"to rout the Devil's entire phalanx." And while to those who don't
scrutinize things precisely his answer seemed to be out of sequence,
if a person is attentive, they would see the martyr's wisdom in this
too. For the person who says "I am a Christian" has revealed both
their country and family history and occupation. Let me explain
how. The Christian does not have a city on earth, but the Jerusalem
in heaven. "For the heavenly Jerusalem, which is our mother," scripture says, "is free" (Gal 4.26). The Christian doesn't have an earthly
occupation, but arrives at the heavenly way of life. "Our citizenship,"
scripture says, "is in heaven" (Phil 3.20). The Christian has as relatives and fellow citizens all the saints. "We are fellow citizens of the
saints," scripture says, "and God's own" (Eph 2.19). In consequence,
with a single statement he taught precisely who he was and from
where and of whom and what he spent his time doing. And with this
utterance he quit his life and departed safe and sound for Christ,
bringing [with him] his deposit and through his experience advising those after him to resist and to fear nothing except just sin and
denying [Christ].

9   Knowing these things, then, let us too in a time of peace practice the exercises of war, so that, when war does arise, we too might
erect a brilliant trophy. He despised starvation, let us too despise
overeating and suppress the stomach's tyranny, so that, if a time were
to come which sought courage of this dimension from us, through
having practiced in advance in the lesser events, we might appear
brilliant in the wrestling ring. He boldly addressed prefects and
emperors. This, too, let us now do, and even if we are seated among
meetings of rich and illustrious Greeks, let us confess the faith with
boldness. Let us mock their error. Even if they attempt to exalt their
[beliefs] and purge ours, let us not keep silent nor take it meekly, but
reveal their shamelessness and praise in hymns every Christian
belief with great wisdom and boldness. Indeed, just as the emperor

carries his diadem around on his head, let us, too, carry around our confession of faith everywhere. For his crown doesn't adorn him in the same way as our faith and our confession of it usually adorn us. Let us do this not just through words, but also through actions themselves and demonstrate through everything a life worthy of that confession, so that we don't cast shame on our teachings in the poor quality of our works, but rather, in glorifying our Master through everything, enjoy honor both here and there. May we attain all these things through the grace and loving kindness of our Lord Jesus Christ, through whom and with whom be glory, power, and honor to the Father, together with the holy and life-creating Spirit, now and always, and forever and ever. Amen.

On Saint Phocas

That this homily was delivered in Constantinople is evident both from the fact that the emperor and empress will be present when the relics arrive at the martyrs' tomb and from the topography. The waters that immediately surrounded Constantinople played an important role in both imperial and liturgical ceremonial and the displaying of Phocas' remains in procession throughout both the landmass of the city and its waters in a two-day celebration, escorted on this second day by a lamp-lit flotilla of boats, is not untypical for this region.[1] The term used to refer to the imperial couple (*basileis*) and the fact that they are both said to wear a diadem may imply that the empress Eudoxia had already been elevated to the status of *Augusta*, in which case, like *Homily delivered after the remains of martyrs*,[2] *On St Phocas* dates to after 9 January 400 CE. In both these homilies the imperial couple are intimately involved in the ceremonies surrounding the reception in Constantinople of newly translated remains. Since, because of the history of the city, Constantinople had few martyrs of its own, the acquisition of relics and associated establishment of new martyr cults became a significant feature in the life of the city in the second half of the fourth century.

The major question here is the identity of the Phocas mentioned in the homily title. Aside from the information that the martyr came from Pontus, the homily tells us nothing of his life. It is possible that this had been recounted as part of the liturgy on the previous day, in which case John is safe here in assuming that the audience is familiar with the martyr's story. According to *BHG* 1535ff there were two

[1]See W. Mayer, "The Sea Made Holy. The Liturgical Function of the Waters surrounding Constantinople," *Ephemerides Liturgicae* 112 (1998) 459–68.

[2]*CPG* 4441.1: Mayer-Allen, *John Chrysostom,* 85–92.

martyrs from Sinope in Pontus named Phocas, one of whom was the bishop of Sinope, who was martyred under Trajan. It is to the latter tradition that it ascribes John's homily. If this is the case, then the Phocas whose remains are received by John at Constantinople differs from the Phocas, gardener and patron of sailors, celebrated by Asterius of Amasea in a homily delivered c. 400 CE.[3] Dehandschutter, following the editor of that homily, Datema, however, assumes that the Phocas of both homilies is one and the same.[4]

As already mentioned, in this homily John tells us little about the life of Phocas. He begins by talking about the forthcoming events of the day and encourages everyone to participate. The psalm for the occasion then leads him to digress onto the issue of Christ's nature and to address the belief of the Anomoeans that Christ and God are not equal. It is this latter concern which takes up the bulk of the homily. As is typical for a major martyr's festival, the church is full.

Contents:

1. Yesterday a martyr from Pontus was escorted through the main areas of the city; today he is being escorted across the sea to his own resting-place. Not everyone was present yesterday to receive his blessing.

2. John encourages everyone to attend today's festival and make their way to the tomb, where the imperial couple will participate. The power of martyrs is such that it draws people of all backgrounds and is the Church's crown. The martyrs are not honored by the size of the crowd; rather the crowd is blessed by them.

3. Today's festivities involve setting out on the sea with lamps which will reflect in the water. The church is packed. The Church is likened to a merchant ship.

4. Today's psalm leads us into battles against heretics. The attack is not against the person but the heresy. In doing this John imitates Christ.

5. The example of King Jeroboam.

---

[3]Translated in Leemans et al., *"Let Us Die that We May Live,"* 168–73.
[4]Leemans et al., *"Let Us Die that We May Live,"* 167.

6–8. The audience is asked to pay attention, as John is about to wrestle with the heretics. The heretics interpret scripture in a way that suits them. Christ's true nature is not affected by their claims.

9–11. Scripture is not responsible for the heretics' interpretation, but the mind of those doing the interpreting. In their desire to show that the Son is less than the Father, they attribute different labels, saying that "God" refers to the one, and "Lord" to the other. John uses logic to show that "God" and "Lord" are one and the same.

12. The audience is asked to remember what has been said and to take the arguments of the sermon home to their wives for the dinner table.

Translated from PG 50.699–706.

On the very holy martyr Phocas, and against heretics,
and on Psalm 141: "With my voice I cried out to the Lord,
with my voice I made supplication to God."

1   Yesterday our city was magnificent, magnificent and renowned not because it has columns, but because a martyr was in our midst, ceremoniously conveyed to us from Pontus. He observed your hospitality and filled you with his blessing. He praised your enthusiasm and blessed the people present. He blessed those who gathered and shared his sweet smell, and cursed those who kept away. Rather, so that their fault doesn't go uncured, again on a second day we herald him so that those who kept away out of laziness will double with their zeal too the blessing [radiating] from the martyr. For, indeed, I shan't stop saying what I've often said: I'm not demanding an account of their sins; rather, I'm preparing medicines for the sick.[5] Did you keep away yesterday? At least come today, so that you might see him escorted off to his own location. Did you see him as he was escorted through the market place? See him sailing across the sea as

---

[5]For a similar sentiment see *On his return* § 5 (Mayer-Allen, *John Chrysostom*, 99).

well, so that each of the two elements might be filled with the blessing [that radiates] from him.

2   Let no one keep away from this holy festival. Let no virgin
remain at home, let no married woman stick to the house. Let's
empty the city, and set course for the martyr's tomb. After all, the
imperial couple, too, are joining with us in the festivities. What
excuse, then, does the private person have, when the imperial couple are quitting the palace and taking a seat at the martyr's tomb? For
the nature of the martyrs' power is such that it catches in its net not
just private persons, but those who wear the diadems. This [power
is] a source of shame for the Greeks, this [power is] the censure of
their error, this [power is] the total annihilation of demons. This
[power is] our nobility, and the Church's crown. I celebrate with
martyrs and instead of at [the sight of] meadows skip at the sight of
their trophy, because instead of springs [of water] they poured forth
blood. Their bones were consumed and yet their memory becomes
fresher with every day. My point is that just as the sun cannot in any
way be extinguished, so too the martyrs' memory. For Christ himself revealed: "The heaven and the earth will pass away, but my words
will not pass away" (Mt 24.35). But let's put off our praises of the
martyr until the appropriate moment. For truly what's been said is
enough for the benefit of those who ought to assemble and make the
day of the festival renowned. For what I said yesterday, I say again
today, too, namely that while no glory will attach to the martyr from
the attendance of large numbers, the blessing to you from being in
the martyr's presence will be substantial. For just as the person who
looks towards the sun doesn't make that star more brilliant, but
floods their own eyes with light; so, too, then, the person who honors a martyr doesn't make him more radiant, but draws from him
the light's blessing.

3   Let's again make of the sea a church by going out there with
torches, both getting the fire wet and setting the water on fire. Let no
one be afraid of the sea. The martyr wasn't afraid of death and you're

scared of the water? But, we've said enough on that point. Come, and from what's been said today let's furnish for you the customary table. For even if our bodies are packed tight, even so let our minds take wing. I don't even see your discomfort, but your enthusiasm. For a sea billowing with waves is a pleasure to a helmsman, and to a preacher, a church flooding its banks. I say this because in these waters there is neither spume nor rock nor sea monsters, but a sea and ocean brimming with a sweet smell. Here the ship doesn't [sail] from landfall to landfall, but has its course set from earth towards heaven; not with a cargo of money—not gold nor silver— but faith and love and zeal and wisdom.

4   Come, then, with precision let's launch the ship that never perishes nor sustains shipwreck. But pay precise attention to what's being said. For today the psalm leads us out into battle array against the heretics, not so that we might fell them as they stand, but so that we might raise them up from their fallen state. I mean, that's how our battle works. It doesn't make corpses of the living, but fashions living people of the dead, brimming [as it is] with gentleness and considerable kindness. For I don't hound in reality, but pursue verbally, not the heretic, but the heresy. I don't reject the person, but hate the error and want it to be overturned. My fight is not with substance. For substance is a work of God. Rather, I want to set straight the thinking which the Devil destroyed. In this way, too, a doctor in healing a sick person doesn't fight the body, but relieves the body of the impurity. Thus, if I am about to do battle with heretics, I, too, don't fight the people themselves, but want to throw out the error and clean out the putrefaction. It's my habit to be pursued and not to pursue, to be hounded and not to hound. This is the way, too, that Christ succeeded, not by crucifying, but by being crucified; not by striking, but by being struck. "If I have spoken wrongly," he says, "testify to that wrong. If properly, why are you laying into me?" (Jn 18.23). The Master of the world speaks in his own defense against the high priest's servant, even though the mouth from which he

uttered words and curbed the sea and raised Lazarus from the dead
after four days had been struck: [the same mouth] which put evils
to flight, which dissolved sicknesses and sins. This is the miracle of
the one who was crucified. For indeed, although capable of releas-
ing a thunderbolt and shaking the earth and shriveling the servant's
hand, he did none of these things; instead, he spoke in his own
defense and achieved success with mildness, teaching you, who are
a human being, never to fight back. In consequence, even if you're
crucified, even if you sustain a beating, say like your Master: "If I
have spoken wrongly, testify to that wrong; if properly, why are you
laying into me?" Truly, observe his loving kindness: how for that
which affects his servants he retaliates, while that which relates to
himself he lets pass.

5   There was once a prophet and he countered a king who was acting impiously, and he went and said: "Altar, altar, listen!" (3 Kgs 13.2).
For when King Jeroboam was standing and offering a sacrifice to the
idols, the prophet went up and addressed the altar. What are you
doing, prophet? You've dismissed the man and are addressing the
altar? "Yes," he says. For what reason? "I'm dismissing him, because
the man has become more insensate than a stone, and I'm addressing this (altar) so that you may learn that the stone listens, but the
man does not." "Listen, altar, listen!" and at once the altar shattered.
The king stretched out his hand, wanting to grab the prophet and he
wasn't able to contract it. Do you see that it was rather the altar that
listened than the king? Do you see that he dismissed the being with
reason and addressed the one without reason so that through its
obedience he might correct [that man's] insensibility and wickedness? The altar shattered and the king's wickedness did not shatter.
But see what happened! The king stretched out his hand to grab the
prophet and at once his hand shriveled up. Seeing that he didn't
improve through the penalty paid by the altar, he was taught obedience to God through his own particular punishment. "For I wanted
to spare you and release my rage on a stone, but since the stone didn't

become your teacher, you take the penalty!" And he stretched out his hand and in an instant it shriveled up. From that point the prophet's trophy[6] stood firm and the king couldn't contract [his hand]. Where was his diadem? Where his purple robes? Where his breastplates? Where his shields? Where his army? Where his spears? God gave the command and all of that was destroyed. The satraps stood next to him but couldn't assist; they were simply observers of the blow. And the king stretched out his hand and it shriveled up. When it became dry, then it bore fruit. I ask you to consider the example of the tree in paradise and the wood in the cross.[7] My point is that just as the first tree, though green, bore death, the wood of the cross, though dry, gave birth to life. So, too, in the case of the king's hand, when it was green, then it bore impiety. When it became dry, then it employed obedience. See the incredible affairs of God!

6   But, as I was saying, when [Christ] was struck he did nothing bad to the person who struck him. But when his servant was about to be physically abused, he punished the king, teaching you that while he retaliates in regard to God's affairs, he lets his own pass. "Just as I let my own affairs pass, but retaliate in yours, so you, too, retaliate in mine, but let your own pass." But, please, strain your ears (for where a time for contests [arises], it requires an audience who has their ears at alert) so that you may know precisely how I imprison, how I forgive the sins of my opponents, how I wrestle, how I strike. After all, if the people seated in the theater crane their necks at two wrestlers, straining their sight and physique in order to watch wrestling matches full of shame, to watch wrestling bouts which mimic shame, by far the more should we pay attention to hearing the divine scriptures. My point is that, if you praise the athlete, why don't you become an athlete? If you're ashamed of being an athlete, why do you mimic the praise of them? But here there aren't

---

[6]In battle, symbols of the enemy's defeat (such as spears, helmets and shields) were erected on the battlefield as a public advertisement of the winner's victory.

[7]The Greek noun *xylon* is used throughout this passage, which bears the sense of both "wood" and "tree."

those kind of wrestling matches; instead, they are open and useful to everyone, both to those who speak and those who listen. My point is that I wrestle with the heretic so that I might turn you, too, into athletes, so that not just by chanting psalms,[8] but also in conversation you might snatch away their tongue.

7   So what does the prophet say? "With my voice I cried out to the Lord, with my voice I made supplication to God" (Ps 141.1). Pay attention! Doesn't it seem that the lection offers a pretext for wrestling matches? Watch how I weave the crown and the basis for the contests. "With my voice I cried out to the Lord, with my voice I made supplication to God." Summon the heretic here for me, whether they're present or not. I say this because, if they are present, let them learn from my voice. And if they're not present, let them learn through your listening. But, as I said, I don't hound them when present, but welcome them when hounded [here], not by us, but by their own conscience, according to scripture: "The impious person flees although no one is pursuing" (Prov 28.1). The Church is mother of her own children, and she welcomes them and wraps her bosom around strangers. Noah's ark was an open theater, but the Church is even better than that. For while it took irrational animals and preserved them as irrational animals, this [theater (sc. the Church)] receives irrational animals and transforms them. For example, if a heretical fox enters here, I make that person a sheep. If a wolf enters, for my part I make them a lamb. But if they're unwilling, it's nothing to do with me, but due to their obstinacy. Since Christ, too, had twelve disciples, and one became a traitor, but not due to Christ, but to his damaged mind. Since Elisha, too, had a greedy pupil (4 Kgs 5.20ff),

[8]This may be an allusion to the night-time processions at Constantinople instituted by John to counteract those held by the Arians. The Arian practice of processing through the city singing pro-Arian propaganda arose after the Arians were banned from worshipping within the city precincts in the early 380s by the emperor Theodosius I. An important feature of the Nicene processions was the singing of anti-Arian material, in which presumably the psalms featured, as they did during the processions associated with martyr festivals (see, e.g., *Hom. delivered after the remains of martyrs*, Mayer-Allen, *John Chrysostom,* 91).

but not due to the teacher's weakness, but the pupil's laziness. I throw down the seeds. If you who receive the seeds are fertile land, you yield mature ears of grain. If you are sterile rock, it's nothing to do with me. Whether you listen, whether you don't listen, I shan't stop singing you a spiritual song, bathing your wounds, lest I hear on that day: "Wicked servant, you should have invested my money with the bankers" (Mt 25.26). "With my voice I cried out to the Lord, with my voice I made supplication to God."

8   What are you saying, heretic? About whom does the prophet speak, and whom does he call Lord and God? For the statement concerns a single person.[9] I say this because they (sc. the heretics) twist the scriptures on their head and are constantly searching for pieces of argument contrary to their own salvation and so don't notice that they're thrusting themselves into a pit of destruction. My point is that neither the person who hails the Son of God makes (him) more glorious nor does the person who defames [him] do [him] harm. For the bodiless substance[10] has no need of our acclamation. Rather, just as the person who says the sun is brilliant doesn't add anything to its light nor the person who says [it's] dark diminish its substance, but instead provides clear proof of their own physical disability, so the person who says that the Son of God is not Son, but a created being, provides demonstration of their own madness, while the person who recognizes his substance demonstrates their own sound judgment. And neither the latter benefits him nor the former harms him, but the one person contests against their own salvation, while the other contests for the benefit of their own salvation. But as I was saying, twisting the scriptures they ignore everything else while they look to see whether they might locate a piece of argument that seems in some way to agree with their sickness. And don't tell me that scripture is responsible. It's not scripture that's responsible, but their lack of

[9]Gr. *prosōpon* is a technical theological term used in the arguments concerning the relationship between Christ and God within the Trinity. John moves here to address the claim of the Arians and semi-Arians that the Son and the Father are not equal.

[10]Gr. *ousia*. Again a technical theological term central to christological debates.

judgment, since honey is in fact sweet, but the sick person thinks it bitter. But that's not the fault of the honey, but an indictment of the illness. So, too, those who are mentally disturbed don't see what's visible, but the fault lies not with what's visible; rather it's the damaged mind of the person who is mentally disturbed. God made the heavens so that we might see the work and adore the Creator, but the Greeks made of the work a god. Yet it's not the work that's responsible, but their lack of judgment. Indeed, just as the person with poor judgment is helped by no one, so the person with sound judgment is helped even by themselves. What is equal to Christ? Yet Judas was not helped. What's more wicked than the Devil? Yet Job was crowned. Indeed, neither did Christ help Judas, since he had poor judgment, nor did the Devil harm Job, since he had sound judgment. I make these comments so that no one slanders the scriptures, but the poor judgment of those who interpret badly that which is stated well. For even the Devil conversed with Christ from scripture.

9   But it's not scripture that's responsible but the mind that interprets badly what's stated well. My point is that, in their desire to show that the Son is less than the Father they (sc. the heretics) go around fiddling with strange labels, and say of "God and Lord" that the Father is "God," but the Son is "Lord" and divide the labels and assign "God" to the Father, but "Lord" to the Son, with the result that they are dividers and distributors of the godhead. Does scripture address the Son as "Lord"? Does it say these things? How didn't you hear the psalm addressing one person today: "With my voice I cried out to the Lord, with my voice I made supplication to God?" In fact, then, it names him both Lord and God. Whom do you want God to be—the Son or the Father? Absolutely you'll say that these labels are the Father's. Therefore "God" is the Son, and "Lord" the Father. Why, then, do you divide the labels and in that case throw them together, but in this divide (them)? Indeed Paul says (would that you listened to Paul and were blessed): "But we have one God the Father from whom all things [exist], and one Lord Jesus Christ, through whom

all things [exist]" (1 Cor 8.6). Did he call the Son "God"? Well, what? "Lord." Tell me, why is "God" more reverent than "Lord," and "Lord" less than "God"? Please, pay close attention! Thus, if I were to show that "Lord" and "God" are one, what do you say? Do you say that "God" is greater, "Lord" less? Listen to the prophet who says: "This is the Lord who made heaven, this is God who constructed the earth" (Is 45.18). "Lord" [made] the heaven and "God" the earth. He (sc. Isaiah) situated Lord and God in the same person. And again: "Hear, Israel, the Lord your God is one Lord" (Deut 6.4). Twice "Lord" and once "God;" and first "Lord" and then "God," and again "Lord." If the first [label] is inferior, the second greater, he wouldn't have placed the lesser first in addressing great substance and greater divine rationality, but would have been content to mention the greater [label] and wouldn't have thrown in the lesser.

10   Have you understood what I've said? I instruct [you] again. For this isn't a spectacle for display, but preaching directed at contrition, not so that you go away unarmed, but so that you'll leave ready for battle. You say, heretic, that "God" is greater and "Lord" lesser? I showed you the prophet who says: "It's the Lord who made heaven, God who constructed the earth." I showed you in turn Moses, who says: "Hear, Israel, the Lord your God is one Lord." How [can he be] one, if there are two labels, the one of lesser, the other of greater substance? For substance isn't greater or lesser than itself, but equal and connected. "The Lord your God is one Lord." Indeed, let me show you that the label "Lord" is God. In sum, if "Lord" is inferior, but "God" is greater, what sort of label ought his to be? "Lord," which is less significant, or "God," which is greater? If he were to say: "What kind of label is mine?," what do you say, heretic? Do you say that "Lord" belongs to the Son, "God" to the Father, as more appropriate? So, if I were to show you that "Lord," which is insignificant, is capable of imparting knowledge of him,[11] what do you do? "Let it be known that

---

[11]Gr. *gnōristikon.* Throughout this latter part of the homily John borrows extensively from the vocabulary of Neoplatonic philosophy.

your name is Lord" (Ps 82.19), says the prophet. He didn't say "God?"
And yet if "God" is greater, why didn't the prophet say: "Let it be
known that your name is God"? For if "God" is natural and appropriate to him, while "Lord" is foreign to him, on the grounds that it's
inferior, why did he say: "Let it be known that your name is Lord"—
the insignificant, the lesser, the (label) inferior in dignity—and does-
n't mention that great and lofty [label], that [label] worthy of his
substance? Indeed, that you may learn that this [label] is not insignificant nor inferior, but has the same force: "Let it be known that your
name is Lord, you alone are the most high over all the earth."

11   But still you don't step away from the fight, but say again:
" 'God' is greater, 'Lord' lesser." So, if I were to show that the Son is
addressed by the greater label, what do you say? Do you end the
fight? Do you step away from your competitiveness? Do you come
to a sense of your salvation? Are you released from your madness?
Have you understood what I've said? After all, they attach the label
"Lord" to the Son, but "God" to the Father on the grounds of [its]
being greater. If, then, I were to show you the Son addressed by the
greater name of "God," the fight would be ended. For with your own
weapons I subdue you, and with your own flanks I subvert you. You
said that "God" is greater, "Lord" lesser. I want to show that the lesser
didn't fit the Father, if he was greater, and the greater didn't fit the
Son, if the Son was lesser. Listen to the prophet when he says: "This
is our God. No other [God] will be considered in addition to him.
He discovered every path of knowledge. After these events he
appeared on earth, and lived among human beings" (Bar 3.36–38).
What do you say to this? Do you contest these words? But you can't.
For the truth persists and sends forth its own radiance and blinds the
sight of the heretics who don't want to believe in it.

12   Certainly the wrestling matches are complicated and the heat
considerable, but the sermon is greater and overcomes the listeners'
distress and soothes the heat with the dew of preaching. Even if we
gather (only) once or twice a week, the listener shouldn't get lazy. For

if you leave here and someone says to you: "What topic did the preacher pursue?," you should say: "He addressed heretics." If the person says to you: "What topic did he pursue?" and you can't come up with it, the shame that attaches to you is considerable. But if you say [it], you bite them and, if they're a heretic, you set them straight, if a friend who's lazy, you drag them along, if it's an incorrigible wife, you make her more modest. For, after all, you are responsible for [your] wife. "Let women," scripture says, "be silent in church. And if they want to learn anything, let them question their own husbands" (1 Cor 14.34–35). If you enter the house and your wife asks you: "What did you bring me from church?," say to her "No meat, no wine, no money, nor cosmetics that make the body beautiful, but a message that improves the mind." When you go indoors to your wife, set the spiritual table. Speak first, while the memory is fresh. Let us [first] enjoy the spiritual [table], and then enjoy the table we can see. For truly, if we look after our own affairs in this way, we shall have God, too, in our midst blessing the table and crowning us. Let us give thanks for all these blessings to the Father himself, together with the Son and the Holy Spirit, now and always, and forever and ever. Amen.

On Saints Juventinus and Maximinus

Despite the general belief that it was preached in Antioch shortly after 24 January 388, since in the opening words of the homily John says that Babylas and the three youths recently caused the audience to assemble at the present location (presumed to be a reference to John's homily *On Babylas* [*CPG* 4347]),[1] the sermon *On saints Juventinus and Maximinus* is unfortunately not so easily dated. As argued in relation to *On Babylas*, there is now some dispute about the sequence of the group of homilies in relation to which the latter is usually dated, which casts uncertainty on the traditional belief that this latter homily was delivered in 388.[2] At the same time, in the present homily John clearly mentions that the festival that drew them to the present location a short while ago included the three youths from the fiery furnace. While there is indeed an association between Babylas and these "martyrs" in the early martyrologies,[3] there is no mention of them in *On Babylas*. While it is not impossible that John could preach about the one and not the others on a festival that celebrates both, the silence in that homily counsels caution in assuming that it must have been the homily delivered on the occasion referred to. At the same time, John's remark in § 2 that he recently spoke about the same impious emperor (in the homily *On Babylas* events in the time of Julian feature prominently) does not necessarily add weight to this possibility since the destruction of the temple of Apollo in the time

[1]For the consensus see Mayer, *The Homilies of St John Chrysostom–Provenance*, Table 13b (*CPG* 4347).

[2]Leemans et al., *"Let Us Die that We May Live,"* 141.

[3]See M. Vinson, "Gregory Nazianzen's Homily 15 and the Genesis of the Christian Cult of the Maccabean Martyrs," *Byzantion* 64 (1994): 174 n. 26. The Syrian martyrology, which is early in date and close to the time of Chrysostom, locates the three boys with Babylas on January 24 (Wright, 424).

of Julian is central to Babylas' history and was probably related annually. On the other hand, the information that the present festival occurred shortly after that of Babylas does suggest that the date for the festival of Juventinus and Maximinus that appears in two Syriac Jacobite calendars (29 January) is plausible.[4]

Like Lucian, who had been a presbyter of Antioch, Juventinus and Maximinus have a close connection to the city. They were imperial shield-bearers who were based in Antioch at the time of their death, as a result of the emperor Julian's residency there (361–363). Theodoret records that they were overheard making a comment at a drinking party, which was construed as hostile to the emperor's religious policies. One of their companions at the party took note and informed the emperor. The two soldiers were interrogated, confirmed their comments and their status as Christians, and were charged with insulting the emperor. The harsh tortures meted out resulted in their death (*HE* 3.15). John's account is more specific, in claiming that they were beheaded. Theodoret further says that the city of Antioch embraced them as martyrs, placed them in a splendid tomb, and that they were still honored annually with a festival early in the fifth century.

It is curious that in the case of this festival the liturgical celebrations do not appear to have been held at the tomb of the martyrs, as usual, but in the Church of St Babylas. Two factors suggest this. In the opening of the homily John says that Babylas recently drew the audience to the same location, and in his closing remarks he encourages the audience to visit the relics of Juventinus and Maximinus regularly, referring to them not as "here," but "there." Since he usually refers to the coffin or relics as "here" in festival homilies preached at a specific martyr's tomb, this comment reinforces the notion that we are at present in the Church of St Babylas and that the two soldier saints are buried locally, but elsewhere.

[4]There is no report of their festival in earlier calendars or martyrologies. See P. Peeters, "La date de la fête des ss. Juventin et Maximin," AnBoll 42 (1924): 77–82.

Contents:

1. While Babylas was the occasion for the recent gathering at this location, today a pair of soldier saints is the attraction. Their martyrdom is recent, and occurred after the time of persecution, but is no less enthusiastically honored.

2–3. Before relating their death, John explains the emperor Julian's strategy at the time, which was aimed at avoiding creating martyrs of those who disagreed with his religious policies.

4–5. In that climate the martyrs happened to attend a military drinking party at which they bemoaned the emperor's adoption of Greco-Roman religious practices over Christianity. They were overheard and their words reported to the emperor, who had their assets confiscated, and the two soldiers stripped and taken to prison.

6–8. Having contact with them was forbidden, but everyone defied the command and met regularly with them in prison. In response the emperor sent covert agents to talk them out of their stance and wear them down. When they were unsuccessful, he had the two soldiers led away in the middle of the night and beheaded.

9–10. People who hunt relics rescued the bodies and had them buried together in a single coffin. John encourages the audience to visit their tomb constantly to receive the blessings that flow from them.

Translated from PG 50.571–578.

*Homily of praise of [John Chrysostom] on the
holy martyrs Juventinus and Maximinus who were
martyred under Julian the Apostate*

1   Blessed Babylas, along with three children, recently drew us together here. Today it is a matched pair of soldier saints that has stationed Christ's army in battle array. Then [it was] a four-horse team of martyrs; now [it is] a matched pair of martyrs. They are different

in age, but one in faith. Of different kinds are their wrestling matches, but their courage the same. Those are old in time, these young and recent. Of such a nature is the Church's treasure, containing young and old pearls. But the beauty of all of them is one and the same. Their bloom doesn't fade, it doesn't flow away with time. By nature this brilliance doesn't succumb to age's rust. For whereas physical riches fade and pass away with the passage of time—indeed, clothes wear out and houses collapse and jewelry rusts, and with time the entire essence of these riches we see and touch perishes and vanishes—in the case of the spiritual treasures it is not like this. Rather, the martyrs always and perpetually remain brilliant in equal vigor and youth, brightly reflecting the glory of their innate brilliance. What's more, knowing this fact, you do not honor the old ones in one way, the new ones in another. Instead, you honor and welcome them all with the same eagerness, with the same love, with the same disposition. For you don't scrutinize time, but look for courage and a pious spirit and unswerving faith, and an excited and keen enthusiasm, and such qualities as those who today draw us together displayed. I mean, they so bubbled over with a longing for God that without persecution they were able to weave for themselves martyrdom's crown, without battle to erect a trophy, without war to invoke victory, without engaging to snatch the prize. As to how they did it, let me tell you. But [first] bear with me as I go back a little in the story.

2   There was an emperor in our generation, who outdid all those who came before him in impiety, about whom I spoke to you recently as well. This emperor, on seeing that our affairs were famous on this account—I mean, the death of martyrs: and not just men, but also tender children, and unmarried virgins and, in a word, every age group and gender each leaping at being killed for the sake of piety—was stung and grieved, [but] unwilling to sound the battle openly. "For," he said, "everyone will come flying at martyrdom like bees at a honeycomb." In fact, he had learnt this not from someone else, but from his own predecessors. It is indeed the case that tyrants

made war on the Church and peoples perpetually rebelled because the spark of piety was still slender. But even so, it wasn't extinguished, nor destroyed. Rather, it was they themselves (sc. the tyrants) who were destroyed, while that spark grew and rose up high and took hold of the entire world, even though all the faithful were being slaughtered, burnt, thrown over cliffs, drowned, [or] handed over to wild animals. Indeed, they trod on the coals as if they were mud, and viewed the sea and its waves as if they were meadows, and ran to meet the sword as if it were a diadem and crown, and condemned every form of torture not just by enduring it nobly, but also by [doing so] with pleasure and eagerness. For just as irrigated plants naturally grow in size, so too our faith when embattled blooms all the more, and when harassed multiplies. Indeed, irrigating with water doesn't usually make orchards thrive in the same way as the martyrs' blood naturally waters the Churches.

3   And so, because of his knowledge of all these facts and more than these, he (sc. the emperor) was afraid to wage the war against us openly. "Lest we lay the groundwork," he said, "[for them] to erect trophies thick and fast and effect victory after victory and weave crowns." So what did he do? Consider his wickedness! He ordered doctors and soldiers and sophists and orators all to desist from their professions or renounce on oath their faith.[5] He launched a missile strike against us in this fashion, so that if they gave in, their defeat would be laughable, in that they didn't honor piety over money; while, if they stood their ground nobly and proved superior, their victory wouldn't be very brilliant, nor their trophy remarkable. For it's no big deal to despise a trade or profession for the sake of piety. And he didn't just stop there. But also, if there was any person who in the preceding period, when emperors were pious, had destroyed

---

[5]The reference here is at least in part to the famous Education edict of 17 June 362 (*CTh.* 13.3.5), in which Julian required moral excellence of teachers and that their appointment be approved by the city councils. The edict itself is less offensive than the reaction it provoked at the time suggests (see R. Browning, *The Emperor Julian* [London: Weidenfeld and Nicolson, repr. 1977], 169–74).

altars or demolished temples or taken votive offerings or done anything else of this kind, they were dragged off to court and put to
death—not just the perpetrator of this kind of act, but even the person who had simply been accused of it.[6] And he devised countless
other devious pretexts for cutting down all who were living in piety.
In truth, he did all these things with the intention of eclipsing the
crown of martyrdom, so that, although the killing might be to his
advantage and deaths occur, the martyrs' prizes might not appear
brilliant. But it didn't go his way at all. For in no way were those who
suffered these things going to receive their crown as a result of his
decision or his wicked plan, but as a result of the incorrupt judgment—I mean, the one in heaven.

4   In the meantime, while affairs were in this state and he (sc. the
emperor) was laboring to carry out his war and afraid of defeat, it
happened that there was a military drinking party[7] in which the
martyrs who gathered us here today took part. And since, as is usual
at a drinking party, there were many stories being exchanged and
people conversing one with another, these men mourned the present evils and declared the preceding period blessed and said to themselves and to those who were present: "Is it really worth living any
more? [Is it worth] breathing or seeing this sun, when the sacred laws
are being trampled, piety abused, creation's common Master
despised? Everything is full of the smell of burning fat and smoke,
everything [full] of impure sacrifices, and we can't breathe pure air."
Please don't just skim over what they said. Instead, consider the
occasion on which these remarks were uttered, and look at the piety
of those who spoke [them]. For if at a military drinking party, where

[6]From early in 362 Julian began to promote legislation aimed at restoring the
temples of Greco-Roman religions at the personal expense of those who had previously gained financially from the appropriation of temple property or building materials, but there is no indication that he actively pursued the death of Christians via
such legislation (see R. Smith, *Julian's Gods: Religion and Philosophy in the Thought
and Action of Julian the Apostate* [London: Routledge, 1995], 211–18).
    [7]Lit. "symposium." Symposia were all-male affairs, associated with heavy drink-
ing and crude behavior.

there is undiluted wine and heavy drinking and one-upmanship over total debauchery, and competition over acting drunk and disorderly, they groaned in this way, they mourned in this way, what would they have been like when they were at home and alone in each other's company? What would they have been like at prayer, who at the very moment of overindulgence were so restrained and demonstrated apostolic fortitude? Others fell, and they mourned. Another behaved impiously, and they burned. They weren't conscious of their own health, because of the sickness of their brothers. Instead, as if they had been assigned as common patrons of the world, in this way they grieved and wept over the evils that were taking place.

5   What they said didn't escape notice. On the contrary, out of a desire to cultivate the emperor one of [the soldiers] who shared that table, a dissembler and flatterer, reported to him everything that was said. He (sc. the emperor), on finding what he had been looking for, for a long time, and having at hand a pretext that enabled him to strip them of martyrdom's rewards, ordered that all their assets be confiscated, charged them with tyranny on the basis of these remarks and commanded that they be escorted naked to prison. They were happy and rejoiced. "What's wealth to us," they said, "or an expensive robe? After all, if we had to shed our very last piece of clothing for Christ—our flesh— we wouldn't hang on to it, but would give it up too." And from that moment their military standards were at home and all their possessions were seized. Indeed, just as people on the point of migrating to a country that's situated a long distance away often liquidate their household and send it on ahead, so it happened in their case too. When they were on the point of migrating to heaven, their assets were sent on ahead, while it was their very enemies who facilitated the exportation. For it is not just the money given in relation to charity that is transferred to heaven, but also whatever those who attack the faith and persecute those who live in piety seize, that too is stored away there. On the point that the one is not less than the other, listen to what Paul says: "And you cheerfully

accepted the seizure of your possessions, in the expectation that you would have greater and lasting property in heaven" (Heb 10.34).

6   So then, the martyrs were in prison, and the entire city flowed together there. And yet, anyone who might approach and converse or share words with them was under threat of major terror, intimidation, and danger. But the fear of God pushed aside all those [anxieties] and because of them (sc. the soldier martyrs) many people at that time became martyrs, despising this present life for the sake of spending time with them. Indeed, many rushed together and celebrated continuous psalm-singing and holy night-long vigils, meetings filled with spiritual teaching and, while the church was locked up, the prison from that point on became a church. My point is, it wasn't just those who came in from outside, but even those spending time on the inside, who received a substantial education in virtue and moderation from the patience and faith of these saints. On hearing this the emperor was further upset and, out of a desire to outwit them and to break up that enthusiasm, set certain foul fellows and sorcerers to treachery. If they happened to find them alone, they would frequently sit down together with them and, as if they were offering advice off their own initiative, not as if they'd been sent by the emperor, counsel them to step back from piety on the one hand and to swap over to impiety on the other. "For by quelling the emperor's rage in this way you won't just evade the danger that lies before you, but will also attain greater honor and a more powerful office. Don't you see that others of your rank have done precisely this?"

7   But the [martyrs] said: "It's for precisely this reason that we will nobly stand firm, so that we might offer ourselves as sacrifices for their lapses. Our Master loves humankind. When he receives even a single sacrifice he is capable of forgiving the whole world." And just as the three children said: "At this moment there is no magistrate, or prophet or governor, or holocaust, or sacrifice, or place for offering fruits before you, or finding [your] mercy; but may we be accepted in [our] contrite heart and spirit of humility" (Dan 3.38–39), in this

way too the martyrs, on seeing the altars razed to the ground, the churches locked up, the priests driven out, all the believers put to flight, hastened to offer themselves to the Master in place of everything. Indeed, they quit military ranks and hastened to integrate themselves into choirs of angels. "Even if we do not die now," they argued, "we will at any rate die for certain a little later, and it is precisely this that convinces us. It is better to die for the King of angels than for a human who commits these sort of impieties. It is better to lay down our weapons for the country above than for the one below that we walk on. Here, even if a person dies, they receive from an emperor nothing worthy of their readiness. For at that point what gift could a human bestow on the person who has died? And so, often, not even rewarded with a tomb, they lie exposed to the mouths of dogs. But if we die for the King of angels, we will abandon our bodies with greater glory, we will return with a great deal of fame, and will carry off far greater rewards and crowns for our efforts. Let's take up spiritual weapons, then. We have no need of arrows or bows, no need of any other perceptible weapon. Our tongue is sufficient for everything," they said. For truly the saints' mouths are a quiver, that shoots incessant, successive strikes at the Devil's head.

8   These and similar remarks were reported back to the emperor. He did not desist, but set to work again, setting his baits via those men. And so, at any rate, this is what the rotten, treacherous, and criminally skilled [emperor] set up, so that, should they get worn down and give in, he might escort them out in full view of everyone and so from then on get them to sacrifice. But, if they persisted in demonstrating their excessive courage and nobly stood firm in the face of battle, the circumstances of their victory might not be obvious, but rather he might lead them away on a pretext of "tyranny" and kill them. But he who reveals deep and hidden things didn't allow the ambush to escape notice, nor the plot to be unobserved. Instead, just as the Egyptian woman once got hold of Joseph in her

private chamber with no one else in sight and expected that she would escape everyone's notice, but didn't escape the notice of the unsleeping eye[8]—and not just that, but not even of people who came after that—instead, what she said to Joseph, with no one present (Gen 39.7–18), is sung all over the world, so too, while this [emperor] hoped to avoid attention when he was conversing in prison via those fake advisers, he didn't escape notice. Instead, everyone afterwards learnt of the ambush, the plot, the victory, the trophy. For as a great deal of time wore away and flowed past, and the number of days didn't destroy their enthusiasm, but rather stretched their eagerness further and created more enthusiasts, at that point he ordered that they be led away to the pit in the middle of the night. And in thick darkness the light-sources were escorted out and beheaded.

9   From that time on their heads were even more terrifying to the Devil than when they emitted sound, since John's head too was not as terrifying when it could speak, as when it lay voiceless on the platter (Mt 14.1–11). For, in fact, the saints' blood has a voice that is not heard through ears, but received through the conscience of those who destroy it. And after that blessed slaughter, those who hunt such remains on the basis of their own salvation, took away those warriors. Indeed, though alive, they too were martyrs. For truly, even if they weren't beheaded, nonetheless they would have preferred to suffer this, and in this way embarked on hunting for the bodies. And so, those who were present at the time and were fortunate enough to see these bodies freshly killed, say that, when they were lying next to one another in front of the tomb, a certain grace bloomed on their faces, of the kind which Luke says came upon Stephen when he was about to defend himself to the Jews (Acts 6.15), and there is no one who at the time stood near them without trembling. So did this sight

[8]The concept of the ever-watchful eye of God occurs a number of times in John's homilies and treatises. For another example in a martyr homily see, e.g., *On Pelagia* (Leemans et al., *"Let Us Die that We May Live,"* 156), where it is used as a deterrent from certain unacceptable behavior.

amaze everyone who was watching, and everyone cried out that which was said by David: "In their life they were not separated, and in their death they are not divided" (2 Kgs 1.23). For together they both confessed and lived in prison and were taken away to the pit and lost their heads, and one coffin contains both their bodies. Just so will a single dwelling receive them (sc. their bodies) again in heaven, when in future they are taken up with a great deal of glory. It is fitting to address them together as pillars, and lookouts, and guard-towers, and light-sources, and bulls. For truly like pillars they hold up the Church, and like guard-towers they wall it in, and like lookouts who beat off every plot, they create a great deal of calm for those inside. And like light-sources they drove away the darkness of impiety and like bulls in body and soul, with equal enthusiasm, they dragged Christ's trusty yoke.

10   And so, let's constantly spend time visiting them, and touch their coffin and embrace their relics with faith, so that we might gain some blessing from them. For just as soldiers, showing off the wounds which they received in battle, boldly converse with the emperor, so too these [martyrs], by brandishing in their hands the heads which were cut off and putting them on public display, are able easily to procure everything we wish from the King of heaven. Let's, then, walk there with a great deal of faith, with lots of enthusiasm, so that from the sight of these saints' memorials, and from thinking about their contests and receiving numerous, substantial treasures from every direction, we may also be empowered to finish the present life according to God's will and sail into that harbor with a great deal of merchandise and attain the kingdom of heaven, through the grace and loving kindness of our Lord Jesus Christ, with whom to the Father, together with the Holy Spirit be glory, power, honor, and adoration forever and ever. Amen.

On the Holy Martyr Ignatius

The Ignatius who is the subject of this homily was possibly an associate of the apostles and was one of the earliest bishops of Antioch, having oversight of the see in the first decades of the second century. Very little is known of his life beyond his correspondence with various Churches in Asia Minor. On his way to Rome, where he was martyred in the time of the emperor Trajan, he visited with Polycarp, bishop of Smyrna, another famous early martyr. That the present homily was delivered by John at Antioch is clear from his comment towards the conclusion of §2 to the effect that Ignatius governed the Church "in our community." Later he says that the remains of Ignatius were "brought back to us" from Rome and indicates that he is preaching at the site of Ignatius' burial, which is within walking distance of the city. This information matches that of Jerome (*De viris illustribus* 16), who says that in his time the relics of Ignatius lay in the cemetery outside the gate to Daphne. Evagrius (*HE* 1.16) later reports that in the time of Theodosius II (prob. the 430s) the relics were translated to a church inside Antioch named after the martyr, which had been converted by the emperor from the old temple to Fortune (the Tychaeum). On that occasion a new festival was established which, Evagrius says, was still celebrated in the sixth century, having been newly promoted by the then bishop of Antioch, Gregory.

In the opening to the homily John tells us that the present festival occurs not long after that of Pelagia (8 October). The Syrian Martyrology locates it on 17 October, suggesting that in this instance the Syrian martyrology accurately reflects Antiochene practice at this time.

Contents:

Translated from PG 50.587–596.

On the very holy martyr Ignatius who was a God-bearing archbishop of Antioch the Great and had been taken away to Rome and martyred there, and in turn brought back from there to Antioch

1   Among those who host banquets, the biggest spenders and the most status-conscious hold banquets thick and fast, at one and the

same time showing off their own wealth and letting their benevolence towards their dependents be seen. So too the grace of the
Spirit, providing for us a demonstration of its own power and showing off a great deal of benevolence towards God's friends, is furnish-
ing martyrs' tables for us without a break one after the other.
Recently, at least, a quite young and unmarried girl, the blessed martyr Pelagia, had us to dinner with a great deal of festivity. Today again
this blessed and noble martyr Ignatius succeeds her festival. Their
persons are different, but the table one and the same. The wrestling
matches are completely different, but the crown one and the same.
Their contests are varied, but the prize the same. My point is that in
the outside games, since the labors involve bodies, it is with reason
that only men are admitted. But here, since the entire contest
involves the soul, the stadium is open to each sex, the spectators con-
sist of each kind. And neither did just men strip off, so that the
women, taking resort in the weakness of their gender, mightn't seem
to have a plausible defense; nor did just women act like men, so that
the male gender wouldn't be put to shame. Instead many people
from both this and that [gender] were heralded and crowned, so that
you might learn in practice that "in Christ Jesus there is no male, no
female" (Gal 3.28), that neither gender nor physical weakness nor
age nor anything else of the sort could impede those running the
race of piety, if noble enthusiasm and an alert mind and fervent and
passionate fear of God were rooted in our souls. For this reason both
young girls, and women, and men, and young and old, and slaves
and free, and every status, and every age, and each sex stripped off
for these contests, and nothing of any kind disadvantaged them,
since they brought a noble inclination to these wrestling matches.

2   And so the time [of year] calls us now to relate the good works
of this blessed man. But my argument is confused and in turmoil,
without a grasp of what to say first, what second, what third. So great
a crowd of speeches of praise flows around us from all sides. Indeed
our experience is the same as if someone on entering a meadow and

seeing a large number of roses, a large number of irises, so great a number of lilies, and other spring flowers of varied and diverse forms, were at a loss what to view first, what second, since each of the items they view is calling their eyes to itself. For truly, we too, on entering this spiritual meadow of Ignatius' good works and viewing not spring flowers but the very fruit of the Spirit, of varied and diverse forms, in this man's soul, are in turmoil and at a loss, without a grasp of where we should direct our argument first, since each item we view draws us away from its neighbors and invites the soul's eyes to view its own particular attractiveness. For consider! He governed the Church in our community nobly and with as much precision as Christ wishes. For that limit and rule of oversight which he (sc. Christ) said was greatest, he (sc. Ignatius) displayed in practice. Truly, when he heard Christ saying: "The good shepherd lays down his life for his sheep" (Jn 10.11), he gave it up for his sheep with every ounce of courage.

3   He was genuinely in the company of the apostles and enjoyed their spiritual streams. What kind of person is he likely to have been, then, seeing that he was raised alongside them and was in their company everywhere, and shared with them experiences both well-known and secret, and, in their opinion, deserved so great an office? Once again there occurred a time that required courage and a soul that despises everything to do with the present, and bubbles over with divine passion, and values things unseen over things seen. And he shed his flesh with as much ease as a person might take off a piece of clothing. What, then, shall we mention first? The apostles' teaching, which he demonstrated in everything, or his disdain for the present life, or the scrupulous virtue with which he administered his role as head of the Church? Whom shall we praise in song first? The martyr, or the bishop, or the apostle? For the Spirit's grace wove a triple crown and in this way wreathed that holy head. No, rather, it was multi-layered. For if a person were to unwind each of the crowns precisely, they would discover that they were shooting forth other crowns for us too.

4   And if you like, let's go first to praising the bishop. This doesn't seem to be just a single crown. Come, then, let's unwind it in our sermon, and you will see two or three or more being born for us out of it. My point is, I don't marvel at the man just because he was considered deserving of so great an office, but because he was entrusted with this office by those saints, and the hands of the blessed apostles touched his holy head. For this is no small subject for a speech of praise: not because he attracted more abundant grace from above, nor because they caused the Spirit's action to descend upon him more generously alone; but because in him they witnessed every possible human virtue. In what way, let me explain. Paul was writing to Titus at the time—when I say Paul, I don't mean just him, but also Peter and James and John and their whole company. For just as in a single lyre the strings are different, but they make a single harmonious sound, so too in the company of apostles the persons were different but the teaching one and the same, since there was also a single artist, the Holy Spirit, who was setting their souls in motion. And this Paul made clear when he said: "Whether it is they, then, or it is I, so we proclaim [the gospel]" (1 Cor 15.11). So then, he was writing to Titus and showing what kind of person the bishop should be, and he said: "As God's steward, the bishop should be without reproach, not stubborn, not quick-tempered, not an excessive drinker, not given to brawls, not greedy for gain, but hospitable, a lover of goodness, of sober character, upright, devout, self-disciplined, a person who sticks closely to the trustworthy word in accord with what was taught, so that he is capable both of advising others with sound doctrine and of refuting those who argue against it" (Tit 1.7–9). And again when he was writing to Timothy on the same issue he spoke more or less as follows: "If anyone puts up his hand for episcopal office, he desires a fine task. The bishop should therefore be blameless, a husband of one wife, a teetotaler, of sober character, well-behaved, hospitable, instructive, not given to brawls, not an excessive drinker, but mild, peace-loving, not interested in money" (1 Tim 3.1–3).

5   Did you see how much precision in respect of virtue is required of the bishop? For just as a master painter mixes various colors and so renders with absolute precision whatever picture he is about to produce as an archetype of the imperial form, so that all those who copy it and paint from it have an image that is portrayed accurately in every detail. So too indeed blessed Paul, as if painting an imperial image and producing its exemplar, has mixed the various colors of virtue and sketched for us in complete form the distinctive features of the episcopal office, so that each person ascending to this office, by looking at it (sc. the image or exemplar), might administer every aspect of themselves with as much precision. With confidence, therefore, I would say that with precision blessed Ignatius impressed every aspect of this image on his own soul, and was blameless and without reproach and neither stubborn nor quick-tempered, nor an excessive drinker, nor given to brawling, but peace-loving, uninterested in money, upright, devout, disciplined, a person who stuck close to the trustworthy word in accord with what was taught, a teetotaler, of sober character, well-behaved, and the rest that Paul required. "What's the proof of this?," you ask. The same men who made these statements ordained him, and those who were advising others so precisely to subject to scrutiny those about to ascend to the throne of this office would themselves not have done this cursorily. On the contrary, if they hadn't seen all of this virtue planted in this martyr's soul, they wouldn't have entrusted this office to him.

6   My point is that they knew precisely how much danger there is in store for those who perform such ordinations carelessly and at random. Indeed again making this same point clear Paul, in writing to the same Timothy, said: "Lay hands on no one swiftly, nor join in the sins of others" (1 Tim 5.22). What do you mean? Another person sins, and I share the charges and the punishment? "Yes," he says, "since you placed your authority at the service of impropriety." Indeed, just as when a person entrusts a sharpened

sword to someone who is raving and out of their wits, whatever murder the insane person commits, that person who handed over the sword takes on the responsibility, so too a person who places the authority that stems from this office at the service of a person engaged in impropriety draws all the fire for that person's sins and enterprises on their own head. For the person who supplies the root is responsible in every way for what grows out of it. Did you see how it is meanwhile clear to us that the crown of the episcopal office was two-fold, and the status of the men who ordained him made the office more brilliant, in that they gave witness to every proof of virtue in him?

7   Would you like me to reveal to you yet another crown that shot forth from this very thing? Let us give consideration to the time at which he was entrusted with this office. For it is not the same to administer a church now as it was then, just as to travel in the steps of numerous travelers a road that's compacted and well constructed is not the same as [to travel] one that's right on the point of being cut for the first time and has chasms and rocks and is full of wild animals and hasn't yet received a single traveler. My point is that at present by God's grace there is no danger for bishops, but instead profound peace everywhere, and we all enjoy calm and the word of piety has extended itself to the ends of the world and those who rule over us keep a close and precise watch over the faith. But at that time there were none of these things. Instead, wherever one looked, [there were] cliffs and pits and wars and battles and dangers; and governors and emperors and peoples and cities and races—both domestic and foreign—were plotting against the believers. And it wasn't just this that was terrible, but that many of the believers themselves too, in that they had just for the first time tasted strange teachings, were in need of considerable accommodation, and were still rather weak and were often caught out. And it was this that grieved the teachers no less than the external wars; rather it [grieved them] far more. For while the external battles and plots actually provided them with

much pleasure because of the expectation of the rewards stored up—truly, this is why the apostles turned away from facing the council, rejoicing that they had been whipped (cf. Acts 5.40–41), and why Paul proclaims: "I rejoice in my sufferings" (Col 1.24) and everywhere boasts in his afflictions—the wounds of their own people and the lapses of their brothers and sisters didn't allow them to catch a breath, but instead like an extremely heavy yoke unrelentingly compressed and dragged down their souls' necks.

8   At any rate listen to how Paul, who so rejoices in his [own] sufferings, bitterly grieves over them. "Who is weak," he says, "and I am not weak? Who is made to stumble and I don't burn?" (2 Cor 11.29). And again: "I am pretty much afraid that, if I come, I won't find you in the state that I wish and that I too will be found by you to not be as you wish" (2 Cor 12.20). And a little later: "[I fear] that when I come again God will humble me before you, and I will mourn for many who have sinned beforehand, and won't repent of their uncleanliness and sexual immorality and licentiousness they have practiced" (2 Cor 12.21). And in every situation you always see him in tears and in mourning because of his own people, and afraid and trembling over those who believed. And so, just as we marvel at a captain not when he is able to save the passengers when the sea is calm and the ship is being carried along by a fair wind, but when he is able to set the vessel to rights with complete safety when the sea is raging, the waves are towering, the marines on board are mutinying, a great storm is besieging the passengers from without and within; so too should we be struck with far greater amazement and wonder at those entrusted with the Church at that time than at those who govern it now—[a time] when there was much warring without and within, when the shoot of faith was still rather tender and in need of considerable care, when like a new born babe the bulk of the Church required considerable forethought and some extremely wise soul to next look after it.

9   Indeed so that you may learn more clearly how many crowns those who were then entrusted with the Church deserved, and how much effort and danger it was to take on the matter in the opening moments and at the start and to come to it first off the rank, I produce as a witness for you Christ, who puts his vote behind these statements and confirms the opinion we've expressed. For on seeing many people coming to him, and desiring to show the apostles that the prophets expended much greater effort than they, he said: "Others have put in the hard work and you have come in on their hard work" (Jn 4.38). And yet the apostles expended much greater effort than the prophets. But since the latter were the first to sow the word of piety and drew people's uninstructed souls toward the truth, he attributed the bulk of the hard work to them. My point is that it is not, absolutely not, the same for a person who comes after many other teachers to teach and for that person to sow the seeds for the first time. For what has already been practiced and has become a habit for many, is easily taken on board. But what is now being heard for the first time confuses the mind of the audience and throws up many issues for those doing the teaching. At any rate this even confused those among the Athenians who were listening, and because of this they turned away Paul, with the accusation: "You're introducing something foreign to our ears" (Acts 17.20). My point is, if being at the head of the Church at present provides hard work and considerable effort for those who steer it, consider how the effort was at that time double, or triple, or many times more, when there were dangers and battles, and plots, and constant fear. It isn't, it absolutely isn't possible to come close in theory to the unpleasantness which those saints endured at that time. Rather that person alone will know it, who has had actual experience.

10   Let me mention a fourth crown too, which emerges for us from this episcopal office. So, what is it? That he was assigned our country. I mean, it is labor intensive to be at the head of just a hundred or five hundred men. But to be entrusted with so large a city and a

population stretching into the 200,000s, of how much virtue and wisdom do you imagine that to be proof? For truly, just as in the case of armies the more experienced generals are entrusted with the praetorian legions with their larger body count, so too in the case of cities the more capable magistrates are assigned the larger, heavily populated ones. And, in any case, this city was of considerable interest to God, as he in fact revealed through his actions. At least, [God] ordered Peter, the commander-in-chief of the entire world, to whom he entrusted the keys of heaven, to whom he assigned control of everything, to spend a considerable length of time here. To him our city was thus the equivalent of the entire world. When I recalled Peter, I saw a fifth crown being woven from it too. It was he (sc. Ignatius) who succeeded to this office after him. For just as, if a person removes a large stone from foundations, they for sure hurry to insert in its place a second [stone] equivalent to it, lest they be a step away from shaking the entire building and making it less sound; so too, when Peter was about to move away from there, the grace of the Spirit inserted in his place a second teacher equivalent to Peter, so that the construction that was already there wouldn't become less sound through the poor quality of his successor.

11   And so we have counted up five crowns: from the magnitude of the office, from the status of those who ordained him, from the unpleasant nature of the time, from the proportions of the city, from the virtue of the person who handed the episcopal office on to him. After weaving all of these I could have mentioned a sixth or a seventh or more than these. But, so that we don't waste the whole time on a discussion of his episcopacy and so be deprived of the tales about the martyr, come, for the rest let's move to that contest.

12   A cruel war was once stirred up against the Churches and, just as if an utterly cruel tyrant had got hold of the earth, everyone was snatched away from the midst of the marketplace, accused of nothing out of the ordinary, except that, free of error, they raced towards piety, that they resisted the worship of demons, that they recognized

the true God and adored his only-begotten Son. And, on account of those [virtues] for which they should have been crowned and marveled at and honored, on their account everyone who had taken on the faith was punished and overwhelmed with countless tortures, but the heads of the Churches to a far greater degree. For the Devil, being a criminal and clever at devising such plots, anticipated that if he removed the shepherds, he would easily be able to scatter the flocks. But the one who catches the clever in their trickery allowed this to happen, with the intention of showing him that it is not humans who steer his Churches, but he himself who in every instance shepherds those who believe in him. [He did this] so that whenever [the Devil] saw the matters of piety not diminishing, despite [the shepherds'] removal, nor the word of the message being extinguished, but rather growing, he might learn through experience—both he himself and all who serve him in these matters—that our affairs are not human, but that the basis of our teaching has its root above in heaven, and it is God who guides the Churches in every respect, and that it isn't possible for the individual who fights God to ever overcome him.

13   It's not just this piece of chicanery that the Devil put into effect, but also a second of no less magnitude than this. For he didn't allow the bishops to be killed in the cities which they headed, but first escorted them to a foreign country and then did away with them. He did this simultaneously out of a haste to get them stripped of necessities, and from the hope of rendering them weaker from the hardship of the journey, which is precisely what he did in the case of this blessed man. For he summoned him from our city to Rome, imposing upon him longer laps of the race, in anticipation that he (sc. the Devil) would depress his (sc. Ignatius') spirits both through the [sheer] length of the road and the vast number of days [involved], not knowing that on so long a journey [Ignatius] had Jesus as a fellow merchant and migrant. Instead, [Ignatius] became stronger, and provided ample proof of the power that was with him, and trained up

the Churches in a major way. I mean that the cities along the road raced together from all directions[1] and anointed[2] the athlete and sent him on his way with a large quantity of supplies, offering him assistance through their prayers and intercessions. And they (sc. the cities) received no ordinary comfort when they saw the martyr running to meet death with as great an enthusiasm as was fitting for a person summoned to the royal palace in heaven. And they learnt from experience, from the enthusiasm and brilliance of that noble man, that it was not death toward which he ran, but a migration and translation, and ascent to heaven. After teaching these things in every city through what he said, through what he did, he would take his leave.

14 And what happened in the case of the Jews when, in shackling Paul and dispatching him to Rome, they thought they were sending him off to his death, but in fact sent him as a teacher to the Jews who lived there, this very thing happened in the case of Ignatius too with a certain abundance. For he went away as a marvelous teacher for not just those who inhabit Rome, but also for all the cities lying in between, persuading them to despise the present life and consider as nothing what can be seen, and to love the future, and look towards heaven, and pay heed to none of the disasters in the present life. He traveled, in practice teaching them these [virtues] and more than these like a sun rising from the east and running its course towards the west. Rather, he was even more brilliant than that. I mean that while this [sun] runs its course above, bringing perceptible light, Ignatius shone from below, sending an intelligible light of instruction into their souls. And while when that [sun] goes off to the regions of the west, it is hidden and at once introduces night, when this [sun] went off into the regions of the west, it rose more brilliantly from there, and benefited everyone along the road in the greatest possible way. And when he reached the city (sc. Rome), he

[1]From Ignatius' letters it is evident that at the very least he passed through Philadelphia, Sardis, Smyrna, Troas, Neapolis, and Philippi, while representatives of the cities of Ephesus, Tralles, and Magnesia came to meet him in Smyrna.

[2]I.e., helped to get him ready, encouraged him, spurred him on.

taught her to practice philosophy too. Truly, it is for this reason that God agreed that he lose his life there: so that his death would be an instruction in piety for all who inhabit Rome.

15 My point is that, while by God's grace you are no longer in need of any proof, since you were firmly rooted in the faith, the inhabitants of Rome, in that at the time there was a great deal of impiety there, needed greater assistance. It's for this reason that both Peter and Paul and this man after them were all sacrificed there. This [occurred] on the one hand so that they might purify with their own blood the city stained with the blood of idols, on the other, so that they might provide practical proof of the resurrection of the crucified Christ, by persuading the inhabitants of Rome that they wouldn't have despised the present life with such great pleasure if they themselves had not been utterly convinced that they were about to ascend to the crucified Jesus and see him in heaven. For this is truly a substantial proof of the resurrection, that the murdered Christ exhibited such great power after death that he convinced living human beings to ignore their country and household and friends and relatives and life itself for the sake of confessing him, and to choose whips and dangers and death instead of the pleasures of the present. My point is, these deeds were not those of a dead person nor a person still in the tomb, but of one risen from the dead and alive. After all, how could one account for the fact that when he was alive all the apostles in his company became weaker from fear and betrayed their teacher and fled away, but when he died, not just Peter and Paul but also Ignatius, who hadn't even set eyes on him nor enjoyed his company, displayed such great enthusiasm for him that they even laid down their very life for him?

16 So then, so that all the inhabitants of Rome might learn these things in practice, God allowed the saint to end his life there. And that this is the reason, I'll guarantee from the way he died itself. For he didn't receive the condemning vote outside the walls in a pit, or in a court of law, or in some corner. Instead, in the middle of the

theater, with the whole city seated in the stands,[3] he endured the way of martyrdom via wild animals dispatched against him, so that by erecting his trophy against the Devil under everyone's gaze, he might make all the spectators enthusiasts of his own struggles, not just through dying so nobly, but also through dying with enjoyment. For he viewed the wild animals irreverently in this way—not as someone about to be torn away from life, but as someone summoned to a better and more spiritual life. What makes this clear? The words that he spoke when he was about to die. For when he heard that this type of torture awaited him, he said: "Bless those wild animals!"[4] Of such quality are those who passionately love. Whatever they suffer for their loved ones, they accept with pleasure and seem to be full of passion precisely whenever what is happening is far more cruel; which is what happened, then, too in the case of this man. For he strove to emulate the apostles not just in his death but also in his enthusiasm. And on hearing that they had been whipped and yet departed with joy (cf. Acts 5.41), he too wanted to imitate his teachers not just in his death but also in his joy. It's for this reason he said: "Bless the wild animals!" Indeed he thought that their mouths[5] would be much more gentle than the tyrant's tongue. And rightly so. For while the latter called him to hell,[6] their mouths sent him off to the kingdom [of heaven].

17   Well then, when he lost his life there—no rather, when he ascended to heaven—from that moment he returned crowned as victor. Truly this was a feature of God's management: to bring him back to us and distribute the martyr between the cities. For while she (sc. Rome) received his dripping blood, you were honored with his

[3]Lit. "above."

[4]The Roman martyrdom of Ignatius (§10; Lightfoot II.2, p.533 ll.20–21) records Ignatius as saying: "I am God's grain and I am ground by the teeth of wild animals, so that I might become pure bread." Both traditions express the idea that Ignatius embraced the manner of his death.

[5]Gr. *tomata*, which appears here in Montfaucon's edition, appears to be a misprint for *stomata* (mouths).

[6]Lit. "Gehenna."

relics. You enjoyed his episcopacy; they enjoyed his martyrdom. They saw him competing and winning and being crowned; you have him perpetually. God removed him from you for a short time and happily gave him [back] to you with greater glory. And, just as those who borrow money pay back whatever they receive with interest, so too God, after using this valuable treasure among you for a short time and showing it to that city, gave it back to you with greater brilliance. My point is that you sent away a bishop, and received a martyr. You sent [him] away with prayers, and received [him] with crowns. And not just you, but also all the cities in between. For how do you think they felt when they saw the remains being escorted back? How much pleasure did they reap? How much did they rejoice? With how many acclamations did they bombard the crowned victor from every direction? For just as the spectators immediately welcome a noble athlete who has wrestled down all his competitors and exited the arena with magnificent glory, and don't allow him to set foot on the ground but escort him home in a litter and bombard him with countless words of praise, so at that time too in succession the cities welcomed that saint from Rome, and carrying him on their shoulders sent him along as far as this city, praising the crowned victor, praising in song the President of the games,[7] mocking the Devil, because his trick backfired with opposite effect, and what he thought he was doing to the martyr's detriment happened in his own case. And whereas at the time he (sc. the martyr) benefited and uplifted all those cities, from that time even up to the present day he continues to enrich your city. And, just like a perpetual warehouse that is drained day after day and does not run dry, and makes all who share in it more prosperous, so indeed too this blessed Ignatius sends back home full of blessings, confidence, noble thoughts, and a great deal of courage those who come to him.

---

[7] I.e., Christ. The image of Christ as the president of the games in which the martyrs compete against the Devil and win is a common one in martyr homilies of this period. See J. Leemans, "Gregory of Nyssa and the Agonothetes: An Exploration of an Agonistic Image to speak about God and Christ," forthcoming.

18   Let's, then, not walk to him just today, but also every day, and reap spiritual fruit from him. For it's possible, absolutely possible, for the person who's present here with faith to harvest great blessings. My point is that not just the bodies but the saints' coffins themselves, too, are full of spiritual grace. For if this happened in the case of Elisha and a corpse that touched his coffin shattered the bonds of death and came back to life (4 Kgs 13.21), it is even far more possible now, when grace is more generous, when the Spirits' energy is more abundant, for a person who touches a coffin to draw from there a great deal of power. Indeed, it is for this reason that God allowed us [to have] the saints' relics, out of a desire to guide us towards the same enthusiasm as them and to provide a harbor and a secure consolation for the evils that constantly beset us. For this reason, I encourage all of you, whether a person is depressed or ill or suffering abuse, or is in some other condition of life, or deep in sin, let them be present here with faith, and they will put aside all those [troubles] and come back with much pleasure, having rendered their conscience lighter from the sight alone. Rather, it isn't essential for only those who are in trouble to be present here; no, even if a person is in cheerful spirits, even if they're in glory, even if they're in power, even if they address God with a great deal of boldness, let that person not despise the benefit. For on coming here and seeing this saint, they will render the good things [in their life] unchanging, persuaded by the memory of his good works to moderate their soul and not allowing their conscience to be aroused to any swell-headedness by the good things they do. It is no small thing for those doing well not to become puffed up over their happy state of existence, but to know how to bear doing well in a measured way. In consequence for everyone the warehouse is useful, the inn convenient—for those who have stumbled, so that they may be free of temptations; for those in a happy state, so that the good things might stay secure for them; for those who are sick, so that they may return to health, for those who are healthy, so that they won't fall sick. On taking all these factors into consideration, let's value spending time here above every

enjoyment, every pleasure, so that at one and the same time rejoicing and profiting we may be enabled through the prayers of the saints themselves to become housemates of these saints and share their lifestyle, through the grace and loving kindness of our Lord Jesus Christ, with whom to the Father be glory, together with the Holy Spirit, now and always, and forever and ever. Amen.

On Eleazar and the Seven Boys

It is not certain where this homily was preached, although the weight of the evidence favors Constantinople slightly.[1] If this is the case, then it is possible that the location at which the festival proper was held on the next day is the shrine of the Maccabees mentioned in the *Life of St Dalmatius*. This is said to have existed in the vicinity of Constantinople in the time of Bishop Nectarius, John's immediate predecessor.[2] The relationship of this shrine to the church of the Maccabees located across the Golden Horn in the suburb of Sykae in the seventh century, as mentioned in the *Chronicon paschale* under the reign of the emperor Heraclius, is uncertain. It is noteworthy that John says that people are still struggling at this point with the idea that the Maccabees can legitimately be venerated as Christian martyrs, suggesting that the Christian adoption of the cult was not yet widely accepted at the present location. If the homily was indeed delivered at Constantinople, then it was preached on 31 July, since in the East the festival of the Maccabees was celebrated on 1 August by this point.[3] Since John was ready to launch into a follow-up to the topic he engaged with in a recent sermon, it seems likely that this sermon was not delivered at a liturgical gathering that was part of the festival itself, such as a vigil, but preached at an ordinary regular worship service. If this is the case and if it was indeed

[1]See Mayer, *The Homilies of John Chrysostom–Provenance*, 498–504.

[2]J. Pargoire, "Les homélies de s. Jean Chrysostome en juillet 399," *Échos d'Orient* 3 (1889–1890): 160 n. 2.

[3]Vinson, "Gregory Nazianzen's Homily 15," 188, points out that the original feast day of the Maccabees fell in December, when the Jews celebrated Hanukkah, but that the Christian celebration was consciously shifted to 1 August to distinguish it, the shift occurring during the reign of Theodosius I.

preached at Constantinople, then the homily dates to either 398 or 399,[4] the first or second year of John's episcopate.

The text itself presents a few problems and is one reason why this homily has not been available in translation before. In the manuscript that Montfaucon used, Ottob. gr. 431, the scribe somehow interpolated a long passage from another homily. Montfaucon's text, which is in addition missing the conclusion to the homily, is reproduced by Migne (PG 63.523–530). On the rediscovery of Stavronikita 6 in the 1950s, Wenger found in this valuable codex a complete version of the homily, recognized that the ill-fitting section of the text published by Montfaucon belonged in fact to the homily which immediately follows it in Stav. 6 (*CPG* 4441.14), and eventually published the missing sections.[5] As yet, no complete edition of the homily exists and one is obliged to reconstruct the text from both Migne and Wenger. The translation which follows provides the reader with the first opportunity to enjoy the homily in its entirety.

Contents:

1. John praises the elderly preacher who has preceded him and explains that, out of modesty, he had resolved not to preach.

2–4. John has been persuaded by the audience and the "old men" to preach. Recently he preached on a difficult topic, which was nonetheless enthusiastically received. Today he would like to finish off that topic, but it is the day before the festival of the Maccabees. He sets out to correct those who do not consider the Maccabees Christian martyrs.

5. Not only are they equal to the rest of the martyrs, but the Maccabees are even more prestigious, because they died at a time when death was unconquered. Even patriarchs, prophets, and apostles feared it. The Maccabees therefore displayed greater courage.

---

[4] See W. Mayer, " 'Les homélies de s. Jean Chrysostome en juillet 399': A Second Look at Pargoire's Sequence and the Chronology of the *Novæ homiliæ* (*CPG* 4441)," *Byzantinoslavica*, 60/2 (1999): 285–7.

[5] A. Wenger, "Restauration de l'*Homélie* de Chrysostome sur Eléazar et les sept frères Macchabées (PG 63.523–530)," in J. Dummer, J. Irmscher, F. Paschke, and K. Treu, eds., *Texte und Textkritik. Eine Aufsatzsammlung*, Texte und Untersuchungen, 133 (Akademie Verlag: Berlin 1987), 599–604.

6–15. John sets out to prove that the Maccabees suffered for Christ's sake, as well as the law, since they died when Christ was about to appear, and Christ gave the law. He explores the relationship between the old and new covenants.

16. Since it is evident that Christ gave the law and that therefore those who died for the law, died for Christ, John urges everyone to attend the festival of the Maccabees with enthusiasm.

Translated from PG 63.523–530 and Wenger 1987: 601–604.

Homily of (John) preached on the topic of Eleazar and the seven boys, after another very old preacher had spoken first

1   How at its peak is this spiritual olive tree! Although its branches are elderly, it has provided us with mature fruit. For the plants of the earth are not of the same kind as the trees of the Church. I mean that, when the former reach old age, they then shed the majority of their leaves and, whatever fruit they bear, they produce out of season and undersized. But when these trees reach old age, it is then especially that they sink under the weight of their fruit. This is exactly what one can see in the case of the person who spoke today. Indeed, for that reason I resolved to be silent. For, when there are so many old men present who are experienced at preaching, a young man should keep quiet. So in fact do the divine scriptures instruct us. For when they talk with a young man, they say: "If you must, young man, speak scarcely twice, if you are questioned. Encapsulate a lot in a few words" (Sir 32.7–8). But [when they talk] with an old man it is not with restrictions of this kind. Instead they leave that same man alone and allow him to run without such constraints, and, marveling in turn at the pleasure of what is said, when it is said with intelligence, say as follows: "Speak, old man, for it is proper that you do, but in precise understanding, and you will interfere with music" (Sir 32.3).[6]

---

[6]The citation of Sir 32.3 (*kai empodiseis mousika*) differs from the standard LXX

What is "and you will interfere with music?" [Scripture] shows by this that flute and cithara and pipes are not so pleasurable to the audience as an old man's preaching presented with precise understanding. For it compares pleasure with pleasure and says that this [pleasure] is much more commanding than that and that the one exerts control, while the other yields to it. For this reason [scripture] also says "you will interfere with music;" that is, you won't allow it to be apparent, you will obscure it, you will cast it in the shade.

2   It is because of these [instructions] that we should be silent and listen, and that he should preach and instruct. But I will say now too what I have often said. I can withstand neither your tyranny[7] nor their pressure.[8] It is for this reason that I'm stripping off again for the accustomed races (a laborious task, preaching) and take it up with a great deal of ease, not because of my own ability, but because of the enthusiasm of you, the audience. Indeed, when it was driven into such great depths recently, my sermon didn't drown, and when it crossed so broad a sea, it didn't sustain shipwreck on your account at any point. The reason is that nowhere were there rocks or hidden obstacles or cliffs. Rather, in every place it found the sea calmer than a harbor. And with your desire to listen fixed like a breeze at the stern, it was conveyed towards a tranquil harbor. For as soon as it leapt forth from our tongue, you all welcomed it with upturned hands, even though it conveyed considerable difficulty. For such was the nature of the concepts [we preached] recently. Yet even so, through both the excessive nature of your enthusiasm and your keen and precise

text (*kai mē empodisēs mousika*: "and don't interfere with music") in this last phrase, resulting in the opposite meaning. That this reading is found in the text that John is using and is not the result of scribal error is clear from his interpretation of the phrase in the lines that follow.

[7]John often speaks of the "tyranny" of the audience's love for him.

[8]The "they" who are said to have exerted pressure on John to preach on this occasion are likely to be the older, experienced preachers mentioned in § 1. At Antioch this could refer to more senior presbyters but, if he is indeed preaching in Constantinople in this instance, then the older, more experienced preachers are more likely to be visiting bishops.

attention you provided consolation for our effort and rendered what was difficult easy. My point is that you didn't let it fall on rock or on thorns or on the path, but welcomed it all into rich and productive plow-land, into the depths of your mind. As a result, day after day we see the crop waving, nourished by the Spirit's winds instead of a breeze, and our theater day after day becoming magnificent.

3   For these reasons today too I was wanting to take up what was left [of the topic]. But what can I do? The chorus of the Maccabees stands before my eyes and, illuminating my mind with the splendor of their singular wounds, summons our tongue towards their singular beauty. But let no one condemn the odd timing of my sermon, in that, although the day of their wrestling matches is tomorrow, we are weaving their crowns today and proclaiming the trophy in advance of the time of battle. For if, when weddings are being celebrated, those who gather for them prepare the bridal chambers and decorate the houses with garlands and draperies even in advance of the appointed day, we shall do this far more, in as much as this wedding is even more spiritual—not where a man [marries] a woman, but where God marries humans' souls. One would thus not be amiss in calling the martyrs' soul a bride—a spiritual bride—since they contribute their blood as a dowry, a dowry that is never exhausted.

4   But let the time for speeches of praise await us tomorrow. Instead today we shall correct the weaker among our brothers and sisters. I say this since many of the more naïve, due to a mental incapacity, are being swept along by the Church's enemies [and] do not hold the appropriate opinion of these saints, nor, in the same way, do they number them in the rest of the chorus of the martyrs, saying that they didn't shed their blood for Christ but for the law and the edicts that were in the law, in that they were killed over pig's flesh (cf. 4 Macc 5ff). Come then, let us correct their way of thinking. For it would be truly shameful for them to celebrate a festival in ignorance of the festival's basis.

5   So, then, that those who suffer from such a sickness are not the only ones suffering in the midst of everyone's mutual enjoyment, but rather grasp their combatants with a pure mind and see them with clear eyes, by purging their close mental attachment today, we'll prepare them to go off to the spiritual festival tomorrow with a pure intellect and clear mind. For I don't hesitate to count them (sc. the Maccabees) with the other martyrs, to the extent that I declare that they are even more brilliant. For they competed at a time when the bronze gates had not yet been shattered, nor the iron bar removed, when sin still ruled and the curse flourished and the Devil's citadel stood and the path of this kind of virtue was as yet untrodden. My point is that in the present time both rather young men and numerous delicate and pre-marital virgins all over the world have stripped off against death's tyranny. But at that time, before the coming of Christ, even those who were extremely just trembled in fear of it. At least, Moses fled through this fear. And Elijah consequently ran away on a journey lasting forty days. And because of it the patriarch Abraham advised his wife to say: " 'I am his sister' and not his wife" (cf. Gen 12.13). And what should one say about the rest? I mean, Peter himself was so afraid of death that he couldn't even take a doorkeeper's threat. For [death] was so terrifying and unavoidable; its sinews hadn't yet been cut out, nor its power destroyed. But even so, at that time when it breathed so terrifyingly, these men competed against it and wrestled it to the ground. My point is that it happened when the sun of righteousness was about to rise, as occurs in the case of day. I mean that, just as the dawn appears bright to us when the sun has not yet appeared (although the rays are not yet clearly visible, the light from the rays actually illuminates the world from afar), so too did it happen at that time. For when the sun of righteousness was on the brink of coming, from then on he dissolved the darkness of fear, and although he was not yet present in the flesh, he was nonetheless close at hand and on the verge, and from then on had a hand in what was happening.

6   So then, that they displayed considerable courage by competing in those times is absolutely clear. That they received their wounds for Christ's sake, this I will now attempt to demonstrate. Tell me, for what reason did they suffer? "Because of the law," you say, "and the edicts that lie within the law." If, then, it is apparent that it was Christ who gave that law, is it not clear that, by suffering for the law, they displayed all of that boldness for the lawgiver? Come, then, let us demonstrate this today: that it is Christ who gave the law. So, who makes this claim? The one who clearly understands these matters, both old and new—Paul, the teacher of the world. For when writing to the Corinthians, he states as follows: "I don't want you to be ignorant, brothers and sisters, that all our fathers were under the cloud, and they all passed through the sea, and were all baptized into Moses in the cloud and in the sea, and they all ate the same spiritual food (he means, manna), and they all drank the same spiritual drink (he means, the water from the rock)" (1 Cor 10.1–3). Next, showing that it was Christ who performed these miracles, he adds: "For they drank from the spiritual rock that followed. And the rock was Christ" (1 Cor 10.4). And rightly so. For it was not the rock's nature that released the water and those rivers, but Christ's energy which, when it hit the rock, made it release the springs. For this reason he even called it a spiritual rock and said that it followed. While the visible rock didn't follow, but was fixed in one place, nonetheless the power that was everywhere present and performed all the miracles in fact smashed the rock. But if the Jew cannot endure these words, come, let's capture him with his own weapons, engaging him in debate with nothing from Paul or Peter or John, but from the prophets, so that he might learn that while the facts are on his side, the meaning is on ours.

7   So then, which of the prophets states this: that he gave the old covenant? Jeremiah, who was sanctified from the womb, who shone in his childhood. Where and when? Listen to his words and learn clearly from what is said. What, then, are these words? "Behold, the

days are coming, says the Lord" (Jer 38.31). Right at the beginning he alerts the listener, and arouses the thinking processes of his audience, showing that the words are not his, but God's, who sent him. "Behold, the days are coming." Next he shows that he speaks to us about future events. "If he is speaking about future events," you ask, "how then did he (sc. Christ) give the old [covenant]?" Hang on, and don't get upset, and then you will clearly see the lamp of truth. For when he made this statement, the law had been given and violated, but not yet the new [covenant]. So then, storing these things away clearly in your minds, receive the solution to what confuses many. "Behold, the days are coming, says the Lord (signifying the present time), and I shall make a new covenant with you, one unlike the covenant which I made with your fathers" (Jer 38.31–32). I ask the Jew, I ask the sick brother or sister: who gave the new covenant? Without a doubt, everyone will say: Christ. Therefore he also [gave] the old. For in saying "I shall make a new covenant, one unlike the covenant that I gave," he showed that he himself made that covenant too. Therefore the legislator of both covenants is one and the same. And tell me, when did he make the old [covenant]? "On the day on which I took them by my hand to lead them out of the land of Egypt" (Jer 38. 32). See how he demonstrates too the ease of the exodus, his love, the security of the way of life of the time and that he personally performed all the miracles in Egypt. For by saying "when I took them by my hand to lead them out of the land of Egypt" he signifies all the miracles. After all, that exodus took place because of those astounding signs. "And they didn't remain in my covenant and I didn't take care of them, says the Lord" (Jer 38.32). And so, that the legislator of the old and new [covenants] is one and the same is clear from this.

8   At this point, if someone were to examine minutely what was said, they would know that it is full of no ordinary difficulty. I mean that when he states the reason why he is about to make a second covenant, he calls it "new," that is, "astonishing." "I shall make a new

covenant, he says, one unlike the covenant which I made with their fathers, because they didn't remain in my covenant. And I didn't take care of them, says the Lord." In truth, they should have been punished because of this, and paid the ultimate penalty and sustained unendurable punishment, in that, despite enjoying such great miracles and receiving the law, they didn't in any way improve. But as it is, he didn't demand a penalty of them, but made even greater promises than before. I really ought to introduce the solution to this difficulty today, but since our sermon is pressing in a different direction, and we want to teach you not to learn everything from us, but to also discover it on your own, I leave this to you to look for and find. If we see you looking but not finding, at that point we'll stretch out our hands. In consequence the discovery will become easier for you, and the places in the apostles in which the treasure and the solution to this fresh difficulty is to be found in particular, I already tell you ahead of time. In the epistle to the Romans, and to the Galatians and to the Hebrews, he locates and solves this very topic. All those who like hard work will be able, on approaching these epistles, to discover this solution, if you don't give yourselves up to ill-timed gatherings and mindless frivolity in these intervening days. Instead, stick firmly to thinking over what's been said and dig up the treasure.[9]

9   In the meantime, leaving this question unsolved, let us proceed to the sequel. What is the sequel? "This is the covenant which I shall make with you, says the Lord. I shall place my laws in their mind and engrave them on their heart. And in no way will each instruct their fellow citizen, or each their sister or brother, saying: 'Know the Lord' Because everyone, from the smallest to the greatest of them, will know me: that I shall be merciful to their wrongdoings and I shall no longer store in my memory their sins and their lawless ways" (Jer 38. 33–34). In mentioning the old covenant which he made and in mentioning a new one, he is about to make, he sketches its beauty and shows its essential features and places its hallmarks one after the

---

[9] Lit. "be nailed to thinking over what's been said . . ."

other, so that you may learn how great the difference between the new and the old is—its difference, not its opposition—how great its superiority, how great its brilliance, how great the glittering of its gifts and grace.

10   And so, what are the essential features of the new [covenant]? "I shall place my laws in their mind and I shall engrave them on their hearts." The old law was written on stone tablets, and when the first tablets were broken, Moses chiseled out others in turn and after engraving the edicts there, descended, with the tablets' nature akin to the lack of sensation of those receiving them. But the new [covenant] is not like this, for tablets weren't chiseled out when the new covenant was made. Instead, how and in what way? Listen to Luke telling it. "They were all with one accord in the same place, he says. And suddenly from the sky there was a sound as if there was a violent wind coming. And there appeared distributed among them tongues as if of fire. And it sat on each one of them, and they were filled with the Holy Spirit and began to speak in tongues, just as the Spirit gifted them" (Acts 2.1–4). Do you see how the prophet clearly declared this in advance from the first, when he said as follows: "I shall place my laws in their mind and I shall engrave them on their hearts." For the grace of the Spirit, which God had granted to dwell in their minds, made them living columns.[10] And it engraved everything on their mind with complete ease and stored it all away in the breadth of their soul. Nowhere was there stone or lifeless raw material or edicts chiseled in rock, but instead the Spirit's grace engraved in the apostles' minds. It was for this reason that they were all at once rendered wiser than anyone, like jumping sparks, since they had the fount of teaching welling up in their mind. From this source they both bridled Jews and stitched shut philosophers' mouths and

[10]A column erected in a marketplace or other public location was an important means of publishing information intended for broad dissemination. The image being evoked here is of the disciples at Pentecost publishing the laws engraved on their hearts as if they were columns that had been brought to life. It is at this point that the lacuna restored from Stav. 6 begins.

barricaded orators' tongues and swept their net over land and sea and caught up the old laws and planted the new covenant, not fixing it in one location like those tablets but spreading it all over the earth and proclaiming to all what was engraved in their mind.

11 So, ask the Jew what Jeremiah points to when he says: "I shall place my laws in their mind and engrave them on their heart." For he makes this statement as something new and astonishing compared to earlier, indicating the events of the present, and, by informing us of the singularity of this covenant, he made it clear that the way in which it was made is more brilliant than before. "And in no way will each instruct their fellow citizen, or each their sister or brother, saying: 'Know the Lord!' " What's this? After promising great things and lifting us up with hope and indicating that the signs are brilliant, he for some reason added this comment: "And in no way will each instruct their fellow citizen, or each their sister or brother, saying: 'Know the Lord!' " This is the fruit of such substantial grace: not to be instructed; this is the successful outcome of the new covenant: not to learn. He says this in order to show the easy digestibility of the knowledge and the swiftness of the proclamation. For just as when the sun appears we don't need people to instruct us and show us the light, since the ray of light makes itself obvious, nor is there anyone who says to the person next to the them: "Look at the sun!," so is the knowledge brilliant and manifest and more obvious than the ray of light itself. As a result we don't need instruction but all, off our own initiative, swap to the truth and welcome the proclamation with a great deal of speed.

12 That's exactly what happened. As a result he also added the following words: "Because everyone, from the smallest to the greatest of them, will know me." For that reason there was no need for instruction or catechesis. He says this to contrast it with what was said just before, namely that, whereas countless teachers and prophets took the Jews and molded them day after day, yet didn't train them as they ought, in a short time they (sc. the apostles)

caught up the entire world with considerable ease. As a result teachers weren't required; instead, the Word raced swifter than light itself.
For even if the apostles did instruct, even so everyone welcomed the
Word with considerable ease: on the first day, at least, three thousand, then five thousand, then tens of thousands, then the entire
world was won over to the truth in a short space of time. And so,
what he is saying is this: that because of the impetus and the grace
that was lavished [on them] and the obvious nature of the knowledge there was no need of effort or time; instead, of their own accord
everyone will arrive at knowledge of the truth. And so, he (sc. Jeremiah) established this [hallmark] not to do away with teaching but
out of a desire to show how easy the instruction was by actually winning ahead of time the teachers' students. That's why he added:
"everyone, from the smallest to the greatest of them, will know me."
Which is what another prophet says, too: "All the earth shall be filled
with knowing the Lord just as considerable water covers the sea"
(Hab 2.14). For just as water carried along by a great force
approaches everything with considerable speed, so too the Word of
the proclamation raced over the entire world, encircling everything
like a river.

13   So, at this point, too, ask the Jew when this happened in the old
covenant. But he couldn't point to it. For how (could he) in a situation where, despite the occurrence of such great miracles and signs,
a nation wasn't even corrected. I mean, even with prophetic pro-
nouncements sounding day after day in their ears, they bowed down
to idols and worshipped groves and trees and stones, despite being
instructed in the details of the law for thousands of years and much
longer. But this did not occur in grace; instead at one and the same
time the Word of the proclamation rose up and shone light on the
entire world. Indeed, Paul made this clear since those times when he
spoke, "while the good news was being proclaimed in all of creation
under heaven" (Col 1.23). And again, just as [the Word] is bearing
fruit and multiplying, he also hits out at the foolishness of the Jews

and says: "But, I ask: didn't they hear? Indeed they did. Their voice went out into all the earth and their words to the ends of the world" (Rom 10.18). In saying this he actually means a second hallmark of the covenant. Of what nature? "That I shall be merciful to their wrongdoings and I shall no longer store in my memory their lawless ways." What did he mean? Here he indicates baptism and forgiveness through grace. This happened not under the law, but under the new covenant. For under the law there was punishment and torture and penalty punishing those who transgressed its edicts. Under the new [covenant], grace and forgiveness of wrongdoings and absolution. That's why Paul also said: "Because God in Christ was reconciling the world to himself, not counting up their faults against them and placing on us the ministration of that reconciliation" (2 Cor 5.19). Which is what the prophet says too: "I shall be merciful to their wrongdoings and I shall no longer store in my memory their sins."

14   And so he establishes three distinguishing features of the new covenant: one, that it wasn't given on stone tablets but that it was given on tablets of flesh, our hearts; second, that the Word raced with ease and lit up everyone's mind; third, that, when the law was dissolved, no one demanded payment for sins but each received forgiveness for their wrongdoings. See, then, how Paul too established these three [distinguishing marks] with precision, so that you may learn the harmony of the heralds of both the new and the old [covenant]. For when he wrote to the Corinthians he said: "You are our letter, supplied by us engraved not with black ink but the spirit of the living God, not on stone tablets but on tablets of flesh, your hearts" (2 Cor 3.3). Did you see how he both mentioned the distinguishing feature of the old [covenant] and the character of the new when he interpreted the prophet's words: "I shall place my laws in their mind and I shall engrave them on their hearts?" This is why he also said: "not on stone tablets but on tablets of flesh, your hearts." And, moving ahead, he again says: "But our suitability is from God, who made us suitable as administrators of the new covenant, not of

edits, but of the spirit. For the edicts kill, while the spirit creates life" (2 Cor 3.5–6). At this point he again interpreted that statement: "I shall be merciful to their wrongdoings and I shall no longer store in my memory their sins and their lawless ways."[11] But the prophet is outlining for us the brilliance of the old [covenant], while the apostle, since he was doing battle with Jews, places each side by side. While he said above: "not on stone tablets but on tablets of flesh, your hearts," here [he says]: "not of edicts, but of the spirit. For the edicts kill, while the spirit creates life."

15   On the Sabbath someone gathered wood and was stoned. Did you see how the edict killed, that is, the law punished? Learn how the spirit creates life. A person enters full of countless wrongs, having prostituted themselves, thieved, defrauded, committed adultery, guilty of every evil, already deadened by sin. The Spirit's grace receives them in the baptismal pool and renders the person who has prostituted themselves a son of God and restores life in the person deadened by sins. This is: "the spirit creates life." How does it create life? By not demanding an account of their wrongdoings, in accord with what the prophet said: "I shall be merciful to their wrongdoings and I shall no longer store in my memory their lawless ways." Again, ask the Jew: where did this occur in the law? But he couldn't point it out. For truly the person who gathered wood was stoned, and the prostitute burnt down to ash, and because of a single sin Moses was thrown out of the promised land. But under grace, when those who have committed countless crimes enjoy baptism they are restored to life and no penalty for their wrongdoings is demanded of them. For this reason Paul too says: "Don't stray! Neither prostitutes, nor effeminate males, nor homosexuals, nor adulterers, nor thieves, nor defrauders, nor drunkards, nor those who hurl verbal abuse, nor robbers will inherit the kingdom of God. Some of you were these things. But you were washed clean, you were sanctified, you were

---

[11] At this point the lacuna and interpolated passage in Montfaucon's text ends. Translation resumes from PG 63.529 ll.46.

justified in the Lord Jesus' name, and in our God's spirit" (1 Cor 6.9–11). Did you see how the words of the prophet: "I shall be merciful to their wrongdoings," shine? How the saying of the apostle: "the spirit creates life," glitters? Do you want to learn yet another, the apostle Paul saying how it encircled the entire world in a brief space of time? Listen when he says: "From Jerusalem to Illyricum I have fulfilled the good news" (Rom 15.19). And again: "Now since I no longer have a reason for being in this area and I am keen to see you, whenever I travel to Spain I hope to see you, once I have enjoyed your company for a little" (Rom 15.23–24). If a single apostle raced through the bulk of the world in a short space of time, consider how others too cast their net over all of it. For this reason he said too: "the good news was being proclaimed in all of creation under heaven." He was interpreting that prophetic statement: "Because everyone, from the smallest to the greatest of them, will know me."

16   Well, that Christ gave the law is clear from these [passages]. And that people who were killed for the law, shed their blood for the giver of the law, is also clear. I ask of your love that from now on you go off to the festival with considerable enthusiasm. Like bees from the hives leap off to the martyrs' wounds and embrace their tortures, with no one balking at the length of the journey. For if Eleazar, an old man, braved fire, and the mother of those blessed [youths] endured so much pain in extreme old age, what defense could you have, what excuse for not even traversing a few stades[12] for the sake of viewing those wrestling matches?[13] For this reason I ask of your love that you all attend—old women, in order to view a woman of like age, young women to take the old woman as a teacher, men in order to see the woman crowned, old men so that they too might be

---

[12]The stade is a Greek unit of measurement equivalent to c. 202 yards or 185 meters. John is typically vague in his homilies about the measurement of both time and distance. It is interesting to note that the verb he uses here (*diaperōntes*) tends to have the specific meaning of crossing a body of water.

[13]At this point the text used by Montfaucon ends. The remaining lines are restored from Stav. 6.

amazed at Eleazar, and young men at the chorus of youths. For truly for each gender and each age group there are examples of wrestling matches and competitions and victory and trophies and crowns to see. So then, so that we may enjoy this lovely sight, let us go off with considerable enthusiasm, so that we may see wrestlers becoming victors and heralded when crowned and may be considered worthy of sharing with them there too their holy dwellings.[14] May we all be worthy of these things, through the grace and loving kindness or our Lord Jesus Christ, to whom be glory and power and honor and adoration forever and ever. Amen.

[14]John here shifts seamlessly from his encouragement to attend their festival at a martyrium on the following day to the common closing wish that the audience and he be held worthy to share the eternal dwellings of the martyrs in heaven.

Homily 1 on the Maccabees

The story of Eleazar, the seven Maccabean brothers and their mother is recorded in 4 Maccabees in the Septuagint and provides the background for the following two homilies. Although all of the martyrs involved were Jews, there are strong parallels between their experience and that of Christian martyrs. Their deaths occurred in the second century BCE under Antiochus IV, at a time when the king was attempting to impose Greek religious cults upon the Jews in Palestine. All of the martyrs refused to eat the meat that had been sacrificed, which in their case was doubly abhorrent, as it was pork. Eleazar, an elderly rabbi, spits out the meat, refuses the compromise that is offered and deliberately provokes his execution with inflammatory comments witnessing to his faith in God and the law. Similarly the seven brothers and their mother were arrested for refusing to eat such meat, were whipped and scourged and killed one by one from the eldest to the youngest. The mother was killed last. As each dies, they express various noble sentiments, while the remainder console each other as the king's frustration and the severity of the tortures increase. Gregory of Nazianzus also preached a sermon on these martyrs (*Or.* 15), which is the first surviving homily on the topic, and which, like John's, closely follows the biblical account.[1]

As already mentioned, adoption of the Maccabees as Christian martyrs was a relatively recent phenomenon, which occurred at Antioch in the second half of the fourth century, probably during the reign of Julian.[2] Vinson argues that in this city the Jewish and Christian cults probably co-existed harmoniously from the time of

---

[1]Gregory's homily does, nonetheless, contain some significant additions. For these see Vinson, "Gregory Nazianzen's Homily 15," 166–76.

[2]Vinson, "Gregory Nazianzen's Homily 15," 185–8.

Julian to the accession of Theodosius I (early 379), when "vigorous efforts were made to separate the two." It is probably in that period that the Christian celebration of the festival was shifted from December (Hanukkah) to 1 August, on which date it is located in the Syrian martyrology.[3] That the homilies were preached at Antioch is indicated, at least, by the second of the two, in which John, towards the conclusion, says that he will break off so that Bishop Flavian can continue their praise.[4]

In this first of two homilies on these saints, John focuses on the sufferings and example of the mother.

Contents:

1. Today the glory that imbues the bodies of the martyrs lights up the city.

2–4. The contests of the martyrs are different from other athletic games, in that the athletes are not young and vigorous, but old or underage. This serves to demonstrate Christ's power.

5–10. John focuses on the mother, since her gender and age provides a particularly strong example. In being martyred last, after her children, as a mother she suffered twice as much. Yet it didn't weaken her, as the Devil hoped, but made her even stronger.

11. Let us use her as an example for enduring the passions that assail us.

Translated from PG 50.617–624.

[3]Vinson, "Gregory Nazianzen's Homily 15," 188.

[4]For an understanding of the cycle of festivals in Antioch and its surrounding countryside at this time of year, see *On the holy martyrs* (Leemans et al., *"Let Us Die that We May Live,"* 115–26), which was preached at Antioch by John on the day after the festival of the Maccabees. It is possible that the two homilies were not delivered in sequence and belong to different years, in which case only the second of the two can be attributed to Antioch with certainty.

On the holy Maccabees and their mother

1   How bright and festive is our city and how more brilliant this
day than the rest of the year, not because the sun is today sending to
the earth rays that are more visible than usual, but because the holy
martyrs' light is lighting up our city well beyond any lightning flash.
For they are more brilliant than ten thousand suns and more visible
than the major stars. Because of them today the earth is more majestic than heaven. Please don't mention the dust, nor think about the
ash, nor the bones that have been consumed by time, but open wide
the eyes of faith and see God's power that accompanies them, the
grace of the Spirit that clothes them, the glory of the heavenly light
that surrounds them. The rays sent from the sun's orbit to the earth
are not of the same type as the flashes and glitters that bound forth
from these bodies and blind the very eyes of the Devil. For just as
when the leaders of gangs of thieves and grave-robbers see imperial
weaponry lying casually around—a chest-plate or shield or helmet,
gleaming all over with gold—they immediately jump back and dare
neither to approach nor to touch, suspecting great danger if they
were to dare anything of the sort; so too, in fact, wherever the
demons, the true leaders of gangs of thieves, see martyrs' bodies
lying around, they flee and immediately jump back. For they don't
have regard to their interim mortal nature, but to the ineffable dignity of Christ who wore them. After all, these weapons no angel, no
archangel, no other created power has put on, except the Master of
angels himself. And just as Paul proclaimed as follows: "Do you seek
proof of Christ who speaks in me?" (2 Cor 13.3), so they too can proclaim and say: "Do you seek proof of Christ who competed in us?"[5]
For their bodies are precious, since they received blows for their very

[5]The Greek text of Montfaucon published by Migne reads *agnōnisamenou*. This
appears to be a typographic error for *agōnisamenou*, which Migne himself read, as
suggested by his Latin translation *certavit*.

own Master's sake, since they bear identifying marks because of Christ. Indeed, just as an imperial crown decorated all over with a diverse array of gems emits different flashes of light, so too the holy martyrs' bodies, since they are marked with wounds, like precious gems, for Christ's sake, appear more valuable and majestic than any imperial diadem.

2   And so, although in the outside world when the presidents of games set up contests they think it extremely showy when they escort into the arena and into the contests young and vigorous athletes, such that, prior to the display in the wrestling matches, they provide a source of wonder for the spectators from the prime condition of their physique, here it isn't like this, but entirely the opposite. For Christ set up a contest not of the kind that they [do], but one that's terrifying and brimming with fear. For it's not the wrestling of humans versus humans, but the fighting of humans versus demons. And so, when he set up this kind of contest for us, he didn't escort into the wrestling matches young and vigorous athletes, but quite immature youths and with them an old man, Eleazar, and in addition to them an elderly woman, the youths' mother. What on earth is this, Master? You're escorting a useless age group into the arena for the competitive rounds? Who ever heard of a woman competing at such an advanced age? "No one has heard [of it]. But," he says, "I shall confirm this incredible and novel and never-heard-of situation through the events themselves. For I'm not the kind of president of the games to entrust everything to the ability of the competitors. Instead, I stand by and assist and extend a hand to my athletes, and the bulk of their successes occur as a result of my patronage."

3   So, whenever you see a woman, who is shaky, elderly, who requires a walking-stick, entering a contest and destroying a tyrant's rage, defeating incorporeal powers, conquering the Devil with ease, smashing his strength with considerable force, marvel at the president of the games' grace, be astonished at Christ's power. The athletes are not vigorous in the flesh, but they are vigorous in their faith.

Their constitution is weak, but the grace that sustains them is powerful. Their bodies are disabled by old age, but their thoughts are trained by the desire for piety. The contest isn't perceivable. And so don't get to know every aspect of the athletes externally, but enter their reason to find the prime condition of their soul. Get to know every aspect of the strength of their faith, so that you may learn that the person who boxes with demons doesn't require a strong physical shell, or to be at the prime of their life; rather, even if they're quite young, even if they've reached extreme old age, yet have a noble and healthy soul, nothing stemming from their age will cause [them] harm in the contests.

4   And why do I mention old and young, where, at any rate, even women stripped off for these wrestling matches, and wove brilliant crowns? My point is that, whereas in the games in the outside world they scrutinize both age and gender and status, and entry to them is closed off to slaves and women and old men and adolescents, here the theater is opened up with complete safety to every status, every age group, and each gender, so that you might learn in full the generosity and ineffable power of the one who set up the contest, and see that apostolic remark certified in practice: "his power is perfected in weakness" (2 Cor 12.9). For whenever children and old people exhibit unnatural strength, the grace of God who works through them is brilliantly revealed in every respect.

5   Indeed, that you may learn that the athletes' weakness, namely the external one, renders the crowned winners more brilliant, come on, let's dismiss the old man and the children and turn our focus to the weaker among them—the wife, the old woman, the mother of seven children. For truly her labor pains are no small obstacle for these wrestling matches. So, what quality of hers deserves our wonder first? The weakness of her gender, or the maturity of her years, or the fragile state of her compassion? For these truly are substantial obstacles for the race that requires such great endurance. Yet I can mention an even greater one than these, through which we shall

view both the woman's courage and the Devil's malice in full. What is it? Consider the foul demon's wickedness. He didn't drag her into the arena first, but escorted her to the wrestling matches after her children. What on earth for? So that by depressing her will first through the tortures of her seven children, and softening the firmness of her resolve, and with her strength spent in advance on the punishment of her offspring through her watching what was taking place, he might then easily attack her in her weakened condition.

6   Indeed, don't look at that fact—that they received the tortures—but consider this—that she endured the pain more severely with each and every one of them, and was slain with each and every one of them. And all women who've experienced childbirth and become mothers know well what I mean. At least, often when a mother sees a small child burning up with fever, she would choose to suffer anything to transfer the fire of the illness from that body to her own. This is how mothers think—that the sufferings of their children are more unbearable than their own ills. If this is true—as it certainly is true—the mother was punished more severely than her children in her children's tortures, and the martyrdom was greater in the mother than in the children. For if just hearing of the illness of a single child churns up its mother's stomach, what wouldn't she have suffered when she didn't receive what was happening through hearsay but discovered by sight the sufferings of not a single child, but such a large group of children as they were being killed? How wasn't she driven out of her mind when she saw each of them being killed slowly by certain diverse and terrifying tortures? How wasn't her soul ripped out of her body? How is it that from the first sight she didn't leap into the fire to free herself from the rest of the spectacle? For even if she was a philosopher,[6] she was still a mother. Even

[6]John does not mean this in the classical sense. In patristic literature the term *philosophos* has ascetic overtones and refers to a person who leads a life of virtue. The terminology John uses at this point (*philosophos, theophilēs, zēlos*) is usually employed when describing a Christian martyr. Thus, glossing over the Jewish context of the original story in favor of presenting her in Christian terms as a woman of considerable

if she was beloved of God, she was also clothed in flesh. Even if she
was zealous, she also shared a woman's nature. Even if she seethed
with the zeal of piety, she was also restrained by the bond of childbirth. For if often we, who are men [and] who have no duty of
friendship towards the person, when we see a condemned person
being led through the agora with the cord at their mouth, being
dragged to the pit, are shattered by just the spectacle, and yet we have
sufficient comfort that we'll suffer nothing of the sort, since the person has been condemned for their wickedness, what isn't it likely
that she suffered when she saw not one condemned person being led
away, but seven children felled in one stroke on a single day not in a
concise termination, but by various and diverse butcheries? I mean,
even if a person were made of stone, even if her stomach were made
of steel,[7] wouldn't she have been utterly churned up, wouldn't she
have experienced something of the kind both a woman and mother
were likely to feel? Reflect on how we marvel at the patriarch Abraham, because he offered up his own son and bound him hand and
foot and put him up on the altar, and then you will see well how great
the woman's courage [was].

7   O that utterly bitter and utterly pleasurable sight! Utterly bitter
because of the nature of what was taking place; utterly pleasurable
because of the outlook of the woman watching. For she didn't see
the blood that was flowing, but saw the crowns of righteousness
being woven. She didn't look at the ribs that were being pierced
through, but looked at the eternal dwellings under construction. She
didn't see executioners standing around, but saw encircling angels.
She forgot her birth pains, she scorned her [feminine] nature, she
ignored her age. She scorned her nature, a tyrannical thing; nature,
which usually controls even wild animals. At least, many of the wild
animals that are difficult to capture are caught in this way, when they
take no heed of their own safety because of their feelings for their

virtue, John contrasts here the Maccabean mother's devotion to God, from which she
derives an unwomanly strength, to her motherhood and innate feminine weakness.

[7]Lit. "adamant," a stone considered by the Greeks to as hard as diamond.

offspring and, off their guard, fall into the hunters' hands. Indeed there is no animal so weak that it doesn't shield its offspring; no creature so gentle that it isn't enraged when its children are killed. But she dissolved the tyranny of nature that extends both through rational human beings and through irrational animals. And not only didn't she attack the tyrant's head, nor tear his face apart, when she saw her cubs being torn apart, but she displayed so great an excess of philosophy as to even pre-prepare for him his inhuman meal and, while the first [children] were still being punished, to encourage those left to experience the same tortures.

8   Let mothers hear these things, let them emulate the woman's courage, her love for her offspring. Let them raise their children this way. For giving birth is not the defining characteristic of a mother, for that is a matter of nature; instead, a mother's defining feature is raising [her child], for that is a matter of choice. And that you may learn that it isn't giving birth that makes a mother, but raising [her children] well, hear Paul crowning the widow, not because of giving birth, but because of her raising of her children. For when he said: "Let a widow be enrolled who is no less than sixty years of age, who has been observed in good works" (1 Tim 5.9, 10), he added the ultimate in good works. What is it? He said: "If she has raised children." He didn't say: "If she has produced children" but "if she has raised children." So then, let's reflect on what it's likely that the woman suffered—if, that is, one should call her a woman—when she saw fingers shaking over burning coals, a head sailing off, an iron first pounding the head of another child, and skin tearing away, and the child suffering these tortures still standing and talking. How did she open her mouth? How did she move her tongue? How did her soul not fly from the flesh? Let me tell you how. She didn't look towards the earth, but prepared herself for all the [blessings] to come.[8] She

[8]Logically, the questions and answer which follow the comment about the child still standing and talking ought to refer to the child, but since the following sentence clearly refers to the mother, it seems that these comments must also be attributed to her.

feared just one thing: that the tyrant would spare [some] and stop
the contest early, that he would split up the group of children, that
some would remain uncrowned. And because she was afraid of this,
she all but took the last one in her hands and put him in the cauldron, using in place of her hands the comfort and advice of the
words she addressed to him. We cannot hear of other people's ills
without pain, yet she viewed her own without pain. Let us not just
simply hear these things, but let each listener project the entire
tragedy onto their own children. Let each sketch the longed for face
and, outlining for themselves the darlings, paint these sufferings on
them, and then they'll know well the power of what I've said. Rather,
not even by doing this. For no sermon can come close to the sufferings of nature; only experience teaches [them].

9   It's timely following the crown of her seven children to address
to her that saying of the prophet: "You are like a fruitful olive in
God's house" (Ps 51.10). After all, in the Olympic games, although
frequently a thousand athletes enter, the crown is given to just one.
But here from seven athletes there are seven winners crowned. What
estate could you show me that's so productive? What womb so fruitful? What births like these? The mother of the sons of Zebedee
became the mother of apostles, but of just two (cf. Mt 10.2). I know
of no single womb that produced seven martyrs and itself in turn
added to their number, not just in the addition of a single martyr,
but in that of many more. For while her children were just seven
martyrs, their mother's body, though it was just a single body when
added, filled the space of fourteen martyrs, both because she was a
witness[9] for each and every one of them, and because she fashioned
them into such [witnesses], and so bore for us an entire Church of
martyrs. She gave birth to seven children and gave birth to none for

[9]The verb carries the double sense of to act as a witness and to be a martyr. The
sense here was that she herself was a martyr seven times over in the case of each of
her children's deaths, while she was also responsible for having produced each of the
seven martyrs.

the earth, but all for heaven; rather, for the King of Heaven, having born them all for the life to come.

10   And so, the Devil led her to the wrestling matches last for the reason that I started to mention: so that, by first removing her strength in having her watch the tortures, she might be easily overcome when she welcomed the antagonist last. For if people on viewing flowing blood have often felt light-headed and fainted and have required a great deal of care in order to bring back the life that's abandoned them and the body's spirit that's taken flight, what wouldn't that woman have endured on seeing so many torrents of blood flowing from the flesh of not another person, but her own children? How much confusion wouldn't have taken hold of her soul? And so for this reason the Devil, as I started out saying, dragged her to the contests after her children to render her weaker. But the opposite occurred. For, instead, she embarked on the contests with confidence. For what reason and why? Because she was no longer afraid, nor did she have to worry over any of her children who had been left behind her here, that they might perhaps weaken and be deprived of their crowns. Rather, having stored them all away in heaven as if in a theft-proof warehouse and sent them to the crowns above and the steadfast blessings, she confidently stripped off for combat with much pleasure. And as if fitting the costliest gem to a crown, she fit her own flesh to her group of children and traveled off to her beloved Jesus,[10] leaving behind for us substantial comfort and counsel; advice through her actions that we should brave every trouble with a healthy soul and lofty mind. For what man, what woman, what old person, what young person who is afraid of dangers brought against them because of Christ will now attain pardon or will have a defense, when a woman, an old one at that, and a mother of so many children, and one who competed before the coming of

[10]John uses poetic license here to claim that the mother was a virtual Christian, while only a few sentences later highlighting that her sacrifice was even greater, given that it occurred before she had an opportunity to know Christ.

grace when the gates of Death were still closed, when sin was not yet extinguished, nor death defeated, can be seen enduring with such great enthusiasm and courage so many tortures because of God?

11   Taking all these factors into consideration, let us, women and men, young and old, inscribe her contests and wrestling matches on our heart as if on a tablet and have her endurance stored up in our soul as a perpetual counsel for scorning troubles, so that by imitating the virtue of these saints here, we may be able to share their crowns too there, with us displaying as much endurance in the irrational passions as they exhibited philosophy in their tortures, in anger and desire for money, bodies, vainglory and all other such things. For if we subvert the flame of these things just as they did the fire, we will be able to stand near them, and share the same boldness of speech. May we all attain these [blessings] through the grace and loving kindness of our Lord, Jesus Christ, through whom and with whom be glory to the Father, together with the Holy Spirit, now and always, and forever and ever. Amen.

Homily 2 on the Maccabees

In his second homily on the Maccabees, John concentrates on the experience of the seven brothers. That the festival lasted two days at Antioch is indicated towards the beginning of this second homily, when John mentions that yesterday he spent his entire sermon on the mother. Whether or not *Homily 1 on the Maccabees* is the sermon to which he refers, it is clear that at this time of year the topic of the Maccabees occupied two consecutive days.

Contents:

1. Just because we can never praise the martyrs adequately, it doesn't mean that we should fail to do so. Like Christ, they honor the intent of the giver, rather than the size of the gift. The value of the martyrs is overwhelming. Because of this, like yesterday, when we concentrated on the mother, today let's focus on what's manageable—just one of her children. In praising one, we praise them all, and the mother will undoubtedly too come into it.

2–3. Let's look at the youngest, since he wasn't even bound, so enthusiastic was he for the torture. He was anxious not to be left behind.

4–5. His mother, too, encouraged him, all but throwing him into the cauldron with her words. She herself remained unmoved by the tortures, showing that she was their true mother in piety, as well as flesh. But let's stop the sermon at this point to allow our bishop to continue their praises.

6. Let everyone emulate the mother, especially those devoted to the harsh ascetic life. She outstripped them all in discipline. Let us conquer the passions in us, with the assistance of the Maccabees' prayers.

Translated from PG 50.623–626.

1   Well, it isn't possible for a single tongue to praise all the holy
martyrs; but even if we had ten thousand mouths and as many
tongues we would fall short in our praises. In fact, when I look at the
deeds of the seven martyrs I experience the same as if a greedy person were to stand near a spring with seven outlets flowing gold and
try to drain it all, but go away after a great and inexpressible amount
of effort leaving the majority behind. For however much you drain
a spring, the majority is left behind. What then? Shall we be silent,
since we can't offer what they deserve? Not at all. For they who
receive our gifts are martyrs and imitate their Master in their judgment of such largesse. How does [God] do it? When someone offers
gifts he measures the repayment by paying attention not to the size
of what was offered, but to the enthusiasm of the giver. This is how
he acted in the case of that widow. The woman threw down two
cents (cf. Lk 21.2–4) and was honored above those who had thrown
down a lot. For God saw not the paucity of the money, but the rich-
ness of her intent. The money was two cents, but her intent was more
valuable than ten thousand ounces of gold. Let's now undertake the
praises with confidence and, if you're happy, let what we did yesterday happen now too. For yesterday we took the mother aside by herself and spent the entire sermon on her. We did this, not with the
intention of detaching her from her group of children, but of rendering our wealth more secure. Let's do this now too. Let's draw off
one of the children and say a few words about him. For I'm afraid
that like seven rivers the praises of the seven martyrs might come
together all at once and flood our sermon. For this reason let's
take aside one of the youths, not to detach him from his group of
brothers, but to make our burden light. For truly when one is
praised, the crown will be shared too by the others, since they all
shared the same contests too. And certainly the mother will come
into [the sermon] for us today too, even if we don't touch her.
For the progress of the sermon will attract her for sure and she

won't be able to bear leaving her children. For if she didn't stand back from her offspring in the contests, she won't keep away in their praises either.

2   So then, which of the seven athletes would you like us to take aside? The first, or the second, or the third, or the last? Rather, none among them is last. For they are a group, and a group, it appears, has neither beginning nor end. But so that we might make the subject of our praise better known, we mention the last in respect of age. For the wrestling matches are brotherly and the achievements related; and where there is a relationship between achievements, there is no first or second. Let's, then, take aside the last in age and of the same age in mind, not just of the same age as his brothers, but also as the old man himself. He alone of the brothers was led to the torture room unbound. For he didn't wait for the executioners' hands, but anticipated their savagery with his own enthusiasm and was escorted unbound. Moreover, he had none of his brothers as a spectator. For they had all been terminated. But he had a more august theater than his brothers—the eyes of his mother. Didn't I say to you that even without our trying their mother would certainly come into it too? Look, then; the sermon's progress has introduced her. This theater was so august and large that it had even the population of angels itself, rather his brothers too, as spectators, no longer from earth, but from heaven. For they sat crowned, just like the judges in the Olympic games, not judging the wrestling matches, but urging on the victor to get [the crown]. And so he stood unbound and spoke words full of philosophy. For he wanted to convert the tyrant to his own piety. On the basis that he couldn't, he then did what was characteristic of him and gave himself up to the torture. And while [the tyrant] pitied him for his age, he wept for [the tyrant's] impiety. For the tyrant and the martyr weren't looking at the same things. Both had the same eyes, but of the flesh. But the eyes of faith were no longer the same. Instead the former looked at the present life, the latter viewed the future towards which he was about to fly. And while

the tyrant saw the roasting pans, the martyr saw the hell[1] into which the tyrant was about to hurl himself.

3   If we marvel at Isaac, in that, after being tied up by his father and bound hand and foot, he didn't leap away from the altar, nor jump on seeing the knife coming towards him, by far more should we marvel at this youth, in that he was not tied up, nor had need of the constraint of the chains, nor waited for the executioners' hands, but himself became his own sacrifice and priest and altar. For after looking around in a circle and seeing none of his brothers present he was upset, he was spurred on to hurry and catch up so that he wouldn't become detached from this noble group. This is why he didn't wait for the executioners' hands. For he was afraid that the tyrant would spare him and that, out of compassion, he might snatch him away from the company of his brothers. This is why he got in first and snatched himself away from the savage man's philanthropy. For truly there were numerous factors that were sufficient to soften the tyrant: the youth's age; the torture of so many of his brothers, which was enough to satiate even a wild animal (but that tyrant wasn't satiated); his mother's grey hair; that he'd gained no advantage from the punishment of [the brothers] who preceded him. With all these factors in mind, the youth threw himself into a torture from which it wasn't possible to escape, and he plunged into the cauldrons as if into a spring of cold water, considering them a divine washing and baptism. For just as people burning with a fever lower themselves into a canal of cold water, so he, burning up with the desire for his brothers, lowered himself into that torture.

4   His mother too added encouragement, not because he needed encouragement, but so that you might learn in turn the woman's strength. For in regard to none of her seven children did she experience maternal feelings; no rather, she experienced maternal feelings in regard to each one. For she didn't say to herself: "What's this? My

[1]Lit. "Gehenna."

group of children's been snatched away. Only this one's left. In this regard I'm at risk of the consequences of childlessness. Who will look after me in my old age from now on, if he dies? Wasn't I content with having half on hand, and if not half, two parts? Instead, I only have the one left to comfort me in my old age, and I'll have to give him up in turn?" She didn't say any of these things, she didn't think them, but lifting him up by the encouragement of her words, as if by her hand, she threw her son into the cauldron, glorifying God that he welcomed all of the fruit of her womb, and didn't reject any, but harvested the entire tree. In consequence, I would say with confidence that she suffered to a greater extent than her children. For while for them the bulk of their pain and their timidity[2] was then cut short, with her untainted mind and untouched will she received a keener perception of what was happening by virtue of her [feminine] nature.

5   Truly one could see a triplicate fire: the one which that tyrant was burning; that which her nature inflamed; that which the Holy Spirit kindled. That Babylonian tyrant didn't light up a furnace like the furnace which this tyrant lit up for the mother. For while there the fuel of the fire was naphtha and pitch and plant fiber[3] and brushwood (cf. Dan 3), here [it was feminine] nature, the bonds of childbirth, a parent's love, harmony among children. Lying on the fire, they (sc. the three youths) didn't fry as much as she fried because of her love. But she prevailed through her piety, and nature battled with grace, and the victory went to grace. Piety overcame the bonds of childbirth and fire conquered fire—the spiritual [conquered] the physical [fire], as well as the fire lit by the tyrant's savagery. And just as a rock in the sea which receives the assaults of waves itself remains

---

[2]Gr. *leipopsychia*, according to Lampe, PGL s.v. id., a word found only in this homily.

[3]Gr. *stuppion*. According to Migne, in the margin of the Regius ms the scribe notes that this term refers to olive pits, by which he perhaps means the waste matter left over from the process of crushing the olives for oil. In general it refers to the fibrous material of plants such as hemp or flax.

unmoved, while [the waves] readily dissolve into foam and disappear, so too that woman's heart, when it received the assaults of pain like a rock in the sea [does] waves, itself remained unmoved, while it dissolved those assaults with a reason that was strong and full of philosophy. She was eager to show the tyrant that she was truly their mother, they truly her genuine children, not through natural relationship, but through their sharing of her virtue. She didn't consider that she was seeing a torturing fire, but a wedding torch. A mother who's beautifying her children for a wedding doesn't rejoice to the degree that she rejoiced on seeing them tortured. And as if she was dressing the one in a bridegroom's robe, weaving crowns for another, and setting up wedding canopies for another, so when she saw the one running up to the cauldrons, another to the roasting pans, another with his head being chopped off, she rejoiced. And everything was full of smoke and steam, and she received her children's experience through all her senses, seeing with her eyes, hearing through listening to the beloved words, receiving through her nose that sweet and noxious smoke from their flesh —noxious to the unbelievers, but to God and her sweetest of all—that smoke which fouled the air, but didn't foul the woman's mind. For she stood unwavering and unmoved, remaining steadfast in everything that took place. But it's time now to stop the sermon, so that they may enjoy more abundant praises from our common teacher.[4]

6   Let fathers imitate her, let mothers emulate [her], and women and men living in virginity and clothed in sackcloth and wearing collars.[5] For to whatever degree we achieve harsh self-discipline and

[4]A term used commonly by John to refer to his bishop, Flavian.

[5]This final section of the homily offers advice which is rather different in tenor and vocabulary from John's other martyr homilies, and which indeed refers to forms of asceticism which appear to receive mention elsewhere only in Constantinopolitan homilies. It is possible, as suggested by Sever Voicu in a private communication, that what we have here is a homily originally preached at Antioch, with an equally genuine ending from Constantinople added later by an editor to suit a particular need. Had John himself been responsible for the addition, it is likely that he would have found it necessary to strip out the reference to Flavian. On the other hand, it may be

philosophy, the woman's philosophy outstrips our endurance. So then, let no one who has reached a peak of courage and endurance think it beneath their dignity to have the old woman as their teacher. Rather, let us all pray together, both those who inhabit the cities, and those who spend their life in the deserts, and those who practice virginity and those who shine in holy marriage, and those who disdain everything associated with the present and crucify their body, that through invoking the same bold speech as her we can be considered worthy of the same race as her, and of standing near her on that day through the holy woman's and her children's prayers and [those] of the great and noble old man, Eleazar, who helped to complete their group and who exhibited a steely soul during his tortures. We'll be able [to achieve this], if we offer everything of our own along with their holy prayers, by conquering the passions in us before the wars and tortures in [this] time of peace, by pruning the undisciplined stirrings of the flesh, by mortifying the body and treating it as a slave. For if we live our life in this fashion in a time of peace, we shall receive brilliant crowns for our training. If God who loves humankind decides to effect the same contest for us, we shall come to the wrestling matches prepared and shall attain the heavenly blessings. May we all attain them, through the grace and loving kindness of our Lord, Jesus Christ, through whom and with whom to the Father, along with the Holy Spirit, be glory, honor, and power forever and ever. Amen.

that the ending is original to the homily and that we need rather to reconsider our picture of the forms which asceticism took at Antioch.

On Saints Bernike, Prosdoke, and Domnina

The three women celebrated in this homily are a mother (Domnina) and two daughters (Bernike and Prosdoke), who were martyred during the persecutions under Diocletian in 302. Originally citizens of Antioch, they fled for Edessa during the persecution and ended up taking their lives by drowning in the vicinity of Hierapolis to escape being raped by passing soldiers. Their cult developed quite early at Antioch, since Eusebius of Emesa preached a sermon celebrating these women there between 335 and 338 CE. This took place during the episcopate of Flaccillus, one of several Arian bishops who presided over the Church in Antioch in the period after Eustathius[1] was sent into exile. Eusebius himself was a native of Edessa in Syria, who had undertaken exegetical training in Antioch and was present in Antioch at the time that Eustathius was deposed. He then went to Alexandria to further his studies, but developed and maintained a close friendship with Eustathius' Arian successors, particularly Flaccillus. It was under these circumstances that he came to preach his own sermon on Domnina and her daughters in one of Flaccillus' churches in Antioch. At both the opening and conclusion of his sermon he stresses to his audience that these women are "your burnt offering, your sacrifice, the mothers or daughters of [your] Church." That John preached his own sermon on the topic at Antioch is suggested by the statement towards the end of this homily that the bodies of the mother and daughters are buried locally and available for visiting on occasions other than their festival.

---

[1]See the introduction to the homily *On St Eustathius* above.

There is a possible connection between these women and the martyr Pelagia,[2] also a native of Antioch. Ambrose (*On virgins* 3.7.34) mentions Pelagia's mothers and sisters without naming them and says that they died by drowning to preserve their virginity. On the other hand, Eusebius of Emesa draws upon Pelagia as one in a number of examples of a woman killing herself to preserve her virginity,[3] without drawing any closer connection.

The date most generally accepted for the festival of Domnina, Bernike, and Prosdoke at Antioch is 20 April, the day assigned to it in the Syrian martyrology. On the basis that in the opening lines of the homily John says that less than twenty days have elapsed between the "commemoration of the cross" and the current festival, Nardi has located the homily in either 392 or 394, presumably by subtracting slightly less than twenty days from 20 April in order to arrive at a date for Good Friday at the beginning of April.[4] In fact, neither of his dates is feasible, since in both those years Good Friday occurred a little more than twenty days beforehand. Rauschen's proposal of 391 is more likely,[5] as are also the years 386, 388, or 397, since in those years Good Friday fell on 4, 3, 7, and 3 April, respectively. Although John is notoriously elastic with numbers in his homilies, in this case we can be reasonably certain that he preached his sermon in one of these four years, since in all of the others during the period that he was a presbyter at Antioch Good Friday occurs less than ten or more than twenty days before 20 April. For John, "not yet twenty days" is most likely to encompass a range anywhere between ten and twenty.

It is possible that the homily was delivered during a vigil on the eve of the martyrs' festival, since in § 12 John compares the darkness

[2]For John's sermon on Pelagia see Leemans et al., *"Let Us Die that We May Live,"* 148–57.

[3]Eusebius of Emesa, *On a martyr mother and her two daughters* 18.

[4]C. Nardi, "A proposito degli atti del martirio di Bernice, Prosdoce e Domnina," *Civilta Classica e Cristiana* 1 (1980): 245.

[5]G. Rauschen, *Jahrbücher der christlichen Kirche unter dem Kaiser Theodosius dem Grossen. Versuch einer Erneuerung der Annales Ecclesiastici des Baronius für die Jahre 378–395* (Freiburg im Breisgau, 1897), 525.

that accompanied the civil war that spurred the women to martyrdom to "this nighttime darkness." On the other hand, references
to "this daylight" are a common topos in John's homilies and the
comment may have no relevance to the time at which the sermon is
being delivered.

Contents:

1–2. Less than twenty days after Christ's death, his death has born fruit
in a group of virgin martyrs. The weaker sex, whom the Devil used to introduce death, has paradoxically become strong and defeated death. Before
Christ's death it was fearsome even to holy men.

3–10. Abraham, Jacob, and Elijah are adduced as examples of men who
feared death before the time of Christ. Paul, on the other hand, found it preferable. The change in attitude is reflected in the change in our response to death.

11–14. (The focus of the sermon shifts to praise of the martyrs.) The
story occurs in a time of "civil war," with a campaign waged against the
Church in the courts and members of families set against one another. This
spurred the women to leave their country. The journey of the mother and
her two virgin daughters must have been one of considerable hardship, yet
God protected the daughters especially from harm.

15–17. They fled to Edessa, where further decrees were posted, which
encouraged family members to betray each other to the authorities, an event
which God had already prophesied. The husband and father of the women
pursued them there and brought soldiers with him.

18–22. The women made to return. They came to Hierapolis, where a
river flowed beside the road. Deceiving the soldiers, allegedly with the assistance of the husband/father, they avoided the soldiers and the mother
drowned both herself and her daughters to preserve their virginity. In doing
this she became a priest, leading them into marriage with Christ, and performing a new kind of baptism. She avoided capture and being taken to
court through her desire to speed towards martyrdom and heaven. It took
enormous courage for a mother to do this to her daughters.

23. The daughters too displayed courage and deserve praise, particularly
for their kindness in leaving their shoes on the river bank as a silent witness,
so that the soldiers couldn't be accused of being complicit in their escape.

24. Let us embrace the coffins of these women not just today but on other days, since their coffins, as well as their bones, have considerable power, and through their martyrdom they can persuade God on our behalf.

Translated from PG 50.629–640

A homily of praise on the holy martyrs Bernike and Prosdoke, virgins, and Domnina their mother

1   Not yet twenty days have passed since we celebrated the commemoration of the cross and, look, we're celebrating a martyrs' commemoration. Did you see how swift is the fruit of Christ's death? It was because of that sheep these heifers were killed; because of that lamb these sacrifices [were offered]; because of that sacrifice these offerings [were made]. Not yet twenty days have passed and immediately the wood of the cross has sprouted the martyrs' lovely buds. For these are the accomplishments of that death. What's more, observe the proof of what I said on that occasion, which today has turned out to be the case in actual fact. I said then: "He broke off the bronze gates and smashed up the iron bars" (Ps 106.16). Today these statements are demonstrated in reality. For if he hadn't broken off the gates of bronze and had they been shut, the women wouldn't have ventured so readily to enter. If he hadn't smashed up the iron bar, the virgins wouldn't have had the strength to remove it. If he hadn't made the prison useless, the martyrs wouldn't have entered so fearlessly. Praise God! A woman braved death; a woman who brought death into our life—the Devil's own ancient weapon— defeated the Devil's power. The very vessel that is weak and fragile became an unassailable weapon. Women are challenging death. Who wouldn't be amazed? Let Greeks be ashamed, let Jews, who don't believe in Christ's resurrection, hide their face. For, tell me, what greater sign of that resurrection do you seek, when you see that

so great a reversal of reality has taken place? Women are challenging death, something which before this time was frightening and terrifying even to holy men.

2   Learn, then, the fear of it before this time, so that on seeing the contempt for it now, you will marvel at God, who is responsible for the change. Learn its former strength, so that on learning its weakness now, you will give thanks to Christ who cut its sinews completely. Beloved, previously nothing was stronger than it and nothing weaker than us. But now nothing is weaker than it and nothing stronger than us. Do you see how outstanding the reversal is? How God made the strong weak and rendered the weak strong, demonstrating his power to us in both instances? But, so that what I've said isn't just a statement, let me introduce the proof too. Indeed, if you like, let's show first how before this time it wasn't just sinners who feared it, but also holy people, who enjoyed considerable frankness of speech with God, flourished as a result of their good works, and embraced every virtue. I produce these proofs not so that we might condemn the saints, but so that we might marvel at God's power.

3   From what source, then, is it clear that before this time Death's appearance was fearsome and everyone was terrified of it and trembled? From the first patriarch. For the patriarch Abraham, the just man, the friend of God, who left his country and house and relatives and friends and ignored everything in the present because of God's command, was so afraid and feared death that when he was about to enter Egypt he addressed these words to his wife: "I know that you're an attractive woman. And so it will be the case that when the Egyptians catch sight of you they will keep you for themselves and kill me" (Gen 12.11,12). What, then? "Say 'I am his sister,' so that it will go well for me because of you and my life will be preserved for your sake" (Gen 12.13). What's this, holy man and patriarch? Are you turning a blind eye to the abuse of your wife and the wronging of your marriage bed and the undermining of your marriage? Tell me, are

you so afraid of death? You're not just turning a blind eye, but you're even weaving a deception with your wife and co-starring in the spectacle of abuse and contriving everything so that it won't be evident when the Egyptian king attempts adultery, and you've stripped the label of "wife" from her and put the mask of "sister" on her?

4   But I'm afraid lest, in our keenness to paralyze death's power, we appear to be accusing the just man. For this reason I shall attempt to do both: to show death's weakness, and to extract this man from this accusation. It's essential first to show that he feared death, and then to free [him] from the charges. So then, let's see how unbearable and terrible a thing he endured. For to see one's wife abused and to observe her being subjected to adulterous advances is more unbearable than a thousand deaths. Indeed, why do I mention being subjected to adulterous advances? Even if a bare notion of a suspicion about her had taken possession of his soul, life would have been completely unlivable for him. For the passion of jealousy is an invincible fire and flame to him. And a certain [writer] made its tyrannical and implacable nature clear when he said: "Full of jealousy is her husband's rage. He will not exchange his hostility for any compensation, nor be sparing on the day of judgment, nor is he in any way softened by many gifts" (Prov 6.34, 35). And again in another place: "Jealousy is as tough as Hades" (Song 8.6). For just as one can't persuade Hades with money, he says, so neither can one appease or reconcile the jealous man. At any rate, many people on many occasions have even betrayed their own soul in order to discover the adulterer. They would even gladly have drunk the very blood of the man who abused their wife, and would have chosen to do and suffer anything to this end. Yet, even so, the just man put up with this unbearable passion, this tyrannical and implacable [jealousy] to an extreme degree and turned a blind eye to the abuse of his wife through fear of death and finality.

5   Thus, that he was afraid of death is clear from this. It's now time to free him from the accusations and charge in this respect, by first

mentioning the charge itself. So, what is the charge? "He should rather have died," you say, "than turn a blind eye to the abuse of his wife." This is certainly the accusation that some raise—that he chose rather to save his own life, than the modesty of his wife. What are you saying? That he should rather have died than turn a blind eye to the abuse of his wife? What advantage would that have been? For if, in dying, he would have snatched his wife from abuse, your claim would be a good one. But if, in dying, he didn't help release his wife from abuse, why would he betray his own salvation pointlessly and in vain? That you may learn that not even by dying would he have snatched her from adultery, listen to what he says: "And so it will be the case that when the Egyptians catch sight of you they will keep you for themselves and kill me." So then, two monstrous things were about to occur: adultery and murder. It was a mark of no ordinary intelligence to produce at least one advantage out of these two things. For if he would have given up his own life (for I will make the same point again) to free her from abuse, and they, after killing the just man, hadn't touched Sarah, you would have brought a reasonable charge. But if, even though he died, even so his wife would have been abused, why do you accuse the just man, who, since two crimes were about to take place—adultery and murder—prevented the second through his wisdom—I mean that of murder? For on this point he ought even to have been praised, in that he kept the adulterer's hand clean of blood. I mean, you couldn't even claim this, that by her saying "I'm his sister" she incited the Egyptian towards abuse. For even if she'd said "I'm his wife," not even at this would he have desisted. And [Abraham] made this clear when he said: "If they see you, they will say 'She is his wife,' and will kill me, but keep you for themselves." As a result, if she had said that she was his wife, both adultery and murder would have taken place. But since she said that she was his sister, the crime of murder was prevented. Do you see how, although two crimes were about to take place, he removed the second through his wisdom?

6   Do you want to learn how, in as much as he could, he in turn undercut the charge of adultery too, so that he didn't allow him even to be a full-scale adulterer? Listen closely to the same words again. "Say," he says, " 'I am his sister.' " What does he mean? The person who takes a sister is not an adulterer. For the adulterer is judged by their intention. Since even Judah, when he had intercourse with his own daughter-in-law Thamar, was not judged an adulterer (cf. Gen 38.15). For he had intercourse with the woman not as a daughter-in-law, but as a prostitute. So too in this case the Egyptian, since he was going to take her not as Abraham's wife, but as his sister, wouldn't be judged an adulterer. "So what's this say about Abraham," you ask, "who knew that he'd farmed out his own wife and not his sister?" Well, not even this is a charge against him. For if [the Egyptian] would have backed off from the abuse, when he heard that she was his wife, you would have condemned the just man appropriately. But if the label of "wife" wasn't going to protect Sarah at all when it came to beating off the abuse, just as he in fact said ("They will say, 'She is his wife,' and will keep you for themselves"), then we should marvel far more at the just man being able in a matter of such great unpleasantness to keep the Egyptian clean of blood and, in as much as he could, to mitigate the charge of abuse.

7   Let's now steer the sermon also towards his descendent Jacob. Indeed, you'll see him too fearing and trembling death, a man who from a very early age had demonstrated apostolic philosophy. For Paul set down a law for his disciples, saying: "If we have food and clothing, we will be content with these" (1 Tim 6.8). This he (sc. Jacob) also requested from God, saying: "If the Lord gives me bread to eat and clothing to wear, it is enough for us" (Gen 28.20). Yet nonetheless even he, who sought no more than he needed, who ignored his home, who received the blessings, who was persuaded by his mother, who was a friend to God, who through wisdom over-powered nature (for though naturally second, he became first in blessings), who was capable of such great things, who exhibited such

great philosophy, who displayed such great piety, after countless contests, after countless rounds of competition, after countless wrestling matches, and those numerous crowns, when he returned to his country and was on the point of meeting his brother, as if he was about to catch sight of a wild animal and was afraid of him holding a grudge, fell down before God and begged, saying: "Snatch me out of the hand of Esau, my brother because I am afraid that he might come and beat me as well as mother and children" (Gen 32.11). Do you see how he too was afraid of death? How he trembles and begs God concerning this? Would you like me to show you in turn yet another great person who had this very same experience? Consider Elijah, the lofty and divine soul. For he who shut heaven and opened it again, who brought down the fire from above, who offered the wondrous sacrifice, who was zealous about God, he who displayed an angelic life in a human body, who wore nothing more than a sheepskin, who became loftier than any human concern, so trembled at and was afraid of death that after all that, after heaven and the sacrifice, after the sheepskin and the solitude and the philosophy, and such great boldness of speech, he was afraid of a cheap slut and fled because of that. For when Jezebel said: " 'May the gods do thus to me and more, if tomorrow I don't render your soul like the soul of one of the dead.' Elijah was afraid," it says, "and fled along the road for forty days" (3 Kgs 19.2, 3).

8   Do you see how terrifying death is? So then, let's marvel at our Master in that he made what was terrifying to the prophets contemptible to women. Elijah fled death; women fled towards death. He leapt away from death; they actually pursued death. Do you see how great a change occurred all at once? Those in the company of Abraham and Elijah fought against death, while women trampled death under their feet like mud. But let's not condemn those saints. The fault isn't theirs. The weakness belonged to their nature; the blame doesn't lie with their free will. At that time God wanted death to be terrifying so that the magnitude of his grace might be revealed

afterwards. He wanted it to be terrifying, for it was a sentence. He didn't want the threat of the sentence relaxed on the grounds that human beings might afterwards become lazier. "Let the sentence keep on frightening them and having a moderating influence. For there will come, there will come a time, when they will in fact be free of this struggle." Which indeed came to pass. For that he has released us from this struggle, the martyrs make clear and Paul makes clear ahead of the martyrs.

9   Did you hear Abraham saying in the Old Testament: "They will keep you for themselves, but will kill me"? Did you hear Jacob saying: "Snatch me away, Lord, from the hand of Esau, my brother, because I am afraid of him"? Did you see Elijah fleeing a woman's threat because of death? Hear how Paul is disposed regarding this matter—whether he considers it terrifying like they; whether he's distressed when it's approaching, and is afraid. To the contrary, he even thought that the thing was desirable. For this reason he says: "That I depart and be with Christ is far better" (Phil 1.23). To them it was terrifying, to him better. To them unpleasant, to him a pleasure. And rightly so! For previously death led [us] down into Hades. Now death sends [us] on to meet Christ. For this reason Jacob said: "You will draw down my old age with grief into Hades" (Gen 42.38). But Paul said: "That I depart and be with Christ is far better." He said these things not out of condemnation of the present life (heaven forbid! let's watch out that we don't give ground to the heretics' censures), nor from fleeing it as something evil, but through desiring the future as better. For he didn't say that to depart and be with Christ was simply good, but [that it was] better. And "better" is better than "good." My point is, just as when he says: "The person who marries does well, but the person who doesn't marry does better" (1 Cor 7.38), he shows that marriage is good, but that virginity is better, so too [does he do] here. "The present life is good," he says, "but the future is much better."

10   Speaking philosophically about the same matters he said elsewhere on another occasion: "Even if I'm being poured out as a libation over the offering and liturgy of your faith, I am happy and rejoice with all of you. In the same way you too be happy and rejoice" (Phil 2.17–18). What are you saying? You're dying, Paul, and you call on people to share in your pleasure? Tell me, what's going on? "I'm not dying," he says, "but ascending to a better life." Thus, just as people who receive high office invite many to share with them in their excitement, so too Paul, when approaching death, invited them to share in his pleasure. For death is a rest and a release from hard work, and an exchange for one's labors, and a reward for wrestling matches, and a crown. This is why, while in the beginning there was the beating of breasts and wailing over corpses, now [there are] psalms and the singing of hymns. At any rate, the Jews wept over Jacob for forty days; they wept over Moses too for as many more,[6] and beat their breasts because at that time death was death. But now it is not like this; rather [there are] hymn-singing and prayers and psalms, with everyone making it clear that the matter is associated with pleasure. For the psalms are a sign of festivity. "Is anyone cheerful among you?," scripture says, "Let them sing psalms!" (Jas 5.13). So, since we are full of good cheer we sing over our corpses psalms that urge us to feel confident about death. "Commit, my soul, into your rest," it says, "because the Lord has been kind to you" (Ps 114.7). Do you see that death is a kindness and a rest? For the person entering that resting rests from their labors, just as God did from his own affairs.

11   Well, such is the case with death. Come, let's now proceed to the praise of the martyrs, lest you grow tired of listening. For truly these arguments had their basis in the martyrs' praise. But it's necessary to take the story back a little. A cruel war was once stirred up against the Church, more serious than any war. For this war was two-fold: one

[6]This is typical of John's rhetorical manipulation of numbers. At Deut 34.8 it says that the Israelites wept over Moses for thirty days, while at Gen 50.1–3, it says that Joseph was embalmed for forty days, but the Egyptians wept over him for seventy.

internal, one external. One originating from our own people, the other from enemies. One originating from strangers, the other from friends and acquaintances. Mind you, even if the war had occurred on a single front, there would have been unbearable evil, and if they had just attacked from without, the magnitude of the disasters would have been great. But as it is, it was two-fold, and the war initiated by their own side was more cruel than that initiated by external forces. For the acknowledged enemy can easily be guarded against. But the person who bears the mask of a friend, but the disposition of one's enemies, is difficult for those they plot against to capture. And so, the war at that time was two-fold: the one a civil war, the other involving attack by external forces. Rather, if one must tell the truth, each of the two was a civil war. For truly the judges and magistrates and soldiers who attacked from without weren't of another nationality or foreigners or from another administrative district or kingdom, but dwelt under the same laws, inhabited the same country, shared the same way of government. The civil war was thus the one initiated by the judges, while the crueler war, the one that was novel and beyond calculation and filled with a great deal of savagery was that initiated by relatives. For truly brothers betrayed brothers and fathers children, and husbands wives and all the just aspects of relationships were trodden on, and the whole world was in revolt, and at that time no one respected anyone. For the Devil held sway to considerable excess. And so, in that uproar and war these women—if, that is, one must call them women; for although in a female body, they displayed a male mind; rather, they didn't just display a male mind but exceeded even nature itself and clashed with the bodiless powers. And so these women abandoned city and household and relatives and changed over to a foreign [city].[7] "For when Christ is dishonored," they said, "let nothing be either valuable or essential to us." For this reason they abandoned everything and left.

[7]There is probably a double meaning here. In the literal sense, they exchanged their life in Antioch for one in Edessa, while at the same time, they abandoned their life on earth and migrated to heaven.

12   Indeed, just as when a house is burning to the ground in the middle of the night, when those who are asleep inside become aware of the uproar, they swiftly jump out of bed and leap out of the house's front doors, taking nothing from inside—for they have a single focus, to get their own body away from the flame first, and they anticipate the course of the fire, and exit with considerable haste—so these women did too. For when they saw the whole world set aflame, they immediately leapt out and jumped out of the city's front doors, seeking just one thing—to preserve the salvation of their soul by any means. For there was truly a fierce conflagration then and a deep darkness ruled—a darkness gloomier than this nighttime [dark]. And because of this, just as [occurs] in darkness, friends didn't recognize friends and husbands betrayed wives. Because of this they passed over their enemies, yet beat against friends and household members and there was a vicious night-time battle, and events were filled with considerable uproar.

13   And so at that time the women abandoned their country and went away; and they imitated the patriarch Abraham, to whom it was said: "Depart from your land and from your relatives" (Gen 12.1). For truly the time of persecution recommended to these women this advice: to depart from their land and from their relatives, so that they might inherit heaven. And so the woman departed from her house and took two daughters with her. When you hear that women who were raised freely, who had no prior experience of these troubles, departed, don't simply pass it over, but apply your mind to considering how great the evil was, how much unpleasantness the matter contained. For if people who set out on a moderate-sized journey, who are well-supplied with pack-animals, who take servants, who travel without risk, who are in control of their return, perceive many hardships [and] put up with a great deal of misery; where there is a woman, and virgins, and a lack of servants, and betrayal by friends, and uproar and confusion, and unendurable fear, and all kinds of danger in these things, and running for one's

life, and enemies on every side, what account could present the
women's struggles, their courage, their generosity of spirit, their
faith? I mean, if the mother had departed alone, certainly the struggle wouldn't have been so unbearable. But as it is, she brought her
daughters into it too, and they [were] virgins. As a result the struggle was doubled and the added weight of anxiety considerable. For
the greater the possession, the more troublesome its protection.

14 So then, she departed and took virgins, and didn't have the
option of hiding them away in bedchambers. And yet, you know that
bedchambers and women's quarters and doors and locks and security guards and guards outside the door and maidservants and
nurses and a mother's attentiveness and a father's forethought and
much attention by the parents result in virginity's flower being
closely watched, and even so it is scarcely kept safe. But she was
deprived of all this protection. How, then, was she able to keep them
safe? Due to the protection of the divine laws. She didn't have a room
to throw around them, but had the powerful hand that provides
shelter from above. She had neither door nor lock, but had the true
door that walls off treachery. And just as, while Lot's house was
besieged in the midst of the Sodomites, it suffered no harm—for it
had angels inside (cf. Gen 9.10ff)—so indeed too these women martyrs, who were in the midst of Sodomites and all their enemies, and
were besieged on all sides, suffered no harm. For they had the angels'
Master dwelling in their souls. And as they entered the deserted road
they suffered no harm. For they held to the true road that was leading them towards heaven. It is because of this that they walked with
safety in so great a war and confusion, and though threatened by
waves. And what was most astonishing is that the sheep were led
through the wolves, the lambs passed through the lions, and no one
looked at them with lustful eyes; instead, just as God didn't allow the
Sodomites standing near the door to observe their entry, so too at
that time he blinded everyone's sight, so that the virgin bodies
wouldn't be betrayed.

15   And so, they made their way to a city called Edessa, a city more rural than many, but more pious. I mean, which of that city's features did they consider equal to finding refuge in so great a surging sea and having a harbor in such a storm? And the city welcomed the strange women—strangers on earth, but citizens of heaven. And on receiving the deposit, it kept it safe. But let no one despise the women's weakness, in that they fled. For they fulfilled the Master's command that says: "Whenever they chase you from this city, flee to the next" (Mt 10.23). Indeed it was on hearing this that they fled, and in the meantime a single crown was woven for them. Of what kind was it? The [crown] of despising everything in the present. "Whoever abandons brothers or sisters, or country, or house, or friends, or relatives will receive one hundredfold," it says, "and will inherit eternal life" (Mt 19.29). Truly they were women who had Christ dwelling there with them. For if, "where two or three are gathered," he is "there in the midst of them" (cf. Mt 18.20), where the women weren't just gathered, but also fleeing because of his name, how didn't they attract his help all the more? And so, while the women were spending time there (sc. in Edessa), suddenly wicked decrees, full of a great deal of tyranny and barbaric cruelty, were distributed everywhere. For "let intimates betray intimates," they said: "husbands their wives, fathers their children, children their fathers, brothers their brothers, friends their friends."

16   At this point I want you to remember Christ's words and be amazed at his prediction. For he predicted all these events earlier. For he said: "Brother will betray brother, and father child. And children will rise up against parents" (Mt 10.21). He made this prediction at that time for these three reasons. One, so that we might learn his power, and that he is a true God who foresees from a distance things that have not yet happened. For on the point that he predicted what would happen for this reason, hear him saying: "For this reason I have said it to you before it occurs, so that when it occurs you might believe that I AM" (Jn 14.29). Second, so that none of his enemies

might say that these things happened because he was ignorant or weak. For the person who saw it in advance could also have prevented it. He didn't prevent it, however, so that the crowns might be more brilliant. He predicted these events for this reason, and he also predicted them for another third reason. What was it? So that he might make the contest lighter for those in the arena. For while tortures that are unexpected, of whatever kind they are, seem cruel and unbearable, those that are anticipated and prepared for in advance are light and easy. And so when the enemies gave these commands at the time and revealed their own cruelty, they also unwillingly gave witness to Christ's prophecy, and brothers betrayed brothers, and fathers children, and nature was at war with itself, and relationship was split within itself, and all laws were overturned from their foundations, and everything was full of a certain confusion and uproar and at that time the demons filled the houses with the blood of relatives. For the father who betrayed his son pretty much killed [him] too. My point is that, even if he didn't wield the sword, or effect the killing with his right hand, he nonetheless brought the entire matter to completion in intent. For truly the person who betrayed to the murderer the person about to be murdered, himself effected the murder. "So let's make them child-killers," the demons said, "let's make the children patricides through their betrayal." After all, sacrifices of this kind were made to them of old and fathers slaughtered children. And this is what the prophet cried out, when he said: "They sacrificed their sons and their daughters to demons" (Ps 105.37), and drank of that kind of blood.

17   And so, when Christ put a stop to these abominable and foul sacrifices, they strove to renew them again, but while they shamelessly and openly said: "Kill your sons," they didn't dare. For no one was about to obey. On the other hand, they contrived the command in another way and finessed the law, ordering fathers to betray children through the judges. "It makes no difference to us," they said, "whether a person does the killing, or whether they hand over their son to be

killed. For both this person and that one is a child-killer." And so one could see patricides, murderers of children, murderers of siblings. Everything was filled with uproar and confusion. But the women enjoyed profound calm. For anticipation of the things to come walled them around on every side, since even though they were in a foreign city, they weren't in a foreign city. For they had as their true country their faith, they had as their own city their confession, and since they were jointly nourished by excellent hopes they perceived nothing in the present. For they saw only what was to come. While matters were in this state, the father arrived in the city, bringing soldiers to assist in the hunt. The father and husband arrived, father, that is, of the daughters, husband of the woman—if, that is, one should call "father" or "husband" the person who lends his service to these sorts of things. Rather, let's spare him as much as we can. After all, he was a father of martyrs, and a martyr's husband. Let's not make his wound more painful by criticizing him amongst ourselves.

18   Consider instead, I ask you, the women's intelligence. For when they ought to have fled, they fled, and when they should have entered the contests, they stood and followed, bound by their longing for Christ. My point is that just as we ought not to invite temptations, so, whenever they attack, we should compete, so that we might demonstrate from that our goodness and from this our courage. This is precisely what those women did at that point. They both started back and competed. For the stadium was open and the moment was calling them to their wrestling matches. And the manner of their contests was as follows.

19   They came to a city called Hierapolis, and from there they truly raced up to the holy city [8] through the following ploy. A river flowed past the road along which they were returning, and the women avoided the notice of the soldiers, who were having their brunch and drinking. Some claim that the women even took their father as an

[8] I.e. the heavenly Jerusalem. John here plays on the meaning of the name Hierapolis (holy city).

accomplice in deceiving the soldiers, and I believe it. I mean, perhaps he did these things for this reason, so that he might store up in advance for himself at least a small defense for his betrayal for use on the day of judgment: that he worked with them, and assisted, and made the race toward martyrdom easier. And so, since they took him as an accomplice and were able through his services to divert the soldiers, they went out into the middle of the river and gave themselves up to those currents. A mother entered in the company of two daughters. Let both mothers and virgins hear and let the latter in this way obey their mothers, the former in this way educate their daughters, in this way love their children. And so, the mother entered in the middle, restraining her daughters on either side, the woman who possessed a husband [entered] in the middle of those who had never married, and marriage was in the midst of virginity, and Christ in the midst of them. So then, just like a tree's root that has two shoots standing on either side, so too at that moment that blessed woman entered, with her virgins on either side, and lowered them down into the waters, and in this way they drowned. Rather, they didn't drown, but were baptized with a new and astonishing baptism. Indeed, if you want to learn that what happened then was clearly baptism, hear how Christ calls his own death "baptism." For when he speaks to Zebedee's children he says: "Drink my cup and you will be baptized with the baptism with which I am being baptized" (Mk 10.38). With what kind of baptism was Christ baptized after the baptism by John, other than death and the cross? Just as James, then, wasn't crucified, but was baptized with Christ's baptism when his head was cut off with a sword (cf. Acts 12.2), so too these women, even if they weren't crucified, nonetheless were baptized with Christ's baptism when they died by means of water.

20   The mother baptized them. What do you mean? A woman baptized? Yes, women too baptize with baptisms of this kind, just as assuredly that woman too both baptized at that time and became a priestess. For truly she offered rational victims, and her purpose

became her ordination. Indeed, what was most astonishing is that she didn't require an altar when she performed the sacrifice, nor wood, nor fire, nor a knife. For the river became everything—both altar and wood and knife and fire and offering and baptism, a baptism far clearer than this baptism. For concerning the latter Paul says: "We have become united in a death like his" (Rom 6.5). But concerning the baptism of the martyrs he no longer says it's with a death like his (sc. Christ's), but that we are conformed to his death (cf. Phil 3.10). And so the mother led in her daughters, not as if she was going to lead them into a river, but as if she was escorting them under the holy bridal canopy itself. She led them in, restraining them on either side and saying: " 'Look, I and the children whom God gave me' (Is 8.18). You gave them to me; to you I entrust them, my children and myself." And in this way the woman's martyrdom became twofold, no, rather, threefold. For on her own account she was martyred once, and on that of her two daughters twice. Moreover, just as when she was on the point of lowering herself, it took a great deal of resolve on her part, so too, when she dragged her children with her, she employed another just as great resolve, rather, one much greater. For women aren't accustomed to grieve in the same way, when they themselves are about to die, as when their daughters experience this. In consequence, she herself suffered martyrdom greatly on her daughters' account and stripped off against nature's tyranny itself and stood firm against the blaze of her birth-pains, and against the unbearable churning of her stomach, and against the uproar in her womb. For if a woman who sees a single daughter die considers life unlivable, consider what great martyrdoms she exhibited, when she didn't see her two daughters dying at one and the same time, but dragged them to their death by her own hand and endured in reality what isn't even bearable for others to hear.

21   Thus, while the soldiers, since they knew none of this, were still behaving as if they were going to capture them again, the women were from that moment with Christ's soldiers, the heavenly angels.

But those on watch didn't see. For they didn't possess the eyes of faith. And while certainly Paul says about the mother: "She will be saved through bearing children" (1 Tim 2.15), here, however, the daughters were saved through their mother. It is in this way that mothers should give birth. For truly these labor pains are better than the former; although their pain is sharper, they bring greater reward. All women who have become mothers know the sort of labor pains that are involved in seeing daughters die. But to actually be the one who performs the killing with one's own hand, carries an unspeakable excess [of pain].

22 Well, why didn't the woman go to court? She wanted to seize the trophy before the battle, to snatch the crown before the contests, to receive the prize before the wrestling matches, not because she was afraid of torture, but of the lustful eyes of the unbelievers. She didn't fear that someone might puncture her ribs, but was afraid that someone might destroy her daughters' virginity. Indeed, that she trembled with this fear and not that one and that because of this reason she didn't go to court, is clear from the following. She endured far greater tortures in the river. My point, as I started saying, is that it was truly far more cruel and painful than to see flesh scourged, to drown her own innards, I mean her daughters, by her own hand, and to see them suffocating, and it required far greater philosophy than to endure tortures for her to have the capacity to restrain her children's right hands and to drag them along with her into the river's currents. For it was not the same in terms of pain to see [her daughters] suffering badly at the hands of others and to herself act as death's servant, to herself promote their end, to herself stand against her daughters in place of an executioner. Rather, this is more cruel and unbearable than that. And you will bear witness to my account, all you who've become mothers, and have experienced labor pains, and possess daughters. How could she touch her children's right hand? How could her hand not stiffen? How could her nerves not go slack? How come she didn't go out of her mind? How could her

rational mind be subservient to what was happening? For truly what happened was more piercing than countless tortures, utterly scourging her soul instead of her body. But to what end do we strive to pursue the unattainable? For no account could come close to the magnitude of her suffering. Rather, only the woman who has had experience and has competed knows what these wrestling matches are like.

23 These things let mothers hear, let virgins hear—mothers, so that they might instruct their daughters in this way, daughters, so that they might in this way obey their mothers. For one shouldn't just praise the mother who gave such orders, but should marvel at the daughters too, who obeyed such commands. I mean, the mother didn't need chains for the sacrificial victims and offerings, nor did the heifers skip away, but dragged the yoke of martyrdom with equal enthusiasm and spirit, and in this way entered the river, leaving their shoes out on the riverbank. They did this to spare the guards. So great was the forethought of those holy women. For they were keen to leave behind for them a defense to use in court, so that that cruel and savage judge couldn't accuse them of betrayal and that they had taken a bribe and let the women go. For this reason they left behind their shoes as a witness to the soldiers' state of mind, to the fact that they had no knowledge; that instead without their knowledge [the women] defected to the river.

24 Perhaps you have developed a great love for those holy women. So then, with this ardor let us throw ourselves on their relics. Let us embrace their chests. For the martyrs' chests too can contain much power, just as the martyrs' bones, then, too hold great strength. Indeed, not just on the day of this festival, but on other days too let us sit beside them, let us entreat them, let us ask them to be our patrons. For they possess much boldness of speech, not just when they were alive, but also now that they are dead—and far more so now that they are dead. For now they bear the marks of Christ, and when they display these marks they can persuade the King of

anything. So, since they have so much power and friendship with God, by rendering ourselves one of their own through constant attendance and perpetually coming to them, let us embrace through them the loving kindness that comes from God. May we all attain this, through the grace and lovingkindness of our Lord, Jesus Christ, with whom to the Father be glory, together with the Holy Spirit, now and always and forever and ever. Amen.

On Saint Barlaam

The Barlaam who is celebrated in this homily is the same Barlaam whose martyrdom is commemorated in a homily attributed to Basil of Caesarea (*On St Barlaam, CPG* 2861).[1] In the latter sermon Barlaam is a non-Greek-speaking country-dweller who refuses to offer sacrifice to pagan gods during a time of persecution. When none of the usual tortures work, he is stood over a brazier or altar and a libation jar is placed in his hand, in the hope that the flames will force his hand to drop and cause him involuntarily to pour. Barlaam remains motionless as the flames consume his hand, thus avoiding betraying his Christian faith. In John's homily, while the essential story appears to be the same, there is no mention of Barlaam's background, and the libation jar is replaced by burning coals and frankincense placed in his open outstretched palm. The coals burn through the palm of the hand as Barlaam holds it rigid over the altar.

There has been considerable debate about the date of this festival, which is located in some traditions around 16 or 18 November, in the Syrian martyrology on 14 August, and has, on the basis of the assignment of the sermon on St Barlaam by Severus of Antioch (*Hom.* 73; PO 12.372–8) to a Sunday in 515 CE, been located also on 31 May.[2] The latter date has some support in Slavic liturgical tradition. The first of the date(s) must be dismissed, since in another homily John himself says that they celebrated the festival of St Barlaam on

---

[1]There has been some discussion amongst scholars as to whether the homily might not belong to John Chrysostom himself. Both style and vocabulary, however, seem to me to be alien to Chrysostom and it seems best to treat the authorship of the homily as uncertain.

[2]See H. Delehaye, "S. Barlaam. Martyr à Antioche," AnBoll 22 (1904): 136–7.

the previous day and that at the moment they are free of winter and enjoying summer. On the particular day in question there is also a pleasant breeze.[3] The suggestion that winter has only recently passed, in conjunction with the indication that the weather is as yet mild would seem to support the last date, 31 May, especially if it is taken in conjunction with Severus' comment over a century later that the night of the festival is short. Since, however, the Syrian martyrology seems a reliable source for Antiochene practice in a number of other instances, and since one could presumably on occasion experience a pleasant breeze in Syria in August due to a temporary change, and since also all of the nights between late May and mid August could be said to be short, there is, however, no compelling reason to exclude 14 August as the date on which the festival was held at Antioch in John's time. If the date of 31 May for the feast day of St Barlaam at Antioch in the early sixth century is accurate, it is not beyond possibility that the date had in the intervening century for some reason been changed.

While it is possible that the homily was delivered at Antioch, this is by no means certain. John says only that he and the audience are present at more than one martyr's tomb. Given that in his martyr homilies John often refers to the specific martyr's tomb, if the festival is being celebrated at that location, this may suggest that locally there was at the time no martyrium containing a tomb firmly associated with Barlaam. It is rather the circumstantial evidence which suggests that Antioch is the location. Aside from the homily attributed to Basil, in which it is said that Barlaam is buried locally,[4] the rest of the tradition associates Barlaam's martyrdom firmly with Antioch. Theophanes and Malalas mention a Church of Barlaam in the vicinity of Antioch in the later fifth century, although it is uncertain when it was built,[5] and clearly by Severus' time the festival of Barlaam was a fixture in the Antiochene liturgical calendar.

[3]On Paul's saying: "I don't want you to be unaware . . ." (CPG 4380), PG 51.241–2.
[4]Hom. 17: In Barlaam martyrem, PG 31.484.
[5]Theophanes, Chron. ann. 5973; Malalas, Chron. 15.6.

Contents:

1. It is the feast day of Barlaam. The greatest praise of martyrs is to imitate them.

2–3. Even though it is not a time of persecution, we are being persecuted by demons and the Devil. Desire burns us in the same way as Barlaam, who held an entire pyre in his hand.

4–6. Since none of the usual tortures worked, the Devil devised a new strategy for Barlaam. He kept him in prison for longer than usual and then led him out to a tower, which was unexpected. There Barlaam was ordered to stretch out his hand and burning coals and frankincense were placed on it. The theory was that the moment he felt pain, he would turn his hand and the frankincense and coals would fall, causing him to technically make a sacrifice. Barlaam, however, kept his hand unwavering.

7–9. Even if his hand had turned over, the Devil wouldn't have won, since the contraction of his hand due to the heat of the flame would have been involuntary. But Barlaam's hand did not move and the coals and frankincense burnt through. While his flesh withered, his will intensified.

10–12. Let us not just hear the story but take the martyr home in our hearts and imitate him by overcoming wealth and luxury.

Translated from PG 50.675–682.

1 Blessed Barlaam has called us together to this holy festival and feast-day, not so that we might praise him, but so that we might emulate him; not so that we might become an audience for his praises, but so that we might become imitators of his achievements. Whereas, in worldly matters those who ascend to the great magistracies would never choose to see others share in the same precedence—for there jealousy and envy disrupt affection—in the case of spiritual matters it isn't like this, but entirely the opposite. For the martyrs gain a sense of their own honor above all when they see that their fellow servants have outstripped them in sharing their particular blessings. In

consequence, if someone wants to praise martyrs, let them imitate martyrs. If someone wants to extol the athletes of piety, let them emulate their hard work. This will bring the martyrs pleasure no less than their own achievements. Indeed, that you may learn that they sense their own blessings above all when they see that we are secure, and consider the matter an extremely great honor, hear Paul, who says: "Now we are alive, if you're standing in the Lord" (1 Thess 3.8). And before this Moses said to God: "If you forgive them their sin, forgive; but if not, then expunge me too from the book that you have written" (Ex 32.31,32). "I don't sense the honor above because of their ill fortune," he says. "For the fullness of believers is a bodily connection. What use, therefore, is it for the head to be crowned, if the feet are being punished?"

2   "How is it possible," you ask, "for us to imitate martyrs now? After all, it isn't a time of persecution." Yes, I know. Yet while it isn't a time of persecution, it is a time of martyrdom. It isn't a time of wrestling matches of that sort, but it is a time of crowns. Human beings aren't in pursuit, but demons are in pursuit. A tyrant isn't in persecution mode, but the Devil's in persecution mode, crueler than any tyrant. You don't see burning coals lying in front of you, but you do see desire's flame kindled. They trampled on burning coals; trample on nature's pyre. They sparred with wild animals; bridle your anger, the savage and untamed wild animal. They stood fast against unbearable pains; subvert the unnatural and wicked thoughts that swell in your heart. It's in this way you will imitate martyrs. "For our struggle now isn't against blood and flesh, but against the rulers, against the authorities, against the cosmic powers of this darkness, against the spiritual forces of evil" (Eph 6.12). Nature's desire is a fire, a fire that is inextinguishable and constant. It is a rabid and mad dog; no matter how many times you get rid of it, it leaps at you every time and doesn't give up. The flame of the burning coals is savage, but this is crueler—that is, the flame of desire. We never have a cease-fire in this war, we never have a lull in

hostilities throughout the present life; instead, the struggle is constant, so that the crown might be magnificent too. It is for this reason that Paul constantly arms us, since it's always a time of war, since the enemy is always alert.

3   Do you want to learn that desire burns no less than a fire? Hear Solomon, who says: "If a person treads on a fire's coals, don't they burn their feet? So the person who has sex with their neighbor's wife, and every person who touches her, will not go unpunished" (Prov 6.28,29). Do you see that desire's nature competes with fire's nature? For just as it's impossible for a person who touches a fire not to receive a burn, so the viewing of beautifully formed faces attacks the lecherously gazing soul more acutely than a fire. And just like a readily combustible fuel, so stunning-looking bodies lie in front of the eyes of the libidinous. For this reason we shouldn't furnish the viewing of worldly things as fuel for the fire of desire, but suppress and extinguish it in every respect with pious thoughts and, further, bridle the conflagration it effects and not allow it to turn upside down the firmness of our mind. Truly the moment the passions take control every pleasure tends to burn the mind more fiercely than a fire, unless one fights against each of the passions nobly with patience and faith. This is what the blessed and noble athlete of Christ, Barlaam, did concerning his own hand, when he held an entire pyre in his right hand and didn't give in to the pain, but stayed more unfeeling than statues; rather, he did feel pain and suffer—for it was his body that was subjected to this and not iron—but despite feeling pain and suffering he displayed in a mortal body the philosophy of the bodiless powers.

4   But I shall relate his martyrdom from the beginning so that the story will be clearer. Please, consider the Devil's malice. He led some of the saints to roasting pans, some he threw into cauldrons boiling more fiercely than fire. And of some he scourged their ribs, others he drowned in the sea, others her handed over to wild animals, others he led into a furnace, and of some he levered the joints [from their sockets], of others he flayed the skin while they were still alive, of

others he put burning coals under their bloodied bodies, and the sparks leaping at their open sores bit the wounds more sharply than any wild animal. For others he devised other more cruel tortures. And so when he saw all these tortures laughed at and those who were suffering them prevailing with considerable superiority and becoming a major source of confidence to those who came to the same wrestling matches after them, what did he do? He devised a new method of treachery so that the unrehearsed and unusual nature of the torture would deject the martyr's state of mind. "I mean, the one is heard of and is conceivable and, even if it's unbearable, becomes easily despised through being rehearsed by expectation, but the other, in that it's unrehearsed, even if it's lightweight, is more unbearable than anything. And so, let the contest be a new one, let the machination be foreign, so that the new and strange torture might upset the athlete and thus easily trip him up."

5   So, what did he do? He led the saint out of the prison in chains. For truly this was characteristic of his malice, that he didn't employ the cruel machinations right away at the beginning, nor apply the terrifying tortures, but launched an attack using smaller missiles. For what possible reason? So that if those competing were defeated, their defeat would be shameful, in that they couldn't even hold out against the little [obstacles]. But if they were subversive and won, with their strength expended in advance on the smaller obstacles they might be easily overcome at the major hurdles. For this reason he adduced the smaller [obstacles] first, so that whether he caught them or not, he wouldn't lose. "For if I catch them," he said, "I've had the last laugh. If I don't catch them, I've made them weaker in the face of what's to come." And so, he led him out of the prison. But he (sc. Barlaam) went out like a noble athlete who had spent a lot of time exercising in a wrestling school. I mean, to the martyr the prison was a wrestling school, and there by speaking privately with God he learnt all the techniques of wrestling from him. For where there are such chains, there too Christ is present.

6   And so, he went out made stronger by his longer stay in prison. And on his exit the Devil, leading him into public view by means of those who served his lawlessness, didn't bind him to a stake, didn't station executioners around him. For he saw that he longed for these things, and had for a long time been training for them in advance. Instead he led him to the tower—a somewhat foreign, novel and completely unexpected machination that could easily cause his downfall. For this is what he (sc. the Devil) works towards: to trip up the saints in every situation rather than to cause them pain. So then, what was the machination? Ordering him to stretch his hand palm up over the altar, they put burning coals and frankincense on the hand so that, if he felt pain and turned his hand over, they might attribute a sacrifice to him and [consider] the act a transgression. Did you see how malicious the Devil is? Well, see how he who "seizes the wise in their wickedness" (cf. Job 5.13) rendered his machinations powerless, and caused the heightening of his treachery and the variety of his malice to become an addition and an amplification of greater glory for the martyr. My point is that when his opponent has perpetrated countless acts of malice, but then goes away defeated, then the athlete of piety becomes more brilliant, which is what in fact happened here. For blessed Barlaam persisted in keeping his hand inflexible and uninverted, as if he had a hand composed of steel. And yet if his hand had turned, it would have been no fault of the martyr's.

7   At this point, please, all pay precise attention, so that you may learn that, even if his right hand had turned over, what happened wouldn't have been a defeat. Why ever not? Because just as we decide in the case of those whose ribs are being scourged or who are being tortured in some other way, so ought we to judge in this case too. For if they give in and sacrifice, the blame attaches to their weakness, in that they sacrificed because they couldn't endure the pain. While, if they remain steadfast in their tortures and groan over what they suffer, but don't betray their piety, no one holds them responsible for

their groans; instead, we accept and admire them all the more, for the reason that even though they were in pain they endured it and didn't recant. So then, in this case too, if blessed Barlaam hadn't been able to endure being burnt and had promised to sacrifice, he would have been defeated. But if, although he didn't give in, his hand had turned over, this is no fault of the martyr's will. For this happened, not because his will was weak, but because his nerves' character [was affected] in terms of its strength and the saint's hand was involuntarily bent by the fire. My point is that just as we don't blame those whose ribs were scourged because their flesh was ripped apart— rather, let me introduce a closer example. Just as no one would blame those in the throes of a fever or convulsions, if their hands bent—for what has happened is not attributable to their laziness, but because the flame of the illness steals the moisture and then unnaturally contracts the ending of the nerves—so one wouldn't have blamed this saint either, if his hand had turned over. For if, even involuntarily, a fever can contract and twist the limbs of the sufferer, by far more would burning coals lying on the right hand have effected this, even though the martyr didn't give in.

8   Yet even so they didn't effect this, so that you might abundantly learn that God's grace was present and encouraging the athlete, and correcting nature's disadvantage. Nor did it suffer characteristically in this respect; instead, that hand remained unturned as if it was built out of adamant.[6] Who, when they saw this at the time, wouldn't have been amazed? Who wouldn't have trembled? Angels from above peeped down; archangels watched the show. The theater was brilliant and truly exceeded human nature. After all, who wouldn't be eager to see a human being competing, and not suffering what was characteristic of humans? The same person becoming altar, victim, and priest? For this reason double the smoke rose up—that of the burning frankincense and that of the roasting flesh. Truly the latter smoke was more soothing than the former, and this sweet smell

[6]A legendary hard, unyielding mineral.

better than that one. And the same thing happened that also took place in the case of the bramble bush (cf. Ex 3). My point is that just as that bush burnt, but did not burn, so too here the right hand burnt, but the soul wasn't burnt up. The body was consumed, and the faith not spent. The flesh gave up, and the enthusiasm didn't give out. And while the burning coals bored through the middle of his hand and fell out below, the soul's courage was not lost. Yes, the hand was destroyed and drew down, for it was flesh and not adamant. But the soul sought out in turn a second hand, so that it might display its steadfastness in it too. And, just as a noble soldier who, in attacking enemies, decimates the phalanx of his opponents and shatters his sword in the welter of rapidly successive blows, next wheels around and seeks out another, because he hasn't yet had enough of slaughtering the enemy, so too, indeed, blessed Barlaam's soul, when his hand was destroyed in decimating the phalanxes of demons, sought out in turn a second right hand, so that he might demonstrate his enthusiasm in that one too.

9   Don't tell me that he gave up just one hand. But consider this ahead of that: that the man who abandoned his hand, would also have given up his head and exposed his ribs to fire and wild animals and sea and cliff and cross and wheel, and prepared himself to face every torture ever heard of and would have suffered anything in will, even if not in actual experience. My point is, the martyrs don't encounter defined punishments, but strip off for indeterminate tortures. For they're not in control of the tyrants' will, nor do they impose limits and constraints on their tortures. Instead, as many evils as [the tyrants'] inhuman and savage will desires to impose on them, they enter into in a spirit of compliance. Unless, that is, their body in the meantime gives up and leaves the tyrants' desire unsatiated in the middle of it. So then, his flesh withered and his will became more enthusiastic, surpassing the burning coals themselves in brilliance and glowing more brightly than them. For a spiritual fire was kindled within that was much more scorching than this fire. For this reason

he (sc. Barlaam) didn't notice the external flame, since the blazing, red-hot fire of Christ's love was burning inside him.

10   Beloved, let's not just hear these things, but also imitate them. What I said at the beginning, I say now too. Don't let the martyr be admired just for the duration of the present hour, but when they go off home let each person take away the saint and introduce him into their own household—rather, into their own heart through the memory of what I've said. Welcome him, as was said earlier, and position him with his hand stretched out in your heart. Welcome the crowned victor, and never let him leave your mind. It's for this reason that we've brought you alongside the coffins of the holy martyrs, so that you might receive some encouragement to virtue from the sight too, and strip off and set to work at the same zeal. For truly, while even hearing of a warrior lifts up a soldier, much more so does seeing and viewing and especially when, on entering the warrior's tent itself, one sees his bloodied sword, the enemy's head lying there, the spoils hanging up above, the fresh blood dripping from the hands of the person who erected the trophy, spears and shields and arrows and all the rest of his arsenal lying around everywhere. It's for this reason that we too have gathered here. For the martyrs' tomb is a soldier's tent. And if you open wide the eyes of faith, you will see the breastplate of righteousness lying here, the shield of faith, the helmet of salvation, the greaves of the Gospel, the sword of the Spirit (cf. Eph 6.14–17) hurling the very head of the Devil onto the ground. For when you see a person who is demon-possessed lying on their back near the martyr's tomb and frequently lacerating themselves, you see nothing other than the lopped-off head of the Wicked (Demon). For even now these weapons are available to Christ's soldiers, and just as emperors bury their warriors with their weapons, so too did Christ, and buried them (sc. the martyrs) with their weapons so that even before the resurrection[7] he might show all the glory and the power of the saints. So then, learn about their spiritual

[7] That is, the resurrection of the body at the Last Judgment.

arsenal and you will go away from here rewarded handsomely. You too, beloved, have a major battle against the Devil—major and substantial and constant.

11   So then, learn about their wrestling matches, so that you may imitate their victories. Despise wealth and money and all the rest of life's ostentation. Don't consider blessed those who are rich, but bless those who are martyrs; not those in luxury, but those in roasting pans. Not those at a lavish table, but those in a boiling cauldron. Not those at the baths every day, but those in cruel furnaces. Not those who reek of perfume, but those who give off smoke and steam from their roasting flesh. This sweet smell is better and more useful than that. For that [smell] leads those who use it away to punishment, this one towards the prizes and crowns above. Indeed, so that you may learn that luxury is wicked, as also the smearing of perfume and drinking and wine that has no limit, and a lavish table, hear what the prophet says: "Woe to those who sleep on ivory beds and sprawl on their cushions; who eat kids from the flocks and suckling calves from the herds; who drink filtered wine and rub themselves with the finest perfume" (Amos 6.4–6). If these things were forbidden in the time of the old covenant, far more [is it the case] in the [time of] grace, where philosophy is more abundant. I address these remarks to both men and women. For the stadium is shared. Christ's army is not divided on the basis of gender; instead, the company is united. Women too have the capacity to don a breastplate and wield a shield and let fly a shaft, both in a period of martyrdom and in another like it that demands considerable bold speech. Indeed, just as, when an ace archer lets the bolt fly from the string with perfect aim, he throws the entire enemy battle formation into disarray, so too the holy martyrs and all the fighters for truth who oppose the Devil's wiles, let their words fly from their tongue with perfect aim as if from a string. And these, flying like bolts through the air, fall on the invisible phalanxes of demons, and throw their entire battle formation into disarray.

12   This too, then, is what happened in the case of this blessed Bar-laam. Using naked words like flying bolts he confounded the Devil's army. Let us too imitate this perfect aim. Don't you see that those who descend from the theatrical shows have become softer? The reason is that they focus on what happens there with keen interest. After all, when they depart, they do so after storing up in their souls the rolling of eyes, and weaving of hands, and circling of feet, and the impressions of all the images that became apparent in the twisting of the contorted body. How, then, isn't it absurd that while they display so much foresight for the ruin of their own soul, and have stored in their mind a memory of what took place there, we, who are about to be compared to the angels as a result of imitating [the martyrs] here, don't contribute even the same level of keen interest as them in preserving what was said? Don't, I ask and implore, don't let's be heedless of our own salvation in this way, but let's all store the martyrs away in our own minds, with the roasting pans, with the cauldrons, with the other tortures. And, just as painters wipe clean a painting that has often become dimmer with smoke and soot and time, so too you, beloved, use the memory of the holy martyrs. When worldly concerns attack and are about to dim your mind, wipe it clean through the memory of the martyrs. For if you keep this memory in your soul, you will not admire wealth, will not weep over being poor, will not praise glory and power, and in general of human affairs you will suppose that nothing joyous is great and nothing grievous unbearable. Instead, you will be above all those things and will have the viewing of this painting as a constant instruction in virtue. I mean, the person who sees soldiers acting like men every day in wars and battles, won't ever desire luxury, won't admire the soft and dissolute life, but the harsh and tense and competitive one. After all, what do drinking and fighting have in common? To pamper the stomach and to act like a man? Perfumes and weapons? War and partying? You are a soldier of Christ, beloved; take up arms, not cosmetics. You are a noble athlete; act like a man, not a fashion statement. In this way let us imitate these saints, in this

way let us honor the warriors, the crowned victors, the friends of God, and, by walking the same road as them, we shall attain the same crowns as them. May we all attain these blessings through the grace and loving kindness of our Lord, Jesus Christ, with whom to the Father be glory, together with the Holy Spirit, now and always and forever and ever. Amen.

On Saint Drosis

Little is known about the female martyr who is the subject of this homily. John tells us that she was martyred by being thrown onto a pyre, but tells us nothing explicit about when she died or at what time of year her festival was celebrated. That the location of the festival is Antioch can be inferred from the homily itself, since John indicates that a person other than himself is the bishop who led the procession to the martyrium. The celebration is clearly taking place at a site which is distinctive in that it holds a large number of burials in addition to those of Drosis and other martyrs. This suggests that the site may in fact be the common martyrium located in the cemetery outside the city walls beside the road leading to Daphne. Of particular interest here is the comment that Drosis has just led the procession to the martyrium. Aside from the instruction in *On Julian the martyr* to take Julian with them the next day when on the second day of his festival they stage a protest at the city gate,[1] this is the only instance in which John makes reference to a martyr herself leading the procession to the martyrium, on an occasion other than the translation of relics. This may refer to the processing of the relics of the martyr at the annual festival and if so, is a rare example from this period. Elements from John's arguments about other martyred women are adopted here, with his emphasis on Drosis' virginity, stress on her masculine courage, and his styling of the martyred virgin as a second Eve.

Contents:

1–4. Visiting the martyrs outside the city is likened to the experience of sheep, released from their pens after winter. While each martyrium refreshes

[1]Leemans et al., *"Let Us Die that We May Live,"* 139.

us like a spiritual meadow, this one does so in particular. The sight of so many tombs reminds us of death, and urges us to adopt moderation and prepare for life in heaven, and is an encouragement to faith.

5–6. The martyrs provide proof that Christ rose from the dead and continues to work in our lives. The response of demons to martyrs' remains also proves this.

7. The celebration of women who are martyrs is special. Drosis, a virgin, defeated death and is an admonition to all men. Her gender was no impediment.

8–10. Drosis was thrown onto a pyre for refusing to renounce her faith. The pyre is at one and the same time a spring, a dye-bath, and a smelting-furnace.

11–12. John takes issue with people's concerns about burial arrangements and explains why Moses took Joseph's bones with him on the exodus.

13–15. People are wrong in their expectations about what it means to die with honor versus dishonor.

Translated from PG 50.683–694.

A homily of praise on the great and holy martyr Drosis, and on remembering death

1   Whenever hardworking shepherds see the sun's rays becoming brilliant and daytime becoming warmer after a long winter, they lead the sheep out of the pen and off to the usual pastures. Imitating them, this good shepherd too[2] has led this holy crowd and Christ's spiritual flock off to these spiritual pastures of the saints. When they stand at the feed-box, the sheep are satisfied. But whenever they're outside the pens they reap a more abundant benefit from the plains; they bend down with much enjoyment and shear

---

[2]A metaphor for the local bishop of Antioch, Flavian.

off the grass with their teeth, and both breathe in pure air and gaze at the sun's clear, bright rays, gamboling beside pools and springs and rivers. The earth too provides them a certain enjoyment, decorated as it is in every direction with flowers. Not just in their case, but in our case too does this hold a great deal of benefit. For although we actually have a table full of spiritual dishes ready for us inside, nonetheless the exodus to these saints holds both a certain spiritual guidance and a reward of no lesser value than the spiritual guidance, not because we breathe in pure air, but because we gaze at the achievements of these noble men and women, gamboling not beside rivers of water, but beside rivers of spiritual gifts. Not bending down and shearing off grass with our teeth, but recounting martyrs' virtues. Not viewing an earth decorated with flowers, but gazing at bodies bursting into bud with spiritual gifts.

2   While each of the martyria, then, provides no small benefit for the assembled, this one does so above all. For the moment a person crosses the threshold, a large number of tombs in every direction immediately strike the eyes and, wherever one looks, one sees the coffins and memorials and funerary chests of the departed. The viewing of these tombs itself contributes no small part [in urging] us towards philosophy. For through this sight, if it's lazy, the soul swiftly becomes moderate, and if it's zealous and alert, becomes more zealous. And if a person bitterly laments poverty, they at once receive comfort from this sight, and if they're arrogant about their wealth, are humbled and deflated. For, even if they're unwilling, the sight of the tombs compels each of the viewers to think philosophically about the matters relating to their own death, and persuades them to think that nothing belonging to the present is secure, nor painful, nor good. The person persuaded of these things will not easily be caught by sin's net. For this reason a certain wise person too gives advice as follows: "In everything you say remember your end and you won't commit sin forever" (Sir 7.36). And another person harmonizes with him and offers advice in these words: "Ready your works for your departure

and prepare for the road" (Prov 24.27), speaking not about the road we can see, but about the departure from this life. After all, if we look ahead to the uncertainty of death constantly and every day, we won't commit sin quickly. For neither will the brilliant things in life be able to puff us up nor what is painful depress or upset us, seeing that each has an uncertain end. For truly, often the person who is alive today doesn't even last until the evening.

3   And so, while it isn't very likely that we'll meditate on such ideas and think philosophically when we're spending time in the city, when we go outside the walls and come to these tombs and view the large number of the departed, we are totally compelled by the sight to adopt these ideas, whether willing or not, and, on adopting them, to become more elevated and be freed of emotional attachment to worldly concerns. Not only shall we adopt such ideas, but we'll also have enough encouragement to spur us on and prepare us for our eternal country, and to put all our own affairs in order for the journey there, knowing that whatever of our own we leave behind here will, when left behind, cause us a loss. For just as whatever a traveler who is traveling a lengthy highway and hurrying back to their own country leaves behind in the inn is completely lost and suffered as a loss, so too everything of our own that we abandon here when we depart, we suffer as a loss. For this reason we should have some things with us, but send others ahead of us there. My point is that the present life is a highway and contains nothing stationary; rather, we travel past both what is painful in it and what is good. I love this place for this reason above all, in that when I come here, not just during a synaxis,[3] but also often apart from a synaxis, I am constantly reminded of these words, while my eyes look around at the tombs in much solitude and quiet, and send off my soul to the departed and their condition there.

[3]Lit. "a gathering." This is a technical term for a Christian service of worship. John indicates here that the martyrium is the site of liturgical services one or possibly more times a year, but that he also comes to the martyrium for private reflection or devotion.

4   For these reasons I admire this noble father too, in that he led us out here when a calm day came up, while blessed Drosis, whose commemoration we celebrate, was in lead out the front and guiding us. For truly, in addition to what I've said there is a second greater reward to be reaped. I mean, whenever we race past the other coffins and come to the funerary chests of the martyrs, our thoughts become more elevated, our soul more zealous, our enthusiasm greater, our faith more fervent. And so, whenever we recount the labors and the contests and the rewards and the prizes and the crowns of these saints, we discover in turn a second more major pretext for humility. My point is that even if a person had achieved great things, they would consider that they had done nothing great, when [they compared] their virtue with [the martyrs'] wrestling matches. And even if they had achieved nothing great or good, they would not despair of their own salvation, having taken from their (sc. the martyrs') courage encouragement to change to virtue, and having thought to themselves that it might at some time turn out that, if God's loving kindness considered them worthy, perhaps they too would leap such bounds and in a single moment ascend to heaven and attain that ultimate boldness of speech. After thinking philosophically about these matters and others more numerous than these, it is possible for us to leave here. For a martyrs' death is an encouragement to believers, Churches' bold speech, Christianity's confirmation, death's dissolution, a proof of resurrection, ridicule of demons, the Devil's condemnation, an instruction in philosophy, advice to disdain the things of the present, also a path for desire for the things to come, a comfort for the disasters that restrain us, and a pretext for patience, a starting-point for steadfastness, and a root and spring and mother of all blessings.

5   Indeed, if you like, we'll demonstrate each of these points and will say how it's an encouragement to believers, Churches' bold speech, a proof of resurrection, and all the rest that I said just now. So, whenever we set in motion contests against Greeks and battles

about points of dogma, and they slander our faith, along with the rest let's hurl this at them too (I mean the martyrs' death), saying: "Who convinced them to despise the present life? If Christ died and didn't rise up, who accomplished these supernatural acts?" For concerning the fact that it wasn't a matter of human power to persuade over so long a time so many tens of thousands of not just men, but also women and unmarried virgins and little children to disdain the present life and to brave wild animals, to laugh at fire, to trample on every form of punishment and torture and to hurry off to the life to come, they won't lack our proofs, but will question themselves and gain a sufficient demonstration of what we say. For since the time when Christ was present, while there have been non-Christian emperors, there have also been Christian [emperors]; but of the non-Christians the majority led the Christians to pits and fires, and cliffs and sea and the raging of wild animals and diverse punishments and tortures, and [tried] by every means to lever the faith out of their soul, and accomplished nothing, but instead went away laughed at, since even though the believers kept being knocked about by every means, their faith kept increasing substantially. But no pious emperor ever chose to punish or torture a non-Christian man, forcing [him] to desist from his error. Yet even so in this way it truly flows away of its own accord and perishes, so that you may learn both truth's strength and falsehood's weakness, since [falsehood] perishes of its own accord and without anyone applying pressure, whereas [truth] grows by means of those who hinder it and is lifted to an indescribable height. The reason is that Christ is both alive and is active in the martyrs' souls. And so when they claim that he didn't rise [from the dead], let's ask them these questions. "So, who accomplished these things? Tell me, [was it] the corpse?" But there have been so many corpses and not one has effected such things. "Well, was he a magician and a sorcerer?" But there have been many magicians and sorcerers and charlatans and they have all fallen silent and their traces don't exist anywhere; instead, the [features] of their trickery too were extinguished along with their life. But those of Christ grow day by day, and rightly so. For what happened did not happen by sorcery, but by divine power. For this reason they don't perish. Rather, from this I don't just prove that his power grows, but that [it does so] both with a view to good and for the salvation of our life. For after his coming those who inhabit the earth developed from wild animals into human beings—rather, all [developed] from human beings into angels—all those who follow him in truth. "But the martyrs were mistaken and drew false conclusions," they claim, "and because of this disdained the present life. Next, the first [martyrs] didn't convince the second ones, nor the second ones the third; instead, to the same extent that the persecutions progressed, this deed too advanced, and throughout this long period of time no one was ignorant of the mistake. How else could one account for these things?"

6   If they were mistaken, how come the demons fear their dust? How come they flee their tombs too? After all, it's not because demons are afraid of corpses that they suffer this. I mean, look, there are countless corpses everywhere on earth, and they sit right next to the demons, and one can see many people who are demon-possessed spending time in deserted places and at tombs. But where martyrs' bones are buried, they flee as from a fire or unbearable punishment, proclaiming with a clear voice the power flagellating them within. Well, it's been demonstrated from this that the martyrs' death is a condemnation of the demons' weakness. But that the matter is also an indictment of their insensibility, is clear from the following. For when they (I mean the martyrs) are subject to the body and natural impulses, and have a substantial crowd of pains and griefs surrounding them, and live the mortal life and spend time on earth, and are seen thus to disdain the present life because of their love for God who created them, while they (sc. the demons), free of flesh and of all this pain and grief, are seen thus to be insolent and to have become ungrateful concerning their benefactor, what kind of defense will they have? What pardon? Absolutely none at all, since

[the martyrs'] virtue condemns their wickedness abundantly. For truly not only do humans condemn humans—the more zealous the more lazy—but now the martyrs' zeal condemns even the demons themselves. And Paul made this clear when he said: "Don't you know that we judge angels? Let alone human affairs?" (1 Cor 6.3), meaning the Devil's angels, the deserters. "And how do we judge them?," you ask. Not by taking a seat and demanding accounts of them, but by condemning their laziness through our zeal. This, then, is the very point that he made clear, when he said: "And if the world is judged in you" (1 Cor 6.2). He didn't mean "in front of you," but "through you." Just as when it says: "The men of Nineveh will rise up and condemn this generation" (cf. Lk 11.32), not on the basis that the Ninevites were demanding an account of those Jews who were unbelievers at the time, but on the basis that their faith was condemning the latter's lack of faith. One can enjoy from the martyrs both substantial [encouragement] to virtue and to despise the things of the present. For when you see them despising every aspect of life, even if you are more insensible and lazier than anyone, you will adopt an exceedingly elevated frame of mind and will laugh at luxury, despise money, and be keen to spend time there. And if you're in ill health, you'll take the martyrs' sufferings as a major pretext for patience. And if you're oppressed by poverty, or something else extremely harsh, whatever it is, when you gaze at the magnitude of the tortures that were unleashed on them you'll have sufficient comfort for all the troubles that have befallen you.

7   This is why I especially love the commemorations of the martyrs; [why] while I both love and embrace them all, [I do so] especially when it happens to be women who are competing. For the weaker the vessel (cf. 1 Pet 3.7), the greater the grace, the more brilliant the trophy, the more famous the victory; not because of the feebleness of the athlete's gender, but because even through those whom the enemy controlled is he captured now. At least, recently the Devil killed Adam because of a virgin; after this through a virgin

Christ conquered the Devil, and the sword that had been sharpened by him against us cut off the serpent's head. This is what happened in the case of David too. For just as at that time that just man ran and cut off Goliath's head with the barbarian's own sword, so indeed now too. Because of a woman he (sc. the Devil) prevailed, because of a woman he was defeated. This was first his weapon, this has now become the instrument of his slaughter, this [has become] an unde-featable implement. The first [woman] sinned and died; this one died, so that she wouldn't sin. The first trampled at that time on God's laws, puffed up by expectation raised by an empty promise; the second despised even the present life, so that she wouldn't deny upon oath her faith in her patron. What defense, then, could there now be for men who have grown soft, and what pardon, when women act like men? When they strip off so nobly for the contests of piety? For neither gender, nor age, nor anything else could hold them back, when enthusiasm is present and zeal and a fired-up faith. Indeed, through all these things we win God's grace, which in fact is what happened too in the case of this blessed woman. For truly she had a weak body, and her gender was vulnerable to injury and her age was rather immature, but grace came and hid the weakness of all these elements, when it discovered that her enthusiasm was noble and her faith unwavering and her soul prepared for dangers.

8   For there is nothing, no, nothing more powerful than the per-son who has the fear of God rooted in them with considerable zeal; rather, whether fire, or sword, or wild animals or anything else of this kind threatens, they disdain everything with a great deal of ease, just as blessed Drosis herself, then, did too. For when the tyrant lit the pyre—my point is, he didn't lead her off to a pit or cut off her head, lest the brevity of the torture make the competition too easy for her; [he lit a pyre] instead from a desire to strike her mind numb with terror and to overpower her unsubdued soul with the sight of the pyre—he threw her into the middle. And so, when he lit up the pyre and the furnace was burning and rising up to a

great height, the blessed martyr herself too, on seeing this, was fired up with enthusiasm and seethed with the fire of longing for Christ, remembering the three boys (cf. Dan 3) and reckoning to herself that she was sharing in their contests and pursuing the same crowns as they. And, just as those who are in a manic rage view nothing that's visible as it is, but if they see a sharpened sword, they readily plunge forward, or if a pyre, or a pit, or a cliff, or a sea, or anything else like that, they fearlessly let themselves loose against it all; so indeed too did she, raging in a frenzy—not of this kind (heaven forbid!), but another [frenzy] more august than all moderation—and dyed by her longing for Christ,[4] view nothing that was visible, but since she'd been redeployed in heaven and had transferred her soul there, she laughed at all her tortures and thought that the fire wasn't fire, but dew.

9   For this reason I call that pyre both an extremely pure spring of water, and an astonishing dye bath, and a smelting-furnace. For truly, like gold in a smelting furnace, so too did that blessed woman's soul become purer because of that pyre. For although her flesh melted away, and her bones were charred to a crisp, and her nerves were burnt away, and the lymphatic fluid in her body flowed out in every direction, her soul's faith became firmer and more dazzling. And while the people who were watching these events thought that she had died, she was purified all the more. Indeed, just as in the case of gold, whereas the ignorant person who stands and watches it liquefying and flowing out and mixing with the ash thinks that it is lost and has perished, the craftsman who truly has a precise knowledge of these matters knows that through this technique it becomes purer, and after its incineration he collects it from everywhere and extracts the gleaming [metal]; so too in her case, while the non-Christians who saw her flesh liquefying and flowing out thought it had become ash and dust, the Christians understood very precisely

---

[4]This unexpected and somewhat mystifying metaphor is explained by John in section 10 below.

that in liquefying she shed every stain and, upon receiving immortality, ascended in a more brilliant state. Indeed, in that very pyre, before the resurrection, she conquered in no usual way the opposing powers. For, when her flesh was released by the fire and emitted a noise, it repelled them with considerable force. Indeed, just as a noble soldier who has dressed himself in bronze armor in fact strikes terror in the more cowardly of his adversaries with the clanging of his weapons, so too then did blessed Drosis put those powers to flight with the noise of her skin, and not just in this way, but also in another no less effective than this. For the moment she entered the pyre smoke rose up to a great height and took hold of the air and suffocated all the demons flying through the air, drove away the Devil, and wiped out the nature of the air itself. My point is that, since it was fouled by the smoke of the idols, a second smoke arose in its place that purified the stain that occurred as a result of them. Truly, the image of a spring would suit that pyre. For as if she had taken off her clothing in the spring and washed her body, so in that flame she shed her flesh more easily than any piece of clothing and shined her soul, while angels wielding torches escorted her to her bridegroom. After all, if angels escorted the Lazarus who had ulcers off to the bosom of Abraham, far more so did they escort this woman in person and depart, taking her from the furnace as if from some holy bridal canopy or bridal chamber, and escorting her up to her bridegroom in heaven.

10   On what grounds did I call that pyre a dye bath too? In that, as if she had become imperial purple in some astonishing dye bath, she was dispatched to the emperor in heaven, and entered the vaults of heaven with considerable boldness of speech, while Christ himself held the martyr's holy head in his invisible hand and baptized her in the fire as if in water. O astonishing pyre! What a treasure that dust and ash contained within, more valuable than any gold, sweeter smelling than any perfume, more precious than any gems! For to the same extent that wealth and gold have no power, martyrs' relics do

have power. For while gold never drove away disease nor put death to flight, martyrs' bones have effected both these things, the one in the time of our fore-fathers, the other even in our own time. And concerning these matters, not just we, but also those who were righteous before Christ's coming know precisely how to think philosophically, seeing that at the time when everyone was exiting Egypt and some took away gold, some silver, Moses took Joseph's bones and brought them instead of any wealth, carrying home with him a very substantial treasure full of countless blessings (cf. Ex 13.19).

11   But perhaps someone might say: "Why did he transfer them from Egypt to Palestine?" For on a martyrs' commemoration it's necessary to examine such things in particular. After all, many people go into precise detail about their burial arrangements and enjoin upon their relatives how, if they happen to die elsewhere, they should bring them home and bury them; next, when they're mocked for this by us on the basis that they're being mean-spirited, they offer us this story in justification, and when we say that it makes no difference whether a person happens to end up at home or in a foreign tomb, they say: "So then, why, if it makes no difference, did Moses take Joseph's bones from Egypt and bring them to Palestine?" But I will mention an even greater issue: that Moses didn't just take them, but that when [Joseph] was dying, he in fact commanded it. For truly this is a greater issue. "God enjoined upon you this oversight," he says, "and you will take up my bones" (cf. Gen 50.24–25). So why did both Joseph speak and Moses obey? For truly what he said deserves investigation. What are you saying? That the patriarch who both despised the present life and disdained everything, whom the world didn't deserve, the "stranger and migrant" (cf. Heb 11.13), who visualized the things in heaven day after day, whose sight was set on the heavenly Jerusalem—that while this man lost both his country and his freedom through fear of God when he was alive, and lived in a prison, and didn't give way at those machinations, when he was about to die, he was so caught up in petty details that he devoted so

much effort to the transportation of his bones and gave orders that his remains be brought back from so great a distance? Really, who would say these things? What was the advantage or of what nature was the benefit to the dead person from the translation of his bones? So why, then, did he command it? Not because he was concerned about his bones, but one could say that he was in fact afraid of the Egyptians' impiety. For when he brought about many great benefits, and was their tutor and patron and found a major relief for the famine and was the first and only person to interpret what was clear to no one and make it public, and when he solved the dreams didn't just reveal the famine in advance but also applied the right dose of medicine to it beforehand, so he also filled Egypt's warehouses so that no one would notice its presence. Thus, so that he wouldn't be considered a god after his death because of the magnitude of his patronage, seeing that those foreigners readily make gods of human beings, he took away the pretext for any impiety and ordered that his bones be taken back home.

12   And so this is one pretext. But one could mention a second indisputable one, too. For indeed it can be guaranteed from scripture. What, then, is it like? Joseph knew, having heard from his father, and his father having learnt a story passed down from his grandfather, that they would be slaves for many years and that the Egyptians would treat them badly. "Your seed will be a resident alien in a foreign land and they will serve it as a slave and will suffer badly for four hundred years," God said to Abraham (Gen 15.13). Thus, so that, when they grew weary at the length of time and couldn't handle the misery, they wouldn't despair of returning home and lose heart, he gave them a substantial guarantee of hope and spoke in advance about the bringing back of his bones so that, by reckoning to themselves that, if the just man hadn't convinced himself fervently and accurately that "We will all go back home," he wouldn't have given instructions about his bones, they might have indisputable proof and a secure expectation of returning to the land that bore them.

And that this is true, and that it was for this reason that he spoke in advance about his bones—not because he was concerned about his burial, but in order to correct their lack of faith—hear what Paul says. "In faith Joseph at his death reminded [them] about the exodus of the sons of Israel and gave instructions about his bones" (Heb 11.22). What is "in faith?" It stands for: "he foresaw what was going to happen a long time later and that his descendants would without a doubt receive their own land." Thus, so that he might make this clear, he said both these things in advance and one could see an amazing and wondrous occurrence at the exodus when his bones were translated. For Joseph, who brought them down into Egypt, again led them out front in person when they were going up [out of Egypt], encouraging them towards patience and hope for the things to come. For when they saw his remains before their eyes, and were next as a result reminded of that entire story, and reflected to themselves that he was plotted against by his brothers, that he was thrown into a pit, that he was at risk of death, that he spent time in prison and everything else that happened to him; then, that after all that he became king and of first rank in Egypt and benefactor and patron of so many people, they had sufficient hope that they would be freed from the troubles that constantly afflicted them, taught by the just man's bones that no one who believes in God and awaits help from him has ever been abandoned. My point is that, even if something painful and disagreeable were to disrupt his promises and intrude in between, it will never be able to dash their hopes of the end result; rather, that which was said in advance will of a certainty turn out as was determined in heaven, making more brilliant those who await with patience everything prophesied by God. It was for this reason that he gave instructions about his bones.

13   So then, let's not focus to such an extent on the petty details of being buried at home, nor tremble at death, but rather at sin. For it's not death that bore sin, but sin that gave birth to our death. Death became a remedy for sin. On the point that one shouldn't fear death,

but rather sin, hear what the prophet says: "Precious in the eyes of the Lord is the death of his saints" (Ps 115.6). And elsewhere: "Evil is death for sinners" (Ps 33.22). Do you see that those who pay attention to their affairs also have the capacity to reap the greatest benefits from it, while those who are careless and lazy, they are the ones who receive the matter (sc. death) in the role of condemnation? I'm not putting forward this argument without reason, but because I often hear many speaking about the means of death and, on the one hand, casting shame on those who don't deserve reproach, while, on the other, not casting aspersions on those who deserve substantial recrimination. For this reason I want to analyze this argument today, too. For this mode of philosophy is appropriate on a martyrs' day, too. I mean, I have heard many people saying: "So and so died in a foreign land with less honor than a dog, with no close friend present, nor anyone to put him in the ground; instead, with barely a few neighbors inviting one another to gather, he was laid out as the result of a quick whip-around and in this way handed over for burial." So, so that these things don't grieve us, it's necessary that this supposition be corrected too. My point, fellow, is that this isn't dying more wretchedly than a dog; rather, dying more wretchedly than a dog is to die in sin, not to quit life in a foreign land. Don't mention to me this corpse that's carried along on a gold inlaid couch, the one that the entire city accompanies in procession, that the people acclaim, that has clothing of silk and inlaid gold heaped up on it with great abundance. For this is nothing other than providing a more plentiful table for the worm. So then, don't show me this corpse, but show me this same corpse being accompanied in procession with such great honor on that day when Christ is seated out front on his lofty tribunal, [show me it] being brought in, being summoned, being asked for an account of what it said, what it did, what it thought. For at that time no one in this crowd will stand by him, nor relieve him of his punishment and penalty, nor will these shouts and acclamations be of help; rather, with his head bowed, denied the right of speech, shamed by the accusation of his affairs, he will be taken away, dragged by the evil powers to the unending punishments that come with the totally cruel gnashing of teeth, from then on wailing to no avail and beating his breast as a result of the unbearable pain.

14   Indeed, although that's what the sufferings there are like, the ones here are by no means tolerable either. For after those public acclamations that were paid for or occurred out of a certain fear, he will hear everyone making accusations in the streets and in the marketplace and at home and in pubs, and in other workshops and on the road and in the countryside, and [will hear] everywhere each traveler conversing with their neighbor with a great deal of fear and mentioning what sort of evils will succeed him, what sort of penalties will arrive, what sort of tortures now await. What advantage is there for him in the present life? What benefit will he reap from his greed? He died and left his money behind for others, while he himself took his sins and was buried; and many accusers from all walks of life sympathize with those he wronged, even those who suffered nothing terrible. I mean, just as in the case of people on the receiving end of patronage, those who get nothing rejoice with those who get something, and praise the benefactor, so in the case of those who experience abuse, those who suffer no injustice grieve with those who suffer badly and curse the perpetrator. It's for this reason [the prophet] says: "Evil is death for sinners," both because of the accusations here and because of the punishments there.

15   So then, this is the person who dies with less honor than a dog, but in the case of the just it isn't like this. Rather, even if they quit life in a deserted place, even if there's no one to lay them out, even if no one's present, they depart in receipt of an adequate shroud—their bold speech with God. They have a wondrous funeral, with angels present and guiding their soul, just as I demonstrated earlier in the case of Lazarus, who left behind innumerable encomiasts of his own life. Even if they leave children behind, everyone who inhabits the city will be their tutors and guardians, focusing on them instead the goodwill towards their father. But the person who dies in sin and

greed, if he dies deserting children, leaves them heirs of his own unpopularity, and abandons them in the midst of his enemies. And if he ends life childless, he leaves behind his own unending accusation in the form of the dwellings, the other possessions which he acquired through confiscation and greed. But the just man is not like this; instead, even when he dies he provides truly great benefits, benefiting all who are alive through the memory of his own virtue and making them better, just as, thus, in this the wicked man too is punished. For not just when he is alive, but also when dead he harms many, leaving them behind everywhere as proofs of his own greed. So then, knowing these things, let us not consider unhappy those [who die] in a foreign land, but those who die in sin; let us not consider blessed those [who depart] in their home, or in their bed, but those who depart with virtue, and let us strive after virtue, but flee wickedness. For while the former benefits both living and dead, the latter causes harm on both sides, both causing them shame and escorting them away to unending punishments. And may God, who brought us together on this blessed day and considered us worthy to strip off and wrestle and win and be crowned, when we've finished the present life along with his commands and laws, deem us all alike worthy to be enabled to approach this holy woman's tents on that day too, and enjoy the unending blessings. May it be that we all attain these things, through the grace and loving kindness of our Lord, Jesus Christ, with whom to the Father be glory, together with the Holy Spirit, forever. Amen.

An Encomium on Egyptian Martyrs

Very little can be said about either where this homily was delivered or on what occasion. The homily itself appears to celebrate martyrs who originated in Egypt but were condemned to the mines, and whose bodies appear to have been buried in the vicinity of the city in which John is preaching. This circumstance has led Stilting to propose that the location is Antioch, since there were mines in that province.[1] His identification is perhaps supported by the remark that the saints form a protective wall about the city on all sides, a comment which is repeated in another homily of probable Antiochene origin,[2] but which fails to appear in any homily that can be assigned with certainty to Constantinople. The connection drawn towards the end of the homily between these Egyptian martyrs and the wilderness may also perhaps point to the Syrian landscape. On the other hand, the remarks about the abundance of Egyptian martyrs and their exportation all over the world, which mirror the first paragraph of the present homily and are found in the homily *On all the martyrs* below, show how tenuous this kind of evidence is and sound a note of caution. The latter homily was without doubt delivered at Constantinople and there the comments explicitly refer to the exportation of bodies rather than live martyrs.

Contents:

1. Egypt produces martyrs, which it exports to other cities all over the world. The bodies of these saints fortify cities like a wall and repel the attacks of demons.

---

[1]J. Stilting, art. "De S. Joanne Chrysostomo, episcopo Constantinopolitano et ecclesiæ doctore, prope comana in Ponto, commentarius historicus," in *Acta Sanctorum Septembris* IV (Antwerp, 1753): 505.

[2]See *On the cemetery and the cross* (*De coemeterio et cruce*: *CPG* 4337), PG 49.393 ll.27–29.

2. The saints' bodies also protect us against God's wrath, since they have earned bold speech with God. While their faith was stored up in their soul, their bodies too shared in that grace and played a role.

3–4. The greater the tortures heaped on the martyrs, the greater their crown. In this case, they were condemned to the mines. It was a foolish idea on the Devil's part. They lit up the wilderness and were more valuable than any metal they dug up.

5. Knowing that all the saints have endured a harsh life, let's follow their example and not pursue a soft and easy one.

Translated from PG 50.693–698.

1   Praise God that martyrs originate even from Egypt—Egypt, the land that fights God and is totally out of its mind,[3] and is the source of godless mouths, the source of blaspheming tongues[4]—[that] martyrs originate from Egypt, yet [are] not just in Egypt, nor in the adjoining and neighboring region, but all over the world, too. Indeed, it's just like the surplus of supply; when the people who live in the cities see that production is more than the inhabitants require, they distribute it to foreign cities, too, at one and the same time demonstrating the kindliness that exists among them and in turn readily purchasing from [the foreign cities] whatever they need in addition to the abundance of those goods. So, too, have the Egyptians done regarding the athletes of piety. When they saw that by God's grace the production among them had become substantial, they didn't lock this great gift of God up in the city. Instead, they sent these ware-

[3]Gr. *mania* (lit. "madness") can also carry the connotation of being under a charge of *superstitio*, a technical legal term that refers to pursuing practices contrary to the true religion (often "magic"). See Boyarin, *Dying for God*, 36–9. In this instance it refers to the heretical tendencies of the Egyptians.

[4]John alludes here to the Arian heresy, which originated in Egypt. Whether there is also a covert play on words which alludes to Alexandria's bishop, Theophilus (*theophilos* = God-lover, *theomaches* = God-fighter), is more difficult to determine.

houses of blessings out all over the earth, both demonstrating their sisterly and brotherly love and glorifying the common Master of all, and also embellishing their city among everyone and making it evident that it was a metropolis of the entire world. I mean, if cheap and worthless resources that reward us with pleasures just for the present life could supply this gift to many of the cities, how isn't it right that the [city] graced with none of these momentary and perishable things, but men who acquired considerable security even after death for the cities who inherited them, that it above all attain this pre-eminence among them. For the bodies of these saints fortify our city more securely than any wall that is of adamant or impregnable. Indeed, just like some towering rocks that thrust forward on all sides, they don't just beat back the attacks of these perceptible and visible enemies, but also the machinations of the invisible demons, and both overthrow and destroy every one of the Devil's wiles as easily as if some noble man were to overthrow and ruin children's toys. And while, regarding the other machinations that occur among human beings, such as walls and ditches and weapons and multitudes of soldiers, and everything that's devised for the safety of the inhabitants, it's possible for enemies to beat them back by other more numerous and substantially excessive contrivances of their own, whenever a city is fortified by saints' bodies, even if [their enemies] spend copious amounts of money, they won't be able to set any mechanism of the sort against the cities that possess them.

2   Beloved, this possession isn't just useful for us against humans' machinations or demons' malicious acts. Rather, even if our common Master were to get angry because of the multitude of our sins, we'll swiftly be able to make him merciful towards the city by throwing up these bodies as a shield. For if those among our forefathers who achieved great things attained some comfort by throwing up as a shield the names of holy men and taking refuge in the citing of "Abraham, Isaac, and Jacob" (Ex 32, Bar 2), and enjoyed great assistance from the memory of these names, by far more will we, when-

ever we throw up as a shield not just names, but also the very bodies
that competed, be able to have God merciful and mild and gentle.
And that what's being said by us is no boast, many of those who are
local inhabitants and those who've come from elsewhere know how
great is the power of these saints, who also give testimony to what's
been said, since they've learnt through experience itself their bold
speech with God. And rightly so! For they didn't fight for truth in the
usual way, but staunchly and zealously resisted the Devil's violent
and intolerable force, fighting as if in bodies of stone and iron, but
not in perishable and mortal ones, as if already converted into the
insensible and immortal nature that doesn't yield to the bitter and
painful necessities of the body. My point is that, like some savage and
cruel and harsh wild animals, the executioners circled their bodies
on all sides and punctured their ribs, lacerated their flesh, excavated
their bones and laid them bare, and nothing stayed them from that
cruel and inhuman behavior. Yet, even though they grabbed spines
and intestines and worked their way right into the innards, they
didn't find a way to steal the treasure of faith that was stored up inside
them. Rather, their experience was the same as if someone were to
besiege a most imperial city that was brimming with a great deal of
wealth and possessed many treasures and bring down its walls and,
on arriving at the treasuries [holding] the money, overturn doors,
smash locks, dig up floors, and, after thoroughly scrutinizing everything, were unable to snatch away its treasure and depart. My point
is that the soul's possessions are like that. They aren't betrayed by the
body's passions, when it (sc. the soul) securely retains them; instead,
if someone were to break up the chest cage itself and take the heart
and cut it open little by little, it wouldn't betray the treasure once it'd
been entrusted to it by faith. This is the work of God's grace, that
organizes everything and enables miracles to be accomplished in fee-
ble bodies. Truly, this is even more amazing. For not only didn't those
who exhibit insanity to this degree spirit away any of the treasures
stored up in them, but they even caused them to be protected with
greater security, and made them both more brilliant and more

opulent. My point is that no longer the soul alone, but even the body itself shared in more abundant grace, and not only didn't throw away what it possessed after it was cut into pieces and often chopped up but also even took on a more abundant and substantial importance. What could be more amazing than this victory, in that those whom they detained and had under their control and imprisoned and scourged with authority, they couldn't conquer, but were instead defeated pitifully and wretchedly by them? For they weren't battling against them, but against God who dwelt in them. It's pretty much obvious to everyone that it's completely inevitable that the person who does battle with God is defeated comprehensively, after paying a penalty for just the attempt.

3   This is what the saints' victories are like. If the contests and wrestling bouts are so amazing and miraculous, what might we say about the prizes and crowns stored up for them on account of their boldness? For they didn't stop at these tortures, nor did they quit the race at this point; instead their bouts were extended further, with, on the one side, the wicked demon expecting to trip up the athletes by the heaping on of torments, and on the other, God who loves human beings acquiescing and not preventing him. The result is that the madness of the non-Christians is revealed more clearly to everyone, and for the [athletes] he weaves more brilliant and abundant crowns. Indeed, it is just as occurred in the case of Job and the Devil. The latter demanded from God more numerous torments against him in the expectation that he'd get around the noble athlete of piety by the heaping on of the disasters. God, on the other hand, acquiesced and granted the wicked demon's wicked requests, so making his athlete more renowned. So it happened in this case, too. For when he chewed their body all over more savagely than any wild animal and bloodied his tongue and mouth, even if it wasn't with the saints' blood, but with those inhuman and pitiless votes,[5] he was defeated by their

[5]The introduction of "votes" at this point is sudden and the reference unclear. The term may allude to the circumstances under which these Egyptian martyrs were condemned to the mines.

boldness and, having more than glutted himself with that inhuman feast and taken his fill, he departed. Consider how great the saints' patience was, which satisfied so great a madness with its own passions. He attacked again, driven to the struggle by his madness and striving to be the ultimate winner over every wild animal by means of a different savagery. My point is that they (sc. the animals) approach this feast through the compulsion of nature and depart when they have had their fill, and even if they see countless bodies they attack but one of them. But this animal (sc. the Devil) actually attacked this food through the wickedness of his choice, and when he'd glutted himself on their flesh, wove another plot against them, betraying these saints to a long drawn-out and extremely cruel death. For he ordered that they labor in the mines in perpetuity.

4   What stupidity! Despite gaining so clear an experience of their courage and patience, he expected to get around them with this [torture]. After all, the saints, who live side by side with the angels, and are citizens of heaven and are now enlisted in the heavenly Jerusalem, lived side by side with wild animals and the wilderness was then more holy than any city. For while in the cities these illegal and tyrannical commands were undertaken day after day, the wilderness rejoiced in immunity from that inhuman liturgy. And while the law courts were full of unholy practices and impious commands, the wilderness contained citizens more law abiding than any other people, who had turned from humans into angels, and the wilderness rivaled heaven as a result of the virtue of the citizens who lived in it. And while the punishment was by nature extremely harsh, through the enthusiasm of the competitors it became easy and light and readily bearable. They thought that they saw the light magnified many times at that time, and they thought that what had been said by the prophet: "the moon will be like the sun and the sun seven times brighter" (Is 30.26), had already obscured the light. For there is nothing, there is nothing more cheerful than a soul considered worthy of suffering for Christ's sake any of these things that we consider terrible and unbearable.

They thought that they had already migrated to heaven and were dancing with the angels. Rather, what need did they have of angels and heaven, when Jesus the Lord of angels was with them in the wilderness? For if where there are two or three gathered in his name, he is there in the midst of them (cf. Mt 18.20), by far more was he in the midst of those who had gathered at that time, who were being punished perpetually not, as it were, in his name, but for his name's sake. For you know, you know clearly that there is no other punishment more cruel than this one and that those condemned to this sentence would choose to endure countless other deaths than to endure the pain that comes from there. They were delivered to the mines where they had to dig up copper, when they themselves were many times more valuable than mineral gold or gold dust, gold not dug up by the hands of condemned people, but discovered by the zeal of men of faith. They who were full of countless treasures worked mines. What is more bitter and painful than that life? They observed the tales told about those great men fulfilled in themselves too, the ones Paul narrated about the saints, when he said: "They whom the world didn't deserve went around in sheepskins, in goatskins, afflicted, set upon, mistreat" (Heb 11.37–38) (wandering in wildernesses and mountains and caves and the caverns of the earth. These events took place even in our generation.)[6]

5   So then, beloved, since we too know these truths, that both now and long ago, since humans came into existence, all those dear to God have been allotted a life that's gloomy and toilsome and full of countless troubles, let us not pursue the life that's soft and dissolute and full of idleness, but rather the toilsome [life], the laborious [life], the [life] that has trials and tribulations. For just as the contestant can't attain the crowns through sleeping and laziness and luxury, nor the soldier the trophies, nor the helmsman the harbor, nor the farmer the full threshing-floor, so neither does the Christian who

[6]The material in parentheses appears in square brackets in Migne's text, indicating that it is an addition in some manuscripts.

spends their life in laziness attain the promised blessings. How, then, isn't it absurd that in all worldly matters we put labors ahead of pleasure, and risks ahead of security, and this when the expected outcome of those labors is of little value and trivial; yet when it's heaven that lies ahead of us and angelic honors and a life that has no end and spending time with angels and the blessings of which one can neither conceive nor speak, we expect to achieve them through laziness and indolence and a dissolute soul and not to dignify them with the same effort as worldly matters? Don't, please, don't let's plan so badly for ourselves and for our salvation, but look to these saints, these noble and brave athletes, who have been given to us in place of torches, and amend our own life to their courage and patience, so that after we depart this life by their prayers we might be able to both see and embrace them and be assigned to their heavenly dwellings. May we attain all these blessings through the grace and loving kindness of our Lord Jesus Christ, through whom and with whom be glory to the Father and the Holy Spirit for ever and ever. Amen.

On the Holy Martyrs

The opening lines of this relatively short homily inform us that it was preached less than seven days after the celebration of Pentecost, a festival which, in the years that spanned John's preaching career, varied in date from between 14 May to 10 June. Thus the homily can be localized to some time in the second half of May or first half of June. Unfortunately there is little else that can be said about its delivery. Despite the title appended to it in the manuscripts, which implies a general martyr festival or festival of all saints, it is unlikely that this homily celebrates all martyrs everywhere, but rather that it is directed at the commemoration of a specific group of martyrs, large in number, whose characteristic form of martyrdom was being roasted on an iron grill, as John describes in some detail towards the middle of the homily. It is noteworthy that in the Syrian martyrology at this time of year there are recorded several festivals dedicated to a large group of martyrs.[1] It is uncertain, however, whether any of them were celebrated at Constantinople or Antioch in addition to the locations listed in the martyrology, and therefore whether any of these might be the occasion on which this homily was preached. There is a vague possibility that the reference in § 6 to the typical behavior of the population when foreign athletes arrive in the city refers to the Syrian Olympics that were held every four years in the provincial capital, Antioch, and that the homily therefore stems from that city, but the

---

[1]The martyrology records on 19 May the commemoration at Alexandria of Serapion and twelve other confessors; on 26 May at Alexandria that of Eucaerius and seventeen other confessors; on 7 June the commemoration of Tirianus (or Trajanus) and twenty-seven other confessors; on 10 June in Tomis that of Marcianus and forty-seven other confessors; and on 15 June at Alexandria, the festival of Hierax, Philip and ten youths who were confessors (Wright 427–428).

evidence is too allusive to admit of any certainty and there is nothing else within the homily to support this suspicion.

Like many of the other martyr homilies, this one too appears to have been delivered at a particular martyrium (see § 7).

Contents:

1–3. It is not yet seven days past Pentecost and it is the festival of a large group of martyrs. Martyrs are comparable to angels and it is death, introduced by the Devil but converted by Christ, which makes this possible. The martyrs are both a dance-chorus and a battalion of soldiers.

4. Despite having the advantage, the martyrs' torturers were defeated.

5. The ladder that they were tied to is like an inversion of Jacob's ladder. Suffering a fever is compared to the flames that tortured the martyrs and the blood that flowed from them was like a rising sun. In imitation of Christ, they suffered being pierced gladly.

6. The martyrs' sufferings are momentary, while nothing can describe the honors that await them in heaven.

7–8. Martyrdom can be achieved even today through despising luxury, suppressing desire, and giving to the poor. Focusing on the benefits of these actions will help overcome the pain of doing them. Prayer vigils are uncomfortable but achievable, if we paint the martyrs' tortures on the walls of our mind and make it a fitting dwelling place for God.

Translated from PG 50.705–712.

Panegyric on all the saints in the whole world who have been martyred

1   Not yet seven days in number have passed since we celebrated the holy festival of Pentecost and again a chorus of martyrs has happened upon us, rather a battle-array and squadron of martyrs, which is in no way inferior to the host of angels which the patriarch Jacob saw (cf. Gen 32.2), but readily comparable and equal to it. For

martyrs and angels are distinct in name only, but come together in works. Angels inhabit the heavens, but martyrs do too. The former are ageless and immortal; this the martyrs will possess too. Yes, but don't the former have a nature that's incorporeal? And so what? For even if the martyrs are enclosed in a body, yet it is immortal. Rather, even before immortality, Christ's death adorns their bodies more than immortality. The sky, decorated as it is with the chorus of stars, is not as brilliant as the bodies of the martyrs, decorated with their brilliant chorus of wounds. As a result, because they died, through this above all they have the greater share and received their prizes before immortality, crowned by death. "You have made it a little short in comparison to angels, but crowned it with glory and honor" (Ps 8.6), says David of the nature shared by humankind. Yet even this short span Christ, when he was here, made up for, by condemning Death to death. But I don't rely on this point, but on the fact that even this diminution became an advantage over Death. For if they were not mortal, they wouldn't have become martyrs. In consequence, if they hadn't been mortal, there wouldn't have been a crown. If death did not exist, martyrdom wouldn't exist. If death did not exist, Paul couldn't have said: "I die daily for your glory, which I have in Christ Jesus" (cf. 1 Cor 15.31). If death and decay didn't exist, he couldn't have said: "I rejoice in my sufferings on your behalf and in my flesh I make up for the defects of the afflictions of Christ" (Col 1.24). In consequence, let us not grieve because we are mortal, but give thanks because the stadium of martyrdom has been opened up to us by death. From decay we receive a basis for prizes. From this we have a pretext for wrestling matches.

2   Do you see God's wisdom, how the greatest of evils, the ultimate disaster for us, which the Devil introduced (I mean death), how this changed into our honor and glory, because it led the athletes towards the prizes of martyrdom? So what? Should we give thanks to the Devil for death? Heaven forbid! For this isn't the outcome of his intent, but the gift of God's wisdom. He (sc. the Devil) introduced it

so that it would destroy, and so that, when he brought it down to earth, he might cut off all hope of salvation; but Christ took it and converted it and, through it, led us back up to heaven. Let none of us, then, cast judgment, if I've called the fullness of martyrs a "chorus" and "squadron," placing two opposing labels on one matter. For a chorus and a squadron are opposites, but here they've both come together. For they (sc. the martyrs) went to meet their tortures with joy as if they were dancing, and as if they were in battle they displayed complete courage and strength and conquered their opposition. If you look at the nature of what took place, what took place was a skirmish and war and engagement. If you examine the spirit of what took place, what happened was dancing and festivities and festivals and utter joy.

3   Do you want to learn how these (I mean the martyrs' acts) were more terrifying than war? What is it that's terrifying in war? Armies stand with their defenses up on both sides, gleaming with weaponry, and illuminating the ground; a cloud of javelins is released from all directions that obscures the air with the sheer number; torrents of blood flow on the ground, and everywhere large numbers keel over as if in a harvested crop of grain—so do the soldiers tumble down, one close on the heels of another. Come, then, let me take you from those battles to this one. Here, too, there are two battle lines—that of the martyrs and that of the tyrants. But the tyrants are armed, while the martyrs fight with a naked body and the victory belongs to the naked, not the armed. Who wouldn't be struck with amazement that the whipped person subverts the person whipping, the person in chains the freed, the one being burned alive the person who set the fire, the one dying the destroyer? Did you see how these events are more terrifying than those? Even if those are frightening, they occur in accord with nature. These exceed all nature and every consequence of things, so that you may learn that the achievements result from God's grace. And yet what is more unjust than this battle? What more lawless than [these] wrestling matches? For in wars

both of the fighting forces have defenses. But it isn't like that here—instead, the one is naked, the other armed.

4   Again, in athletic contests, both [contestants] are able to raise their hands, but here the one is tied up, the other inflicts his blows with authority and, as if on the basis of a certain absolute power, the judges allot acting badly to themselves, but assign suffering badly to the just martyrs, and in this way engage with the saints; yet not even in this way do they subvert them, but depart defeated after this unequal fight. Indeed, it is the same as if one were to lead a battle-thirsty person into battle and, after cutting off the tip of their javelin and stripping off their chest-plate, order them to fight in this way with their body naked, while the person who is being hit and beaten and who receives countless wounds in every part of their body were to erect the trophy. Truly, my point is that, despite leading the martyrs out naked and tying their hands behind their backs and beating and scourging them all over, in this way they were defeated; but those receiving the wounds erected the trophy against the Devil. And just as when adamant is struck it doesn't itself yield, nor is it softened, but shatters the iron that strikes it, so indeed, too, when such great tortures were inflicted, the saints' souls themselves suffered no ill effect, while they destroyed the power of those inflicting the blows and sent them out of the contests defeated shamefully and ludicrously after numerous unbearable blows. For truly they strapped them (sc. the martyrs) to the rack and dug through their ribs, carving in deep furrows, as if they were plowing soil, but not splitting bodies. And one could see cavities exposed, ribs opened up, spines shattered, and those bloodthirsty savages didn't even check their madness here, but took them down from the rack and stretched them out on an iron ladder[2] over glowing coals. And again one could see sights more cruel than before—two drips coming down out of

---

[2] In essence, a type of grill. The primary meaning of the Greek (*klimax* = "ladder") is retained here, because of the comparison between this instrument of torture and Jacob's ladder, which immediately follows.

the bodies, the one of flowing blood, the other of melting flesh. But the saints, lying on the coals as if on roses, in this way viewed what was happening with pleasure.

5   When you hear "iron ladder," remember the envisioned ladder that the patriarch Jacob saw stretching from earth into heaven (cf. Gen 28.13). By means of that one angels descended, by means of this one martyrs ascended. Each [of these ladders] the Lord propped up. These saints couldn't have endured the pain, if they hadn't been fastened to it. But while by means of that [ladder] angels ascend and descend, it's obvious to anyone that by means of this [ladder] martyrs too ascend. Why exactly? Because the first are sent to serve those about to inherit salvation (cf. Heb 1.14), while the second then departed for the President of the games, as if they were athletes and crowned victors liberated from the competitions. But let's not simply listen to what's been said, hearing that burning coals were applied to their scourged bodies, but reflect on what we're like when we've broken out in a fever. We think that life is unlivable, we're beside ourselves, we're don't handle it well, we're ill-tempered like little children, thinking that that fire is no less than hell. But when there was no fever attacking them, but rather flames besieging them on every side, and when sparks were leaping onto their weeping sores and biting their wounds more savagely than any wild animals, these [martyrs], like beings of adamant and people who saw these things happening to other people's bodies, in this way nobly and with a courage that suited them stood fast against the words of confession, remaining unswayed through all those tortures, brilliantly demonstrating both their own courage and the grace of God. Have you often seen the sun coming up just before dawn and emitting saffron-colored rays? The saints' bodies were like that, seeing that torrents of blood flowed around them in every direction, like some saffron-colored rays, and illuminated their bodies far more than the sun does the sky. On seeing this blood angels were happy, demons were scared, and the Devil himself trembled. For what was being

viewed was not simply blood, but saving blood, holy blood, blood worthy of heaven, blood that perpetually waters the Church's beautiful plants. The Devil saw the blood and trembled. For he remembered other blood, the Master's. It was because of that blood that this blood flowed. For since the Master's rib was pierced, from that time on you see countless ribs being pierced. I mean, who wouldn't strip for these contests with much pleasure, when they are about to share in their Master's sufferings, and conform to Christ's death? For this reward is sufficient, and the honor much greater than the labors, and the recompense exceeds the athletic contests, even before [entering] the kingdom of heaven.

6   Let's not tremble, then, when we hear that someone or other has become a martyr, but tremble when we hear that someone or other has gotten soft and lost out on the sort of rewards that lie ahead. If you want to hear what happened after this, too, no account can compare. "Neither has an eye seen," scripture says, "nor an ear heard, nor has there entered a person's heart, what God has prepared for those who love him" (1 Cor 2.9). No human being has loved him to the same extent as the martyrs. Mind you, just because the magnitude of the stored-up blessings exceeds both word and mind, it doesn't mean that we'll therefore be silent; rather, in so far as we are capable of speaking and you of listening, we'll attempt to show you dimly the blessedness that will succeed them there. For they alone will know clearly, who enjoy it as a result of this [very] experience. For while the martyrs suffer these terrible and unspeakable things in a brief moment of time, after their release from here they ascend into heaven, with angels escorting them in front and archangels as a guard of honor. For they (sc. the angels) are not ashamed of their fellow servants, but would choose to do anything for them, since they (sc. the martyrs), too, chose to suffer everything for their Master, Christ. Whenever they ascend into heaven, all those holy powers rush together. For if, when athletes from other regions arrive in the city, the whole population flows around them from all directions,

and circles them and appraises the good condition of their limbs, how much more, when the athletes of piety ascend into heaven do the angels rush together and all the powers above flow around from all directions and appraise their wounds and, as if they (sc. the martyrs) were some warriors returning from war and battle with numerous trophies and victories, so do they greet and embrace them all with pleasure. Next, with a large guard of honor they escort them to the king of heaven, up to that throne that is full of considerable glory, where there are the cherubim and seraphim. And after they arrive there and do obeisance to the one who sits on the throne, they enjoy even more abundant friendliness from their Master than their fellow servants. For he doesn't receive them as servants (even though that, too, is a major honor, of which one can find no equal), but as his friends. "For you are my friends" (Jn 15.14), scripture says. And rightly so. For he said on another occasion: "There is no greater love than this, that a person lay down their life for their friends" (Jn 15.13). And so, since they have exhibited the greatest possible love, he greets them and they enjoy that glory; they take part in the choirs [of angels] and participate in the mystical songs. For if, while they were in the body, at the time of the communion in the mysteries they became part of that choir and with the cherubim chanted the thrice-holy hymn, just as you who have been initiated know,[3] how much more now, when they have regained their fellow worshippers, do they participate with considerable boldness in that praise.

7   Don't you tremble in front of this martyrium? Don't you now yearn for martyrdom? Aren't you now sad that no opportunity for martyrdom is presently available? On the contrary, let us, too, train ourselves for an opportunity for martyrdom. They despised life. You, despise luxury! They threw their bodies on the fire. You, now

[3] An allusion to the Sanctus, which was sung as part of the eucharistic liturgy, and therefore familiar only to the baptized. The unbaptized, including those enrolled as catechumens but who had not yet undergone baptism and the final instruction which occurred in the week following baptism, were dismissed at the end of the Liturgy of the Word and therefore excluded from the eucharistic liturgy and its mysteries.

throw money in the hands of the poor! They trampled on the burning coals. You, extinguish the flame of desire! These things are difficult, but also rewarding. Don't focus on the present obstacles, but on the future benefits; not on the tortures at hand, but the anticipated blessings; not the sufferings, but the prizes; not the labors, but the crowns; not the sweat expended, but the rewards; not the sorrows, but the returns; not the consuming fire, but the kingdom that lies ahead; not the executioners standing all around, but Christ crowned. This is the greatest method and easiest path to virtue, to focus on not just the labors, but also the rewards that follow the labors, but not just individually. So, when you are about to give alms, don't pay attention to the expenditure of the money, but to the collection of righteousness. "He distributed, he gave to the poor. His righteousness endures for ever and ever" (Ps 111.9). Don't look at the wealth that's being emptied, but focus on the treasure that's being increased. If you fast, don't reflect on the discomfort from the fasting, but the release that comes from the discomfort. If you spend a sleepless night in prayer, don't reflect on the misery that comes from the lack of sleep, but the boldness that results from the prayer. Soldiers do this, too. They focus not on the wounds, but the rewards; not on the killings, but the victories; not on the falling corpses, but the warriors who are being crowned. In this way, too, ship's captains focus their sight on the harbors ahead of the waves, on the trading ahead of the shipwrecks, on the post-sea benefits before the disasters at sea. You, too, act in this way. Reflect on how wonderful it is, in the depths of night, when every human being and wild animal and winged creature is asleep, when there is the most profound silence, for you alone to be awake and to converse boldly with the common Master of all. So, sleep is sweet? But nothing is sweeter than praying. If you converse with him one on one, you can accomplish a lot, with no one hassling you or cheating you of your supplication. You also have time on your side with regard to obtaining what you want. So, you're tossing and turning, lying on a soft mattress, and can't bear the thought of getting up? Reflect on the martyrs lying today on the iron ladder, not with a mattress lying underneath, but live coals strewn under it.

8   I want to conclude my sermon here, so that you go away with the memory of the ladder fresh and crisp, and remember it at night and during the day. For even if countless chains restrain us, we'll be able to smash them all easily, and rise for prayer, if we constantly reflect on this ladder. Let's inscribe on the surface of our heart not just that ladder, but the rest of the martyrs' tortures, too. And just like people who make their houses brilliant by decorating them all over with colorful fresco, so too let us paint the martyrs' tortures on the walls of our mind. For while that painting is frivolous, this brings reward. For this painting requires no money, nor expenditure, nor any skill; rather instead of all these it is sufficient to employ enthusiasm and a noble and sober mind and to sketch their tortures by this means as if by a master hand. Let us, then, paint on our soul those martyrs lying on roasting pans, those stretched beneath live coals, the ones plunged into cauldrons, those drowned at sea, others scraped raw, others bent on a wheel, others hurled over a cliff; and some fighting with wild beasts, others led to the pit, yet others losing their life, each in their own individual way. [Let's do this] so that, by making our house brilliant with this painting's rich colors, we may make it a fitting inn for the king of heaven. For if he sees such paintings in our mind, he will come with the Father and, with the Holy Spirit, will make his dwelling-place among us. And from then on our mind will be a royal house and no unnatural thought will be able to enter while, like a colorful picture, the memory of the martyrs is always stored up inside and gives off much reflected light within and while God, the king of all, is constantly dwelling with us. So, by welcoming Christ here, we will be able to be welcomed into the eternal dwellings after we depart here. May we all attain these things through the grace and loving kindness of our Lord Jesus Christ, through whom and with whom be glory to the Father, together with the holy and life-giving Spirit, for ever and ever. Amen.

On Saint Romanus

The Romanus commemorated here is most probably a member of the clergy of Caesarea who was martyred under Diocletian in the early fourth century, when passing through Antioch. According to Eusebius (*On the Palestinian Martyrs* 2), he had his tongue torn out and was strangled in prison. His festival was most likely celebrated at Antioch on 18 November, the date ascribed to it in the Syrian martyrology. As mentioned in the introduction to the homily on St Eustathius, John indicates elsewhere that at Antioch the festival of Romanus closely followed that of Eustathius. Despite the absence of any explicit remark within the homily which ties the martyr to the location at which John was preaching, that the homily was delivered at Antioch seems clear both from the explicit association between the festivals of Eustathius and of Romanus, and is supported by the fact that a martyrium came to be associated with his name at Antioch within the next century and that in the time of Severus his festival was a fixed part of the local calendar.[1]

Contents:

1–3. Today is again a martyrs' festival. Because we are all of the same body, their glory is ours, just as they grieve for our sins and we rejoice in their good works.

4–11. This same depth of love was displayed by Romanus, the martyr we celebrate today. Why was his tongue cut out? At a time when everyone was being forced to sacrifice, Romanus rallied the Christians against that

---

[1]See Severus of Antioch, *Hom.* 35 (PO 36.438–457), delivered on the festival of Romanus, whom he explicitly says was martyred at Antioch; and *Hom.* 1 and 80 (PO 38.255 and 20.324), both delivered in a martyrium of St Romanus. These last two homilies were delivered on 18 Nov. 512 and 6/8 Nov. 515, respectively.

command. His tongue was cut out to put a stop to this, since full martyrdom would only have proved his arguments. Contrary to expectation, he was even more persuasive afterward, since he now spoke with a spiritual voice.

12. John encourages everyone to rejoice together with the martyrs.

Translated from PG 50.605–612.

Sermon 1 of praise on the holy martyr Romanus

1   Again it is a martyrs' commemoration and again a feast day and spiritual festival. They did the hard work, and we rejoice. They wrestled, and we are delighted. Theirs is the crown, and shared is the fame; rather, it is the entire Church's glory. "How could this be so?," you ask. Because the martyrs are parts and limbs of ours. "If a single limb suffers, all the limbs suffer with it. If a single limb is held in honor, all the limbs rejoice with it" (1 Cor 12.26). The head is crowned, and the rest of the body is delighted. One person becomes Olympic victor, and the entire populace rejoices and welcomes him with a great deal of acclamation. If in the Olympic games those who have contributed nothing to those sweaty efforts reap such great pleasure, by far more would this occur in the case of the athletes of piety. We are feet, the martyrs are the head. But "the head cannot say to the feet: 'I have no need of you'" (1 Cor 12.21). Glorious are the limbs, but the superiority of the glory doesn't make them strangers to their connection to the rest of the parts. I mean, through this they become particularly glorious, when they don't shove aside their connection to us. Since truly an eye, which is more brilliant than the rest of the entire body, keeps its own glory intact when it isn't detached from the rest of the body.

2   And why do I speak about martyrs? For if their Master is not ashamed to be our head, by far more are they unashamed to be our limbs. For they possess a love that is firmly rooted, and it is the way

of love to join and bind together what is divided, and it doesn't scrutinize the value. So then, just as they join in grieving for our sins, so we join in rejoicing over their good works. This in fact is what Paul ordered us to do, when he said to "rejoice with those who rejoice," and to "weep with those who weep" (Rom 12.15). But to weep with those who weep is simple, while to rejoice with those who rejoice is not very easy. For we find it easier to grieve together with people who experience disasters than to share in the happiness of those who are in favor. After all, in that situation the nature of the disaster is enough to bend even a stone towards sympathy. But in this instance jealousy and envy of their doing well doesn't allow a person who is not very given to philosophy to share in the joy. For just as love joins and binds together what is divided, so envy divides what is united. For this reason, please, let's practice sharing in the happiness of those who are in favor, so that we may cleanse our soul of both jealousy and envy. After all, nothing so drives out this severe and stubborn sickness as to be bound to those who live in virtue. At least, hear how Paul is at the peak in each of these. "Who is weak," he says, "and I'm not weak? Who is made to stumble and I don't burn?" (2 Cor 11.29). He didn't say: "And I'm not grieved," but "I don't burn," out of a desire to show us via the label "burning" the intensity of his grief. And on another occasion when he was writing to other people, he said: "You have become kings without us; at least, I wish that you did become kings, so that we too might be kings with you" (1 Cor 4.8). And again: "Now we are alive, if you stand in the Lord" (1 Thess 3.8).

3   See how his brothers' and sisters' good repute was very much desired by [Paul], who didn't consider himself alive unless they were being saved. Though a man who'd been snatched into the third heaven and taken away to Paradise and who had taken part in ineffable mysteries and enjoyed such bold speech before God, [Paul] didn't take much notice of those blessings, unless he also saw his brothers and sisters saved with him. For he knew, he knew clearly that there is

nothing either greater or equal to love, not even martyrdom itself, which is the pinnacle of all blessings. As to how [this is the case], listen. For while love creates disciples of Christ even without martyrdom, martyrdom without love wouldn't have the capacity to effect this. What makes this clear? Christ's words themselves. For he said to the disciples: "In this everyone will know that you are my disciples, if you love one another" (Jn 13.35). See, love without martyrdom creates disciples. That martyrdom without love not only doesn't create disciples, but doesn't even benefit the person enduring it at all, hear Paul, who says: "If I hand over my body to be burned, but do not have love, it's of no benefit to me" (1 Cor 13.3).

4   For this reason in particular I love this saint, blessed Romanus, who brings us together today, in that he displayed much love at his martyrdom. In fact, that's why his holy tongue was cut out. For truly it is well worth examining this question: why on earth the Devil didn't lead him away to tortures and punishments and penalties, but instead cut off his tongue. For he didn't do this without purpose, but with a great deal of malice. For truly the beast is villainous, and meddles and stirs up everything against our salvation. So, come on, let's examine why on earth he proceeded to cut out his tongue, at least by going back a little earlier in the story. For in this way we will know both God's loving kindness and the martyr's patience and the Devil's treachery. And when we learn God's loving kindness we will give thanks to the Master, while when we get to know the martyr's patience we will imitate our fellow servant, and when we learn every bit of the Devil's treachery we will escape the enemy. My point is that God granted us to know his (sc. the Devil's) machinations for this reason: so that by hating him in the extreme we might more easily subvert him. Regarding the point that it is possible to know his thoughts, hear what Paul says about the person who had prostituted themselves. For in writing to the Corinthians he pretty much says this: "Confirm your love for him, so that we won't be claimed by Satan. For we are not ignorant of his thoughts" (2 Cor 2.8, 11).

5   What, then, is the reason for which he cut out his tongue? Bear with me as I go back a little in the narrative. A terrible war was once stirred up against the Churches—not when barbarians attacked the cities, nor some other races, but when the very people who appeared to govern our world used their subjects more harshly and cruelly than any barbarians or enemies or tyrants. For the danger then was not over freedom or country, or money or the present life, but over the kingdom of heaven and the blessings stored up, over immortal life, over the confession of Christ. Indeed a new form of captivity was conceived of. For they did not expel people from the city here, but strove to deprive them of the free Jerusalem above, and they compelled each person to sacrifice their soul on the altars and to disown on oath their own Master and to submit to the tyranny of demons, and to worship the demons that are destroyers and enemies of our salvation. This was more cruel and more unbearable than countless deaths and any hell[2] to the Christ-loving souls.

6   While many were going under water at the time, and the storm was raging and many were being shipwrecked, this blessed Romanus came forward into the public eye and didn't immediately consider how he might give himself up to the dangers, but first assembled those who had taken fright, those who'd fallen, those who'd betrayed their own salvation and emboldened them, prepared them to renew the fight, by lifting up the people who'd fallen down, and securing with his prayers and admonition and advice those who had stood firm. He did this by philosophizing a lot about things in the future, about things in the present, showing the transitory nature of the latter, the constancy of the former, by contrasting the prizes to the labors, the crowns to the tortures, the rewards to the pain caused, by teaching the nature of the present life, the nature of the future, and how great a difference there is between the two and that to die is utterly inescapable. "For even if we don't lose our life in this way, we are totally constrained by the law of nature and will in any case give

[2]Lit. "Gehenna."

up these bodies a little later." With this and advice similar to this he raised up the hands that had succumbed, he firmed up the knees that had relaxed, he brought back the fugitives, he expelled cowardice, he banished anguish, he inspired confidence, he made people eager instead of cowardly, instead of antelope and deer he turned them out as ferociously breathing lions, he trained Christ's army, he transferred the shame in our community onto the enemies' heads. And so, when the Devil saw a complete turnaround taking place and those who yesterday or the day before feared him and trembled now laughing at him and acting boldly, stripping off to fight against the dangers, attacking the instruments of torture, and got to know the cause, he dismissed the rest and directed his entire focus from then on against that man, stirring up all his power and rage against this blessed head.

7   What exactly did he do? Consider his treachery. He didn't take him to face tortures; he didn't cut off his head. For the past had taught him that all these maneuvers were pointless and in vain. For not only did they not impede the enthusiasm of those who believed, but they even expanded it further, and made it greater and more fervent. "I strewed coals," he said, "but they ran over them as if [they were] roses. I lit up a fire, but they hurled themselves [into it] as if into streams of chilled water. I scourged their ribs, and cut open deep furrows and produced torrents of blood, but they were decorated in this way—as though covered all over in a golden flow. I hurled them over cliffs and drowned them at sea, but they acted not as if they were descending to the depths but as if they were ascending to heaven itself. Skipping and rejoicing and dancing as if they were in a sacred pageant or playing around in a green meadow, so each seized their tortures, as if they were receiving not tortures but spring flowers and were being crowned, and through the exaggerated state of their own enthusiasm they undercut my tortures." "So what should I do?," he said. "Do I cut off his head? But [if I do that], what he (sc. Romanus) is praying for, is what occurs, and his disciples receive more substantial advice in practice. For truly he advised that a martyrs' death

is no death, but a life that has no end, and that for the sake of this above all one should endure everything, and that one ought to despise death. So then, if I cut off his head, and he bears the event nobly, he will teach them in practice more clearly that they should despise death in this way and he will lift up their spirits all the more and through his death he will inspire them with greater enthusiasm." For this reason he (sc. the Devil) cut off his (sc. Romanus') tongue, so that robbed of the voice which the martyr's disciples enjoyed and deprived of his counsel, and bereft of his advice, they would become more timid and return to their former anguish, without anyone to stir them up, or to arouse and arm them.

8   Indeed, I ask you, consider his treachery. Whereas Herod cut off John's head, he (sc. the Devil) didn't cut off his (sc. Romanus') head, but just his tongue. For what possible reason? Because of much treachery and perversity. "If I cut off his head," he said, "and he dies, he will depart without seeing his own brothers' and sisters' destruction. Instead I want him to stand as witness to his own soldiers' fall and disaster, so that he is strangled by grief when he sees them fallen, but is unable to stretch out a hand and has no way of giving the advice which he did before, seeing that his voice has been cut out along with his tongue." But "he who seizes the wise in their wickedness" (1 Cor 3.19) turned this clever trick back onto [the Devil's] head and not only didn't he deprive them of counsel, but he caused them to enjoy even more abundant advice and to share in more spiritual instruction. For since he (sc. God) was in control of this, the doctor was at that point summoned to perform the surgery and became an executioner instead of a doctor, not correcting the diseased limb, but destroying what was healthy. Yet when he extracted the tongue, he couldn't extract the voice along with it too. Instead, while the tongue of the flesh was cut out, the tongue of grace flew to the mouth of the blessed man. And although nature relinquished its own limb under the irresistible force of the knife, grace didn't permit the voice to be dislocated along with it. As a result, from then on

his disciples enjoyed more spiritual instruction, listening not to a human voice as they did earlier, but a divine and spiritual one more powerful than our nature. And everyone ran together—angels above, humans below—each keen to see a mouth without a tongue and to hear it speak in this way. For a mouth speaking without a tongue was something truly amazing and incredible, bringing much shame to the Devil, much glory to the martyr and substantial comfort and grounds for patience to his disciples.

9   My point is that such has been God's custom right from the start, to turn whatever plots the Devil contrives against us [back] onto that [demon's] head and to set things in place for our salvation. Consider! He (sc. the Devil) expelled humankind from Paradise, and God opened up heaven to them. He drove them from governing on earth, and God gave them the kingdom of heaven, and set our nature firmly on the royal throne. In this way He always gives more abundantly blessings which the Devil attempts to strip away. He does this by rendering the Devil more hesitant in his plots against us, while teaching us never to fear his machinations. This is precisely what happened in the case of the martyr. For God graciously gave [Romanus] the voice, of which [the Devil] expected to strip him, much louder and more majestic [than before]. I mean, it's not the same to speak with a tongue and without a tongue. For while the first naturally follows and is common to everyone, the second exceeds nature and was peculiar to him alone. And yet even if the martyr had stood voiceless after the excision of his tongue, in this way too he would have fulfilled the rules of the contests and his crown would have been made ready. My point is that cutting out his tongue was a major defeat [for his opponent] and a clear proof [of that fact]. For if you weren't afraid of the tongue, you foul and utterly abominable [demon], why did you cut it off? Why didn't you dismiss the basis for the wrestling matches, yet locked up the stadium? In the same way as if a person who was about to compete in the pankration,[3] and

[3]An athletic contest which involved both boxing and wrestling.

who next received unmentionable blows and was unable any longer to stand up and fight, were to order that his opponent's hands be cut off, and were to pummel him in this fashion, there would at that point be no need of further proof to vote the victory to the person with their hands cut off, so too in the case of the martyr the excision of his tongue became a proof clearer than any other of his victory over the Devil. For although the tongue was mortal, even so because it inflicted immortal wounds on the Devil, for that reason he raged utterly against it, putting himself in a situation of greater shame, while making the martyr's crown more brilliant. I mean, just as it's amazing to see a tree without a root, or a river without a source, so too [is it amazing to hear] a voice without a tongue.

10   Where now are those who don't believe in the resurrection of the body? See! His voice both died and rose again, and both these things occurred at a single moment in time. And yet this is a far greater thing than the resurrection of the body. For there, the bodies' elementary substance is a fixed principle, while only the combination of parts breaks down; here the very basis of the voice was removed, yet even so it became in turn more brilliant. And yet, if you remove the reeds of a flute, the instrument afterwards lies useless. But not so the spiritual flute. Instead, even with its tongue removed, not only was it not voiceless, but it released an even more melodious and mystical tune, and to greater astonishment. And again, in the case of a cithara, if one just takes away the plectrum, the player becomes idle, the art useless, the instrument pointless. Yet here it is nothing like that, but entirely the opposite. For truly his mouth was a cithara, his tongue a plectrum, his soul a player, and his confession an art. Yet even when his plectrum was removed—I mean his tongue—neither the player, nor the art, nor the instrument became useless, but everything demonstrated its own capacity. Who effected this? Who demonstrated these astonishing and incredible things? God, who alone performs wonders, about whom David says: "O Lord, our Lord, how marvelous is your name in all the earth, that

your magnificence is elevated beyond the heavens. Out of the mouth of infants and babes you have furnished praise" (Ps 8.2–3a). And so then [it was] out of the mouth of infants and babes, now out of a tongueless mouth. Then [it was] an immature creature, now a vacant mouth. Then the root in the children was tender, but the fruit perfected. Here even the root itself was removed and the production of fruit not hindered. For voice is a tongue's fruit.

11   What happened afterwards is more astonishing than what happened before. Indeed so that these events might not be disbelieved, for this reason we ran ahead of those, so that we might not be confused over these, since our mind was trained in advance in those. These events happened so that those events that are unclear and old might be believed from these that happened openly and recently. Aaron's staff too once burst into bud (cf. Num 17), in the same way as the martyr's mouth burst into bud now. Well, for what reason did Aaron's staff burst into bud then? Since the priest was not held in honor. And why did the martyr's mouth burst into bud now? Since the great high priest, Jesus Christ, was blasphemed. See how great is both the relatedness and superiority of the miracle. For just as that staff wasn't connected to a root, nor drew forth the moisture from the earth, yet despite being bereft of guidance from that source and having lost its fruit-bearing capacity, suddenly displayed fruit, so here too the voice stripped of its root and without any capacity coming from its instrument, suddenly put forth shoots in a dry and barren mouth. In this [lies] its relatedness, in the other its superiority. For the difference between the fruit of each is considerable. Whereas the one could be seen, the other was spiritual and opened up the heavens themselves to the person who produced this voice at that time.

12   For all these blessings let's rejoice together with the martyr, let's glorify God who worked these miracles, let's imitate the patience of our fellow servant, let's give thanks for the Master's grace, let's take sufficient comfort in our trials from what's been said, and, astonished at the power and the mercy of God who created us, let's offer

everything we have and what comes from him will surely follow. Whether human beings, whether demons, whether the Devil himself spars with us, nothing will profit those who war against us. Just let us display our own enthusiasm and offer everything that should be offered by us. For in this way we'll attract God's influence here and enjoy much glory and salvation in the life to come. May we all attain this through the grace and loving kindness of our Lord Jesus Christ, with whom to the Father, together with the Holy Spirit, be glory, honor, and power forever and ever. Amen.

On All the Martyrs

As in the case of *On the holy martyrs*, the manuscript title to this homily is misleading. While the martyrs in general are discussed, the homily was clearly delivered on the festival of a single martyr, who, as we are told later in the homily (§ 11), stems from Egypt. It is also clear that the homily was preached at a martyrium containing the saint's remains and it is almost certain that the homily was delivered in Constantinople. In § 9 John explicitly refers to the emperor and his satellites and indicates that they frequent the martyrium on various occasions. Although he does not say that they are in attendance on the present occasion, his comments are sufficiently concrete that he can only be preaching in the city in which the emperor resides. Since no emperor resided in Antioch during the period of John's presbyterate (386–397)—the last emperor to have resided there being Valens (365–379)—the only possible location is the Eastern capital and current residence of the emperor and his court, Constantinople.

While this much is clear, the significance of John's comments that the martyr flourished only recently in Egypt (§ 11) and that the audience has greeted the martyr enthusiastically after so many years (§ 1) is less easy to determine, although it is likely that the latter remark simply means that it is some time since the martyr died, rather than that it is many years since his festival has been celebrated locally. Without being able to identify the Egyptian martyr who is the subject of the sermon, the date of the martyr's festival and therefore the day on which the homily was preached are impossible to resolve. There is nothing within the homily, either, which might indicate either the year or time of year at which it is being delivered.

Stylistically and in terms of content, there are several parallels with other Chrysostom homilies, which help to establish this sermon's authenticity. Towards the end of § 1 the periphrasis which John employs to indicate that virtually the whole city is present ("Not just people who are free but also slaves . . .") is typical of his opening remarks in other martyr homilies.[1] In § 11 John's comments about Egypt being hostile to God and a source of blasphemers, but a generous exporter of its martyrs, closely reflect those made in the opening section of *On Egyptian martyrs*. At the same time, the language in which he talks about Moses (§ 11) echoes that which he uses in the opening lines of another Constantinopolitan homily, *On his return*,[2] while his description of the powerful effect of martyrs' relics on demons in § 10 reflects those found elsewhere among his sermons. At the same time, John introduces new arguments and material both in relation to the efficacy of the martyrs and concerning the visible power of Christ in the present world. This, combined with his sustained focus in the second half on persuading those who adhere to Greco-Roman religions, makes this homily of particular interest.

Contents:

1–6. A martyr is the source of the large attendance today. This thought sparks off a lengthy discussion of the value of the martyrs. The martyr's victory is the opposite to that which occurs in sport or battle; so too is their reward.

7–10. If these arguments are insufficient to persuade the Greek listener, their own philosophers fled just the anticipation of death, while the martyrs fronted up for limitless tortures and, when their bodies failed, strove to keep on suffering more. The present crowd is also proof, and the ever-increasing memory of the martyrs. So, too, the tomb, which levels all inequality among those who gather on the annual festival and which has a powerful effect on demons. The honors they receive now are nothing compared to what they will receive on the day of judgment.

11–17. John turns to arguments from the present. The change in Egypt with the coming of Christ, and its subsequent exportation of martyrs are

---

[1]See e.g., *A homily on martyrs* (Mayer-Allen, *John Chrysostom,* 94).
[2]Mayer-Allen, *John Chrysostom,* 99.

proof of Christ's power, as too is the work of Paul, who converted an entire world, when Moses didn't convert a single race. The changes to the world and to individuals that Christianity has brought are a powerful proof.

Unedited. Translated from Stavronikita 6, ff.138v–146r.

Homily of [John Chrysostom] on martyrs,
delivered in the shrine of the holy martyr Acacius
while a large audience was present

1   Our theater is brilliant today and the assembly glittering. What on earth is the cause? The martyrs' blood has watered this vine for us. Channels of irrigating water[3] don't cause the trees to flourish as much as the martyrs' blood arouses [our] souls to bearing fruit, and blood which perpetually blooms causes them to hang heavy with fruit. For while all the other dyes become faded with time—the purples of emperors and the yellows of matron's cloaks and the blues and the greens—and pretty much every kind of dye fades and ages with time, the martyrs' blood blooms more readily with time, neither faded nor extinguished by the multitude of days, but rather shining more brilliantly. And your own enthusiasm is witness. For after so many years you have gathered as if you had just seen this holy man yesterday or a few days ago and had him fresh in your memory. You have exhibited every enthusiasm, too—performing holy vigils, [offering] careful listening, warm and genuine attentiveness. Not just people who are free but also slaves, not just young but also old, not just learned but also ignorant, not just men but women, too, not just rich but also poor [have shown such enthusiasm] and neither your tie to your masters nor the weakness of gender nor poverty nor anything else of the kind has prevented [you]. Instead the martyr's fire has overwhelmed all of you and brought you all here; not an

[3]Lit. "irrigating channels of water."

earthly emperor's murder, but perpetual longing for a martyr and the sight of his wrestling matches and the miracle of his competitive bouts and the magnitude of the prizes.

2   Who wouldn't be in awe? Who wouldn't be astonished? Who wouldn't be amazed on seeing human nature, softer than any mud, scourged and not giving in, carved up and not being defeated, burnt and not being beaten, dying and then being crowned, dying and then being heralded most of all, and nature giving in but faith flourishing, the flesh wasted and the will strung taught, the whipped subverting those administering the whipping, and the one getting the better of the many, and the naked and weaponless averting the armed. And yet the form victory takes in other contests is not like this: instead, the aggressors come out on top, while the passive are defeated. But here entirely the opposite is the case. The tyrant who is doing the whipping and scourging and burning and throwing over precipices and hacking into pieces and destroying goes away defeated and disgraced, while the martyr who is being hacked up and burnt and whipped and scourged and dies is the one who departs having put on the crown. Who has seen, who heard of victory in death, a trophy erected in death? In war, whenever the warrior falls, at that point the spear-throwers are less disciplined. But in martyrdom, whenever the martyr is killed, at that moment the encouragement is greater, those who stand in formation with him gain greater confidence. And so before death what relates to the future is unclear, but after death the crown is complete.

3   Did you see how miraculous the contests are? Did you see how novel the wrestling matches are? And how the principle is no different from the victory? That it is victorious over death? That it puts an end to being subverted? That it mimics in a mortal body the impassibility of the bodiless powers? Do you want to see, too, that the magnitude of the prizes is far greater than the apostles' efforts and [far] more brilliant than their labors? Listen to Paul, who says: "The sufferings of the present time do not merit having the future glory

revealed to us" (Rom 8.18). Yet in this instance, too, once again everything happens in a way that is opposite to that in the secular world. For there the crowns are smaller than the labors and the prizes much inferior to the effort expended. After all, to the soldier who faces death countless times what could an emperor repay that matched the value of the dangers? For he cannot fashion a body or impose life, just as that [soldier] has died time and again on his behalf in intent and purpose.

4   What do I mean? There comes a time when [the emperor] will be unable to do anything either small or great to benefit [the soldier], when he loses his life at the frontline. Rather [the soldier] departs, after enduring countless labors and dangers and deaths yet receiving not even the usual reward in return. But in the case of the martyrs that's impossible. Instead, whenever [a martyr] dies, it's then especially that his compensation package will be waiting for that person and their prizes will be more brilliant. For truly after racing through the strait of secular affairs and being set free from the heaving sea and the clashing waves and what lurks below the surface and the submerged rocks and the constant storms, they sail into a calm harbor and go off to a region from which "pain and grief and sighing have fled" (Is 35.10), as the saying of the prophet goes, and are situated above the uncertainty to come. Such a person no longer fears the Devil nor dreads demons. They don't tremble at the readily besetting [nature] of sin, aren't wracked by envy, aren't swollen with desire, aren't besieged by lust, don't look with suspicion at the ambivalent changes [in life], but rather outstare the incorporeal powers, outshine Gabriel in the beauty of their virtue, stand next to the royal throne itself, emitting rays more radiant than the sun, anticipating only blessings that are fixed and free of every change in state.

5   Now, here [on earth] the good things aren't unmixed with sorrows; instead, everywhere [there is] a great deal of mixing up of everything. Next there is the end of them and their total disappearance and, quite apart from the mixing up and the disappearance, in

their presence itself [there is] much confusion, with the anticipation
of disasters disturbing the brilliance of the pleasures at hand. What I
mean is this. For I ought to make it clear. Someone achieves glory
here. But dishonor, too, succeeds it, and the person who today is [rid-
ing] in a carriage is tomorrow in prison. The person who today is
accompanied by lictors is tomorrow circled by executioners. The person who today puts fear into everyone is tomorrow in a state more
pitiful than that of any captive. The person who brandishes the sword
at everyone is himself afraid of this fear and trembles. Here there is
youth; but old age, too, succeeds it. There is life, but termination and
death, too, await. There are honors, but insults, too, attack. There is
safety, but machinations, too, succeed it. There is joy, but grief, too, is
mixed with this in turn. A person enjoys security, but is wracked by
worry, too. And now these things, now those take hold of the person.
There, on the other hand, there is nothing of the sort, but glory alone.
Dishonor is nowhere. [There is] eternal life and no expectation of
death nor doubt about righteousness. For a state of entrenched sin is
impossible.[4] There are a wealth of blessings and no one is afraid of
poverty. There is considerable security for the people who enjoy them
and not a single danger. My point is that in regard to the situation
here it is not just when disasters are present that they cause confusion, but also when they are expected and anticipated. For truly the
rich person fears poverty even when he/she isn't enduring poverty,
and ahead of the experience of it is disturbed greatly by the expectation; and in all the other cases this same phenomenon likewise
occurs. But there each one of those who possess that blessed Word is
free of not just the experience but also the expectation.

6   In addition to what I've said that, too, can be said—that here
even the very things that appear to be good contain much unpleasantness within themselves even before becoming mixed with sorrows
and ahead of the expectation and ahead of the experience. For in

---

[4]The syntax between *hypopsia* ("suspicion") and *ouk eni* ("impossible") is
unclear at this point, but this seems to make the best sense of the Greek.

truth the rich person, even if he/she doesn't become poor, doesn't enjoy unadulterated pleasure, not even in the wealth itself—not because of the expectation of poverty nor because of the transformation into beggardom but, even ahead of the experience and ahead of the anticipation, because of being wealthy itself. My point is, with the state itself there come as a package despondencies, worries, fears, dangers, envies, and incessant machinations, and one is besieged by passions, and a crowd of illnesses come from being wealthy, as if they were carrying around an evil army, and it makes the rich person's soul more cowardly than anything. But for the saints none of these [experiences] occur. Instead they are free of all these [troubles]. As if [they are] on a calm sea and in harbor they sit placidly, enjoying a blessedness which no reasoning nor thought will be able to conceptualize.

7   Well, does the Greek [listener] have no confidence in these arguments? Come, then, let's convince them from the here and now. For the abundance of truth is substantial, obstructing from every direction the mouths of the shameless. After all, the past, too, in particular is sufficient to curb them. I mean the contests and wrestling matches. For while the philosophers among them who prided themselves on their hair were actually expelled from their country and transferred themselves into exile because of just the expectation of death and appeared more cowardly than frogs at that time when their leader drank hemlock and died,[5] these [saints] didn't just despise death but also countless tortures which were more cruel than any death. My point is that while dying brings on an immediate release, to be scourged little by little and to be set up for the insatiable appetites of tyrants, that above all is the mark of a noble and utterly courageous soul. For they (sc. the martyrs) didn't enter [the arena] about to compete against prescribed tortures or awaiting a fixed three-foot measure in punishments, but, as I started out saying, they

[5]John may be alluding here to Critias, Charmides and Alcibiades, who were members of Socrates' circle exiled for various political reasons within a few years of each other at the very end of the fifth century BCE.

stripped off for tyrants' limitless appetites; they were ready to suffer as many of those [tortures] as they (sc. the tyrants) were keen to inflict. So what if nature is the first to give in and the body's feebleness was condemned? Yet fortune remained, keeping their enthusiasm at its peak and while their flesh was being destroyed their enthusiasm wasn't exhausted but blossomed and increased all the more, growing young with longing and keen to find yet other reasons for competing. And just as, after felling many enemies, a noble soldier whose sword has become shattered in the mass of slaughtered bodies turns this way and that looking around for another sword, so that in that act in particular he reveals his courage, so, too, after their flesh was destroyed, the souls of the holy martyrs looked around for other flesh to put on in turn and to reveal their courage in other [contests].

8   So, tell me, are these actions trivial? Don't these actions exceed human reason? Aren't these actions clear even in what is utterly inconceivable, in that they wouldn't occur without God's help? There was thus a certain divine power seated in their souls, stimulating and nerving and equipping them to laugh at all the tortures. Well, you weren't present when they were competing, nor did you see them being hacked to pieces and divided up with knife and fire, and not giving in. Instead, you have heard and understand and know clearly the number and type of tortures the holy martyrs suffered and yet did not give in. But if you want to gain proof of the future from present events, too, please have a look at this crowd here and the people's eagerness and the length of time and consider to yourself why on earth ordinary people who were both insignificant and known to no one before they died, became after their death more prominent than emperors and more famous than any human being and neither length of time nor the tyranny of death which extinguishes everything, nor being unknown to those in honor, nor being humble and insignificant, nor being from another country, nor anything else of this kind extinguished their memory and passed them

on into oblivion. Yet everything else diminishes with time—physical beauty, the greatness of houses, kingdoms, positions of power, glories—and, as if swept away by river currents, departs and is passed on into oblivion. Only the martyrs' memory is beyond all time and higher than these obstacles, and no one can expunge it from eternity. Instead, it increases substantially and, as time goes by, doesn't grow old but flourishes abundantly and blooms all the more.

9   And yet God didn't proclaim that he would grant them these rewards here but in another age. For in the case of the games in the outside world the wrestling matches and crowns, the effort and the prizes take place in the same arena. But it's not the case here. Instead, the effort is allotted in the present life, while the crown is stored up for the life to come. If, then, the honor stemming from their superiority is so great in the time of their labors, when the rewards haven't been announced, consider what kind of repayment they will incur in the time of prize giving. For if what stems from their superiority is like that, of what quality will what is owed them be? On their day[6] an entire city and so great a body of those in office—emperor and consuls and military commanders and everyone—assemble in the martyrs' tomb and cast off the signs of inequality associated with this present life. For neither the rich person nor the poor person, nor the governor nor his subject is seen here. Instead everyone has put aside this differentiation. They enjoy homogeneity because of the esteem and honor directed towards the martyr. Even the emperor takes off his diadem and his bodyguards and shield bearers throw their lances and spears and shields outside and thus approach the martyrs' shrine, and every [dissimilarity] weakens and gives way through awe of these saints. And he who wears the purple and sets everything shaking at his nod often throws himself face down upon the martyr's tomb and calls for that saint's prayers. And if he goes off to battle, he goes away taking him (sc. the martyr) as his ally. And if

[6] That is, on the day each year on which each martyr or group of martyrs is commemorated.

he returns from victory, he calls him to share in giving thanks to the Master and asks [him] to take part in the acclamations over what took place. And often, when a wife looking for her husband who is away from home comes here and pours forth fountains of tears, she has swiftly brought him back from the foreign land. And another person, weighed down by sins and oppressed by despondency, after touching the chest containing the bones has had his conscience lightened and has gone away having achieved a light state of mind.

10   What could one say about the sufferings of demons? For whenever those invisible powers who are terrifying and relentless, who fight against us unannounced, who despise spears and swords and armies and emperors and everything, come and see the martyr's ash and bones, they are frantic, they get upset, they scream, they burst into flame and take a beating and, through their howls, yell out the martyrs' power and against their will abandon the bodies which they besieged from the beginning and, driven to violence by the invisible power, they take to their heels and flee. And so if (for nothing prevents me from saying the same thing again) in the present time, in the time of the competitions and wrestling matches and arenas, the honors for the martyrs are of this kind, consider what kind of crowns they will attain in the time of prize-giving. "Why is it," someone asks, "that their body didn't become immortal or imperishable or impassive?" Because the time for their repayment is not yet at hand. In yet another way on the basis of greater authority the argument curbs your shamelessness. For if [their body] has not yet become immortal or imperishable or impassive, in the dust and ash it displays such great power that it subverts the invisible powers and batters them about and puts them to flight and draws such a large populace and excites cities and attracts emperors and armies and governors and ordinary citizens. When it receives its own lot and enjoys that blessedness, consider how much brightness, how much power it will attain when the only-begotten Son of God arrives from heaven and the population of heavenly powers flows around him

and that terrifying tribunal appears and the book is opened and the rivers of fire flow. For then, then [the martyrs] will stand beside the royal throne, exceeding the sun in brilliance, exceeding the sun's rays in glittering, clothed in inexpressible light, dressed in as much glory as the sight alone can at that moment convey. For at present no verbal account will ever come close.

11   But you don't believe those arguments? So take your proofs from the present and, beyond those things, from the courage which [the martyrs] displayed when they boxed and competed, from the honor which they enjoy although they are located in a strange and foreign land. After all, this martyr who has assembled us today recently flourished in Egypt—Egypt, the land that fights God and is out of its mind,[7] the source of shameless mouths, the source of blaspheming tongues, the source of Pharaoh and Pharaoh's army.[8] Yet even so, so great is the change that took place after the crucifixion that in impiety's acropolis and the demons' tyranny such great piety flourished that entire populations of martyrs appeared. After all, among Egyptians the production of grain is no longer as extensive as the production of martyrs, and what they do in regard to their fruit occurs also in regard to their martyrs. For just as they don't keep their grain locked away at home, but distribute it to both their neighboring cities and those at a great distance (displaying through love of honor their local prosperity), this they did, too, in regard to their martyrs. My point is, when their production of this lovely fruit became substantial, they didn't keep them all at home, but distributed them everywhere as a pledge of love for the cities, shedding the martyrs' bodies in advance everywhere. Even when Moses was in command and split the sea and smashed the rock and trod the air and wrought countless miracles, he didn't convert a single race. But

---

[7] I.e., heretical. See *An Encomium on Egyptian Martyrs*, n. 3, above.

[8] This sentence begins a passage which bears marked similarity to the opening remarks in *An Encomium on Egyptian Martyrs*. Regarding the allusion here to the Arian heresy and possibly also Theophilus, the then bishop of Alexandria, see *An Encomium on Egyptian Martyrs*, n. 4, above.

when the Savior appeared, not Egypt, not just a single race, but all the people who inhabit all the land over which the sun extends changed their position over to the true faith.[9]

12   Where now are those who claim that the Son is lesser?[10] Moses didn't convert a single race, yet Paul, who was sent forth by Christ, caught in his net the entire world, not by breaking up a sea, not by cutting open a rock, but by bringing with him the Savior. Did you see the quality of Christ's achievements? Indeed, I say these things not so that I can show that the Son is greater than the Father (heaven forbid! for that's extreme impiety), but so that by the magnitude of the things achieved by him I might curb the heretics' insanity. For, tell me, how could one who is lesser and more inferior have demonstrated such great strength and greater deeds than those that occurred in the Old [Testament]? My point is, it wasn't in fact Paul who effected everything throughout the world but that one who said: "Look, I am with you all the days until the end of the age" (Mt 28.20). That's why he (sc. Paul) said too: "If you seek proof that Christ calls within me" (2 Cor 13.3). It was he, therefore, who in fact drove out the demons through [Paul] and cleansed the lepers and raised the dead and straightened the crippled and performed all the other miracles.

13   But aren't the Greeks convinced by even these [arguments]? Therefore here, too, let's curb them using the present and let's say nothing of the past or of the future. For while we believe both in the things of the past and of the future—by the past, I mean the signs and miracles; by the future, the kingdom of heaven—for instance, that the only-begotten Son of God will arrive and descend from those heights and resurrect the whole world in a second—in the

[9]Lit. "piety." The word also conveys a strong sense of orthodoxy and the idea that Christianity is the true religion. See Leemans et al., *"Let Us Die that We May Live,"* 189 n. 79.

[10]John here moves from the Greeks, who are in error in their thinking, to Christians who are in error, in this case the Arians. Addressing this error in belief (subordinationism) is a common concern in his homilies. See, e.g., *On St Phocas* § 9–11 above.

blink of an eye—and will magnify everyone's deeds in public and reward each as they deserve, as if he's weighed their sins on a scale and balance. Rather, he won't [reward] every deed as it deserves, but while [he'll reward] sins as they deserve, he won't reward good works as they deserve, but even beyond what they deserve. For this above all is due to his loving kindness, which is a vast and astonishing thing. And so, although I believe and accept these things, since the Greek knows neither what is past nor what is to come, come, let's convince her/him from the present, too.

14 Tell me, what are you saying? He didn't resurrect the dead when he was here? Nor did he cleanse the lepers, nor drive out demons nor did he effect the rest of the things I started out mentioning? Nor after that will he come [down] from heaven and demand of each person an account of their deeds, nor will he resurrect their bodies, nor grant us incorruptibility? Well, does it seem to you that these things are a fairy tale or a heap of words or pure sound? Speak! Surely what is both present and visible doesn't seem to be a fairy tale. For instance, the Churches everywhere in the world that multiply the sea of piety; the choruses of virgins; the ranks of monks; the diverse and perfected social group within the Church of people who conspicuously practice moderation in marriage, of people who practice patience in widowhood; the patronage focused on the poor; the ranks of priests; the obedience of the emperors; the philosophy of foreign people. Surely these things aren't a fairy tale? Surely these things aren't part of the future and the past? (I would gladly address you, the unbeliever, with the signs from the past.)

15 What would you say about this sign that is evident day after day? You didn't see the dead being raised, but you do see the world that was once dead because of false religion,[11] brought to life by the true religion[12] and led by the hand towards the true precision of doctrine. You haven't seen a leper cleansed, but you do see those who are

[11]Gr. *asebeia.*
[12]Gr. *eusebeia.*

weighed down by countless sins shedding them all through Christ's word. I don't mean just in baptism—for perhaps it doesn't allow this—but after baptism, too, through the transformation of [a person's] life. My point is, whenever you see a female prostitute plying her trade even after baptism, then suddenly struck with compunction by Christ's word, and exchanging the church for the theater, clothed in sackcloth instead of silken clothes, smeared with ash instead of perfume, pouring forth fountains of tears instead of laughter, embracing fasting instead of a lavish table, devoting herself to drinking water instead of undiluted wine and various drinks, becoming sallow and wan and uncaring and virtually an animate corpse instead of [wearing] makeup and rouge, letting loose psalmody instead of shameful speech and bawdy songs, running off to the wilderness instead of [frequenting] crowds and the marketplace, deserting countless lovers for the chorus of prophets, taking hold of the future instead of the present, she who is weak and soft becoming harder than iron, she who is weaker than felt [becoming] stronger than adamant . . . whenever you see these things and [see them] happening in a different way again in the case of degenerate men, how do you not bow down and prostrate yourself before the power of the crucified [Lord]? The philosopher who was among you didn't have the power to convert a single tyrant when he sailed so vast a sea, but was transported home after losing his freedom and suffering betrayal.[13] But the power of the cross convinced everyone: Romans, foreign people, fools, ordinary citizens. And whereas before this there were altars and temples and burnt sacrifices everywhere, and cult statues and festivals full of shamelessness and dances of demons and the Devil reveling in the cities, and the tyranny of drunkenness and furnace of licentiousness and the flame of wickedness arose from all quarters, after the cross's power all this was removed.

[13]The allusion is to Plato, who developed a relationship with the tyrant of Syracuse, Dionysius I, and who subsequently traveled to Syracuse in 387 and 362 BCE in the hope of converting Dionysius' son, Dionysius II. In 362 Dionysius II promised to follow Plato's teachings but betrayed him and imprisoned him. Plato remained in prison in Syracuse until the intercession of Archytas secured his release.

16   Tell me, where now is an altar, where a temple, where a seer, where images [of the gods], where cult statues, where demons' celebrations and festivals? Haven't these all been put to flight like dust and thrown out, and everywhere the true religion[14] rules spiritual sacrifices? Hasn't the wilderness, too, become more law-abiding than the cities? Don't you see people competing in . . . ?[15] Subverting the stomach? Controlling desire? Considering money filth? Fleeing cities and bustling crowds and marketplaces and sitting on the peaks of the mountains and shaping their soul? Who showed us so many philosophers and caused natures' essentials to be trampled, and made [us] finish the present life in a mortal and passible body as if impassible? Don't you know what state everything was in the past? Marriages with mothers,[16] sex between men, prostitution, and adultery, and while some things [were considered] law, others were considered religious observance. And unrestrained theatrical shows for men and women and polluted night-long revelries, from which both the comedians' countless plays take their subject matter and every so-called "marriage" gained a starting-point for promiscuity[17]—no bridal canopies were hung, no parents were present to give their daughter away, no bridegroom received the virgin lawfully. Instead, [there were] theatrical shows and drunkenness and night and youths' debaucheries and sex occurring freely and the darkness

---

[14]Gr. *eusebeia*.

[15]The phrase *en kalous* is clearly a textual corruption, but none of the approximate words which are found in similar remarks by John (*kalybais* [cells], *kloiois* [collars]) is sufficiently close in form to warrant adoption.

[16]Almost certainly a reference to the subject matter of theatrical performances (in this case stories such as Oedipus' incestuous marriage with his mother Jocasta), promoting mythology as part of the Greek past.

[17]The image of the theater as a school for immorality is common in John's sermons. See e.g., *On the games and theater* (Mayer-Allen, *John Chrysostom,* 118–25), where he argues that it is a major contributor to the breakup of marriages and entire households; and *On Matthew hom.* 37/38 (PG 57.426–7), where he describes the sexual content of theatrical shows and their effect on marriage in a similar fashion. For a concise description of late antique theater and of John's reaction to it see B. Leyerle, *Theatrical Shows and Ascetic Lives. John Chrysostom's Attack on Spiritual Marriage* (Berkeley: University of California Press, 2001), 13–74.

[acted as] their curtain. And a ring and bedchamber were the symbols of those unholy marriages, and with impunity a drunken youth raped a virgin who was sitting in the theater and, having ruined her, left.[18] And in this way after these things the marriage was concluded. What could be more shameful than these things? What more pathetic? What more irrational? But after the cross all these things were abolished and everything took place in a lawful way. And not just virgins and married women, but not even the more proper of the men would ever enter the theater.

17   Indeed, why do I speak about the theater when the baths, too, at least, were shared by everyone—men and women. Well this custom, too, has been thrown out, and all shameless behavior has been driven away. Modesty and decorousness and reasonableness govern everywhere in the world. When you consider all these things and compare government with government, laws with laws, condition with condition, and precisely scrutinize everything, you will see the power of the crucified [Lord]. You will see the change for the better. You will see the demons' wickedness, you will see God's forethought from these things and receive firm demonstrations and clear proofs concerning the past and the future. Truly, don't be blind in the middle of the day nor, when the sun is illuminating everything, bury yourself in the heart of darkness and blind your mind. Instead, look upwards a little and, guided by what happened in the past and what is happening now, prostrate yourself before the power of the crucified [Lord]. Truly, I could have said this or much more than this to

[18]Throughout this passage John fluidly moves between the theatrical shows themselves and the revels which surrounded them. Here he appears to be referring to the story of Dionysus and Nicaea. Nicaea, daughter of the river-god Sangarius and Cybele and a devotee to Artemis, was distressed by the unwanted attentions of the shepherd Hymnus, whom she shot through the heart in an effort to escape. Eros, in revenge, stimulated Dionysus in his drunkenness to rape her, thus ending her chaste devotion to Artemis. John may be indicating that rape myths, which among other things celebrate the transition of the female from virgin to mother (Nicaea subsequently gives birth to Tetele before killing herself), were closely associated with pre-Christian weddings.

Greeks, but to you Christians[19] let there be said that which has demonstrated the governance that is worth knowing. And after we've become enthusiasts of the martyrs and have bridled our passions and quenched the flame of desire and cast out the besieging of diseases, in this way let us finish the present life, so that in the age to come, too, we may share their holy dwelling. May we attain all these things through the grace and loving kindness of our Lord Jesus Christ, through whom and with whom be glory to the Father together with the Holy Spirit, now and always and forever and ever. Amen.

[19]Lit. "the faithful."

LETTERS CONCERNING
RELICS

Letter of John to Rufinus

This letter is one of several from the period of John's exile (404–407) in which he refers to Christian mission activity in Phoenicia. This activity appears to have taken place under the supervision of the Church in Antioch, but also to have been actively supported by John in his capacity as bishop of Constantinople. John continues to express concern for the viability of this activity and to be actively involved in securing personnel and goods for it within his limited capacity, throughout at least the first year of his exile. The letter is best dated to the summer of 405, since John is clearly not yet at Arabissos and since, as he indicates in the letter, there is a need to act before winter, while the troubles to which the letter alludes appear to be the same that caused the presbyter John to quit Phoenicia at the end of 405.[1]

The letter is of considerable interest for understanding the status of relics and their availability and use at this time. First, the letter assumes that the procurement of relics for a mission endeavor in a region dominated by Greco-Roman religions is a natural part of the conversion process. So basic is this assumption that John gives us no clue as to how it was intended that the relics be used. Given that the focus of the letter is upon fighting and quelling the "Greek" opposition to the planting of Christianity in Phoenicia, several possibilities arise, particularly in the context of the understanding of the power of relics that is expressed by John in his homilies. For John, relics are imbued with the power of the Holy Spirit and have the capacity to repel demons and to throw a protective force field

[1]See R. Delmaire, "Les «lettres d'exil» de Jean Chrysostome. études de chronologie et de prosopographie," *Recherches Augustiniennes* 25 (1991): 135–6 s.v. Iohannes 2 and 156–7.

around a city. They are a constant reminder of the temporal nature of death and a physical prompt for private devotion, particularly penitence and prayer. At the same time they create a virtual *terra sancta* (holy land) wherever they reside. The planting of relics creates a physical link between earth and heaven and the relics thus function as a kind of Christian flag in hostile ground. At the same time, the relics' supernatural powers ensure that they become a protective device for the church in which they are located. In addition to this capacity to drive off the demons of the Greco-Roman cults, they offer an alternative locus of supernatural power to which converting adherents of those cults can turn.

Second, it is of particular interest that a bishop of a remote and small Armenian community has at his disposal numerous relics that are considered authentic. This raises the question: why? Are they of local origin? Did Arabissos suffer heavily during the various persecutions and end up with numerous indigenous martyrs? Or is Bishop Otreius a collector? Is he especially known for his collection of relics and is this why John has no qualms about sending the presbyter Terentius to Otreius to ask him to donate some to the troubled mission in Phoenicia? It is also interesting that John, who at this point has not yet been to Arabissos, has no expectation that Otreius will refuse his request. This may indicate that, despite residing primarily at this time in Cucusus, John has already established a relationship with some of the bishops of other towns in Armenia. Whatever the case, the letter both raises tantalizing possibilities and introduces us to the possession and use of relics in two regions (Phoenicia and Armenia) that are quite different in character from the major Hellenistic cities of Antioch and Constantinople, as reflected in the above homilies.

Contents:

1. News has arrived that the troubles caused by the Greeks in Phoenicia have broken out again and the monks there injured or killed. Rufinus' presence is urgently required.

2. John has every confidence in Rufinus' capacity to address the situation.

3. John is surprised that Rufinus hasn't yet written and urges him to send letters from every point along the way. John will do whatever he can to aid him.

4. Rufinus is to let him know whether he needs more brothers to be sent, but to not worry about relics. John has already arranged for some to be sent to him in Phoenicia by the bishop of Arabissos, who has a large supply. Rufinus is to hurry so that he can finish roofing the churches before the onset of winter.

Translated from PG 52.685–687.

Letter 126—*To the presbyter Rufinus*

1   News has come to us that the troubles in Phoenicia have again flared up and the madness of the Greeks has increased and of many of the monks some have been beaten, others even killed. Because of this I urge you strenuously to take to the road with all haste and take up position in the battle-line. For I know well that if you do no more than appear you will put the opposition to flight, by employing prayer and reasonableness and patience and your accustomed courage. And you will dissolve their madness and revive those who are on our side and effect many blessings. Don't, then, wait or hesitate, but employ all haste and let these reports make you more eager. After all, if you saw a house on fire, you wouldn't withdraw from the scene, but would in fact at that point be extremely anxious to get an early grip on the blaze and would, through your own effort and that of others, do anything that would result in putting out the disaster. Now, too, then, since a fire of this kind has flared up, hurry without delay to get a grip on what's happening there, and that will by all means be something beneficial and very much a correction for these

events. I mean that, while anyone at all can provide Christian instruction in peace and calm when no one is acting hostilely, to take up position nobly and snatch away those human beings who are arrayed with the Devil when he is raging and when his demons are armed and prevent the rest from falling into his hands, this is the mark of a noble man, this is the mark of a sober soul, this is indicative of your lofty and alert mind, this deserves countless crowns, this [deserves] unutterable prizes, this is an apostolic act.

2   Consider, then, that this moment is a moment for establishing your reputation, and a pretext for countless trading and business opportunities and so, please, grab such great wealth and use it with considerable haste. And write to us swiftly when you have arrived there. For should we just learn that you have reached the borders of Phoenicia, from that moment we shall be free of anxiety, we shall relax, we shall spend time feeling secure. For we know what will follow: that like a noble warrior and a person who knows how to act courageously, you will in this way attack everything, awaking the sleeping, fixing and securing the standing, leading back the strays and seeking out and locating the dead, completely thrashing the Devil's entire phalanx. For I know, I know with clarity the sleepless nature of your soul, the anxious nature of your mind, its understanding, its agreeable, its gentle, its courageous, its strong, its patient [character].

3   So then, write to us constantly and before you even catch sight of Phoenicia, send us letters thick and fast from the road, since even now I am astonished at how you haven't sent a letter, when the associates of my lord, the most honorable and worthy presbyter Theodotus, are here with me. So that we don't grieve again, then, at not receiving letters from your honorableness, if at all possible, send us letters regularly from each staging post, so that we may learn how much progress you have made on the journey and if you have come close to those parts. For we are very anxious and concerned and wish to learn these details day by day. Knowing these things, then, my

most honorable lord, do me this great favor and before you depart and when you depart, send letters constantly and make everything clear to us, so that, if there are good outcomes, we may be happy and rejoice, but if there are obstacles, we may attempt to remove them by every means and every effort. For we shan't rest from doing this, either through our own efforts or through the agency of others, in as much as possible, nor resile from this, even if we have to dispatch letters a thousand times over to Constantinople, in order that you may have much ease.

4   Knowing these things, then, make your skills available to us, your sleeplessness, and your zeal. If you require that brothers be sent,[2] make this clear to us, too. And don't worry about the relics of the holy martyrs. For in fact I have just now sent my lord the most worthy presbyter Terentius to my lord the most worthy bishop Otreius of Arabissos. For he has relics that are indisputable and numerous and inside of a few days we shall send them to you in Phoenicia. So then, let none of your honorableness' efforts be lacking. For you can see with how much enthusiasm our efforts have been accomplished. Hurry, so that you can finish off the roofless churches before winter.

[2]It is unclear whether by "brothers" John means monks to replace those who have been injured or killed; other clergy, e.g., presbyters; or simply other baptized Christians.

Letter of Vigilius to John

In this letter we have a rare surviving example of correspondence addressed to John, rather than authored by him. Of even greater interest the letter, written by Vigilius, bishop of Tridentum (Trent) in Italy (c. 385–405), records the gift of a portion of the relics of three very recently martyred Western missionaries, which were conveyed to John in Constantinople via the services of James, a high-ranking intermediary. Such an act, like the one John himself contemplates in the preceding letter, shows that little attention was being paid at this time to an imperial edict promulgated on 26 Feb. 386 (*CTh.* 9.17.7), which forbade the translation of buried human remains and the dividing up or sale of a martyr. The letter itself dates to between John's consecration in February 398 and late 401, since Sisinnius, Alexander, and Martyrius were killed in Anaunia in 397, while the letter makes no indication that James is already *magister equitum*, a position which Claudian's *carm. min. 50* suggests that he held at the time of the invasion by Alaric and the Goths (late autumn 401). While some scholars have located the letter in the first year of John's episcopate,[1] even as early as spring 398,[2] it is more likely that the letter dates to not long after the embassy to the West which reconciled the bishop of Rome and the Western bishops with the Nicene faction led by Bishop Flavian at Antioch. This would situate it in 399 or perhaps 400.

That these are the circumstances in which it was written is suggested by the letter itself. That it is Vigilius who takes the initiative in

[1] E. Menestò, "La lettere di S. Vigilio," *Atti della Accademia Roveretana degli Agiati* 25 (1985): 384.

[2] J. Vanderspoel, "Claudian, Christ and the cult of the saints," *Classical Quarterly* 36 (1986): 248.

sending the relics to John at Constantinople and that their story was unknown there prior to their arrival is clear in both the tone of the opening of the letter and in the level of detail provided. Certainly, it is unlikely that John himself would have solicited the relics from Vigilius, since in the history of Constantinople to that point the relics which had been sought out and procured for the city had tended to be those of high-ranking apostles (Andrew, Luke, and Timothy) or well-known Eastern martyrs (Phocas) who had been dead for some considerable time. Relics of minor Western clergy whose death had occurred only two years previously, leaving little time for them to have developed any status outside of Italy, are likely to have been of only minor interest. If we consider that Vigilius also wrote about the martyrs to Simplicianus, Ambrose's successor as bishop of Milan, the most likely scenario is that Vigilius, the bishop of an Italian see of lesser rank than Milan, Rome, or Ravenna, seized the opportunity afforded by the new concord between the bishops of the West and, via Antioch, Constantinople to promote martyrs local to his region in not just one of the most important Western cities, Milan, but also in a strategically important and increasingly powerful Eastern see.

What we know about these three martyrs is derived largely from the two letters of Vigilius. In this second letter, we learn that Sisinnius, a Cappadocian by birth,[3] was older than the other two, held the rank of deacon, had been responsible for the building of a church, and had initiated much of the mission work in the region of Anaunia. Martyrius and Alexander were respectively lector (one who read aloud the scriptures in the course of the liturgy) and doorkeeper in the church or churches founded in that region. It appears that the Christian mission in Anaunia quietly proceeded for some time before the local inhabitants became antagonized. According to Vigilius, it was the building of a church by Sisinnius that sparked off overt hostilities, to the point that a mob gathered with burning brands and axes

[3]Mention of Sisinnius' Cappadocian origins, which does not appear in the letter to Simplicianus, was probably inserted by Vigilius here in an attempt to make the martyrs more palatable in the East.

and sought out the Christians with the plan of forcing them to sacrifice to the locally worshipped gods. Sisinnius, who was targeted specifically, resisted and was hacked and wounded. Martyrius tried unsuccessfully to tend to his wounds and was himself captured and tied up, after seeking refuge in a garden on church property. Both were killed and their bodies dragged through rough terrain to the site of the church, Sisinnius' with a bell attached. Accompanying the bodies was Alexander, who, although still alive and sensible of what was happening to him, had been tied to the corpses of the other two. Pyres were constructed from the church's roof beams. All three were burnt and their bodies reduced to ash. In the first letter, Vigilius adds that Martyrius, who was an associate of Sisinnius' assistant, embarked on the beginnings of his ecclesiastical profession as a catechumen following military service and that Alexander, whom Vigilius explicitly says was a doorkeeper (in the second letter he only alludes to his status), was a blood relative of Martyrius. Alexander, he also tells us, was taken captive in a hospice or inn.

The Latin is difficult in places and possibly corrupt.[4] Rather than smooth over the difficult passages with an approximate gloss, the awkwardness of the text in those instances has been retained in the translation.

Contents:

1. Vigilius writes on his own initiative because James, a pious man, has asked him for relics of recently killed martyrs to take to John. Vigilius was reluctant to lose them, but has now acceded to James' request.

2–3. The martyrs were missionaries in Anaunia, a hostile region, and different from the locals in race. One of them, Sisinnius, an older man, set off the hostilities by building a church. The locals rose up in procession to the church and attempted to make the Christians perform devilish sacrifices.

4. A digression on the nature of martyrdom occurs.

5–7. The story resumes. At dawn a mob attacked the church and seized several of the priests. The deacon Sisinnius was felled by the axe and laid out

---

[4]See Menestò, "La lettere," 383–8.

on a small bed. Martyrius, a lector, who ministered to the wounded Sisinnius, was himself captured in the grounds of the church and died before they could force him to sacrifice. Last, but not least, the doorkeeper Alexander was bound and dragged with the bodies of the other two to a pyre constructed from the timbers of the church roof.

8–10. The mysteries revealed by the three are discussed. In death Sisinnius' body proclaimed Christ through the bell tied to it, which was intended to demean it. Martyrius witnessed to his name in his martyrdom, and in seeking refuge in the garden copied Christ. Alexander through his name pointed to the region's vices, which reflected the worst of Alexandria and the Egyptian cults. Vigilius himself was a witness to these mysteries.

Translated from PL 13.552–558.

Here begins the letter of holy Vigilius in praise of the most
blessed martyrs Sisinnius, Alexander and Martyrius,
whose relics reached John, bishop of the city of Constantinople,
through the agency of James, a vir illustris.[5]

1   A guest, new to charity, would not otherwise impose on holy ears, or arouse the shame of making the initial approach without an invitation, or initiate contact while he was unknown, unless the reward truly inspired [him]. And so, most dear brother, the contents and fullness of the present letter will begin from an apostolic man, so that you may understand by a simple connection that praises of the martyrs follow. For James,[6] a man of faith with heavenly aspirations, who is about to be released from his officer's rank among the soldiers of Christ, demanded the relics of saints so recently deceased

---

[5]The term denotes a Roman official of high rank, including generals, prefects, high-ranking senators and consuls, depending on the precise period at which the term is being used. It is probable that this title to the letter was added later and may not reflect the status of James at the time that the letter was written.

[6]Lat. *Jacobus.*

that they were still smoking with steam.[7] I said "about to be released"
because a rank that is assigned in the Lord's service cannot be laid
aside. I nearly refused him in the course of my fear, since I was quite
scared and understood too well the reason, having struggled over my
decision so that I was less suited to making such a benefaction. I had
made a debt of what I always owed, like one who lends at interest. I
confess: I much feared loss, robbed of many things by my private
fear, if I hadn't been mindful of James, seeing that he was going to
hand them over to holy John for the reward of veneration, so that—
entrusted with love through the martyrs' pious names—a brother-
hood that is no stranger would be transferred and reforged by
blood.[8] Gladly receiving this sentiment of faith also among others,
which was ridiculing my sorrow, I just delayed, I did not refuse. I
delayed, so that again my slowness betrayed me openly, I who had so
little deserved to follow my companions. I confess: I wanted to, but
the crown of righteousness is not [awarded] for intentions alone.
But now, if a fitting order will not be [too] heavy for thirsty ears, I
will begin from the location of the region or even the road, pursuing the last traces of the matter without aversion, so that, if you come
to the source of the spring with ample love, the flood of rewards will
flow together more rapidly.

2   Now the place which is called by the foreign name of Anaunia,
located twenty-five miles from the city, delivers a kind of spectacle by
its natural scenery: enclosed by narrow ravines, as much by treachery
as by nature, from which one departs by a single access (you could
call it the way of the three martyrs), which lies back on a gentle ridge,
with a valley falling away on either side, and fortresses dotted everywhere on the summit, because its neighbors conspire against it in
perfidy. A reason for the place was lacking, but Christ was a suitable

[7] The image of smoke and steam rising from the altar is a standard feature of the
description of burnt sacrifices. It is probable that Vigilius is invoking it here, the idea
being that the martyrs became a burnt offering to God, after they themselves refused
to offer sacrifice to the local gods.

[8] That is, that a Christian bond will be reforged between East and West.

reason, in order that the Devil's sport should give a procession for martyrdom. May a description of the locale not annoy the ears of the hearer. For it had always had bad company, an echoing hollow place in the mountains. When the army of Christ had first climbed up to it, the ferocious pagans, roused by repeated trumpet calls, were inflamed with jealous rage and cries of war. In truth, the saints had perfected one kind of contest: to withstand everything, to give up those attacked, to endure with patience, to restrain from private mercy [for] those about to suffer public rage, to win by refusing. But predestined glory was greatly pressing [them] on to the honor of a timely death, which the proper order[9] had occasioned. Well, passing over digressions and cutting short long circumlocutions by which the virtue of martyrs is fed, since summary removes the ruin of praise, I will barely refrain from silence.[10]

3   When the name of the Lord was still foreign in the region which I mentioned above, and there was no demonstration of the confession of faith, there were these foreigners, who were at that time singular in number, now in merit,[11] [singular] as much in respect to religious practice as in respect to race,[12] who were preaching not unworthily the unknown God. They were undisturbed in quiet living for a long time, as long as no use for their faith aroused them. But now, if a reason for the rising hatred against the Lord was sought, there was the title of disturbing the peace because one of them, Sisinnius by name, who was older than the other two, [and] whose old age was worthy of honor in its own right, built a church at his own expense. Since he was richer in faith than in resources, wealthy in spirit, but poor in property, he entrusted the fold to a

[9]This is explained below. Order here has the notions both of the different rank of each of the martyrs, as well as the sequence in which they were killed.

[10]That is, by cutting it short Vigilius will avoid spoiling things by overdoing the praise.

[11]"Singular" does double duty here, meaning that they were few in number at that time, but are now distinguished in merit.

[12]That is, they were in a religious minority, as well as not local to the region.

shepherd. He became the guard[13] of what he had established, but the fold was opposed by wolves. The Devil in his fallen state envied the constructed summit. This was the first result of martyrdom, that they killed the sheep while they hunted the lamb. It was counted as a victim, more righteous to God for the following reason, that when they desired to conduct the evil sacrifice of purification around the boundaries of the fields in a funereal parade, and they trampled the young crops as they polluted them, they were also going to crush the seeds of Christ. Crowned with sorrowful adornments, with the Devil's wailing song, with raised banners and processions of various beasts to the Lord's temple, which had recently been converted for their own people, they began to gather to offer sacrifices to the works of darkness. When the servants of the Lord saw this being done scarcely without any guilt of their own, in that the onlookers[14] themselves too were seen to share in the disorderly works, the bodies of the saints were on that day pledged to a mournful slaughter, but the prize of victory was deferred.

4   At this point I want to consider briefly with you the honor of titles, brother, so that martyrdom does not seem to anyone to have been taken up with any common humility: because every good of this world is considered base, since martyrdom is new and wondrous, taken up without the envy of the age, and so perfect that nothing precedes it nor follows it; but it is singular in that it is only finished when consummation has been given. He who guards the sheep from a robber is not a hired man, in my opinion, but is

[13]Reading *excubitor* for *excubator*.

[14]Lat. *assistentes* is translated here by the neutral term "onlookers" because of the difficulty of determining precisely what Vigilius is saying here. *Assistentes* can refer either to the "defenders," that is, the Lord's servants, the soon-to-be martyrs, or to their "associates" (their congregation, perhaps, or other clergy). Reference to the former is awkward, since their being seen (or appearing) to participate is unlikely to have led to their martyrdom, since they were killed for refusing to sacrifice. If it is their associates who participated, then the three might objectively be considered guilty by association. In either case, the second half of the sentence does not follow naturally from the first.

revealed as a follower of Christ; and he who flees is a hired man; he who does not abandon [them] is a shepherd. He who lays down his life lives; he who would save it loses it (cf. Mt 16.25, Lk 9.24, Mk 8.35). For what else did our Master and Lord do, except not abandon those who strayed; or the Lamb, except defend the ewe so that the righteous sacrifice would be consumed instead of the sheep? But I, who am about to enter the gate of sufferings, will not after setting out this complex case stint on another's praise, nor will I steal it; because not to want what belongs to another is characteristic of martyrs; and not to deceive is characteristic of priests—except that I cannot possibly [deceive] when in pursuing these matters I give praise in the telling, and least of all in this, in that I would say less.

5   Well then, after the signal-flag of the devilish lustral sacrifices—which was, as we related [earlier], a sign of glory soon to come—in a single night the ascent was made to the postponed crown. For when the shadow of the sky suddenly gave way to the morning hours of dawn, an unexpected but united band gathered, armed with blazing brands and axes, and whatever weapon[s] the Devil's rage had made for their cleaving. And there, having seized several priests who were singing morning prayer in the church, they made a vast pillaging, and plundered savagely; everything was desecrated, both the secret and divine mysteries, and the final booty was piety. No one should think this struggle was commonplace, as when either lifeless idols are destroyed by the living, or piles of rocks are disturbed along with those who piled them up, so that you are uncertain whom you should judge more harshly: the worshipper or the worshipped. Christ the rock was tried in all circumstances, the cornerstone was rejected by the people (cf. Ps 117.22, Mt 21.42), it had to be tested again; he was about to rebuild a ruin rising from his pure blood (Jn 2.19). Faith had its own spectacle among those events. At that time the body of the deacon Sisinnius was stretched on a small bed, punctured and wounded also by previous injuries, [which had occurred] when he was ordered either to fetch a sheep for the sacrifice or to

become the sacrifice [himself], if he would not agree to the funereal sacrifices. He was struck with the trumpet on which they were playing the Devil's song, a fitting [blow] for the one who had first brought the sound of faith; he was felled by axes, who was defending the axe from the fruitless tree of paganism. And lest I draw out the assertions further—although they are deserved, as we said—he was laid quietly on his funeral bed, having confessed, I believe, that in a secret mystery he would advance more swiftly to the cross in order to release the paralyzed people.

6   Martyrius the lector was also tied by ropes to a stake. He confessed and affirmed at the same time his name, as one who had sung a new song (cf. Ps 39.3, 95.1), then the first and now the only one in that foreign land; among the roaring wild songs of the shepherds, already at that time he rendered praises of sweet language to God, as I mentioned above. And he had administered to the deacon Sisinnius medicine and poultices, in order to heal his pain, although he was about to be wounded [himself]. With extraordinary gasps he was calling back—not to the body, but to suffering—his fleeing soul. But the holy man, already on the martyr's[15] appointed path to Christ, refused a drink of water, because the wine of suffering had come, which had mingled in the offered cup of more truly flowing life. And so, seized by this concern, the one who always cared about the holiness of souls, born not for himself alone, nor surely about to conquer for himself alone, withdrew to the recess of the adjoining garden, that is, he did not withdraw from the church. For there is a garden in the church, as you well know, which is planted with hedges of living laws [of God]. He did not offer his body, which he refused to deny, nor did he assume a bold rashness, out of the confidence of righteousness. Just so do those in parts of Africa carry pride before them who, it is said, are made ready for a voluntary death, which they make without fear. But he who was soon to be a martyr stood his ground, captive, yet free, fearless while confessing [the faith], giving thanks although

[15]Lit. "of martyrdom."

he was wounded, injured physically but safe in his soul, when his head was cut off bathed in blood in a private baptism.[16] No one deserved to follow him, since he planned to flee from the place where to have withdrawn was empty piety and similar to fear.[17] But the prisoner's righteous confession revealed that he stood still only so that they could overcome him; he withdrew so that even his persecutor would perish in his glory. Martyrius was led out from the garden where he had fled. This is a kind of mystery, to have withdrawn, so that the purple flower which is foreign to blooming places would be tinted rose not undeservingly, prefiguring the new martyr; or so that the secret will of life would be declared among the white foliage of lilies, with death falling away for all who have been planted and watered through baptism.[18] He was led to the idol even tied to stocks, but he achieved becoming a sacrifice before he arrived at the Devil's altar.

7   A third crown of the Lord too was fulfilled, which would honor Alexander. With familiarity he found the entrance, he who used to guard Christ's gates (it was when he was guard that the hardened hearts of the pagans severed the temple's curtain). Sought out with zeal by the crowd, because he was well known to all for his zeal for the faith, he was caught but not taken captive; fear[19] he did not fear. The disciple of Christ had often been jeered at, and in this respect his great effort made the punishment more lively among the tortures of martyrdom. And so, in order to balance out the office[20] with an

[16]Or "with baptism having been robbed."

[17]The Latin is awkward at this point. The idea seems to be that had Martyrius withdrawn to the garden for the purpose of escaping his captors his piety would have been empty and he would sought out that place out of fear. Because he withdrew to the garden in order to take a stand and to show up the inhumanity of those pursuing him, the opposite occurred.

[18]Again the Latin is difficult and possibly corrupt. The flower imagery develops out of the idea of Martyrius' capture in the garden and of the blood which caused his body to bloom red at the moment of decapitation.

[19]Reading *timorem*.

[20]I.e., of doorkeeper. The idea here is that, although his office was minor compared to those of Martyrius and Sisinnius, his suffering was greater, so that in martyrdom any inequality was evened out.

excess of suffering, he gained through his fate that he would be in no way inferior among the three [martyrs]. Indeed in the others' case rage did not delay its tortures; [in his case] a lingering punishment saved him for the Lord. He realized that he knew what he was undergoing, as one who observes his own body [from outside], and although the wounds that were inflicted distinguished the above-mentioned martyr from the deacon (sc. Sisinnius), the tortures revealed him as the guard of himself. For while the bodies[21] were joined and bound and dragged through the public [places] in the manner of dogs, but not about to return to their vomit (cf. Prov 26.11), Alexander was led among them still living with his feet bound, on the point of losing some of his quivering limbs among the rocks,[22] until he was led to the end of the place, or should I say of his life. The way led after this to the pious summit, that is, the lofty temple of God. Afterwards the bodies were stretched at full length on the ground, and pyres were made from the consecrated beams in the sight of Saturn, ancient idol of a time long passed. In front of the twin and joined bodies placed on the fire, the wounded Alexander stood his ground, again about to make his confession. The reward of [eternal] life was intended for him, with the result that he would be deprived of life. If he wanted to avoid the present fire, he had to say that he agreed to their darkness. But to him, who guarded the cross-ways and rejected the gifts of the wicked, there was a light before his eyes against that light. Fear of punishment prevented the punishment. Faith's heat repelled the flame. The order of suffering also maintained respect for station. He was taken up last, but he is not crowned lowest among his brothers. Brothers,[23] the mystery of the Trinity was fulfilled in the three servants, even now in the banquet

[21]I.e., those of Sisinnius and Martyrius.

[22]Possibly a reference to stoning, or perhaps, more likely, a reference to the peculiar topography of the location, which is outlined in § 2.

[23]It is uncertain why Vigilius moves from the singular vocative to the plural here, unless he is thinking of the wider audience to whom the letter would have been read aloud. Another possibility is that, in his account of the martyrdom, he is recycling a homily originally preached on the martyr's anniversary.

of heavenly joy, since others too would have suffered as living victims, in a similar fate, if three all together were not deemed the perfect number. For we were perhaps not the least to share in these events, and for their sake we were threatened by the people, nor did we abandon our companions, but station had made its choice.[24]

8   Moreover, many events of the ensuing days of suffering were not so much revealed as described in truth, which we pass over in our précis, so that through these few things which happened, we might more fully make known the mysteries. If, however, you will deign to review patiently with me the account, in fact from his very birth place, Sisinnius was a Cappadocian or Greek by family, once of first rank among you, swift in faith, generous in spirit, an abundant worker, persevering in everything, finishing his course with a victory palm that did not come late, destined to reach the seventh[25] fate of promise, always yoked by the bond of charity, being united in peace, controlling the reigns of spiritual discipline, a yoked subduer of such a people, a sign of Christ. Finally, he is recognized as holding command of the way for the future flock or those of the same blood (just as custom, the master of things, dictates), a bold scout of danger and adviser, so that the troops may follow safely behind. And so in our "sign of faith in the morning"[26] there was primacy in birth and command. Afterwards he led the proven way to life, or led [the way] to glory, he who seduced [people] to salvation and understood the truth, as the prophet bears witness: "and my sign in the morning."[27] And so that the mysteries that occurred would multiply more, and his sign would not lack proof, when they dragged the lifeless body of

---

[24]Vigilius alludes here to his own presence and involvement in the events that took place at Anaunia, which he states more openly in § 11 below. Others could have been martyred, but the divine plan and their rank singled these three out.

[25]The PL editor suggests the emendation *optima*, "best."

[26]See the following scripture quotation in the next sentence.

[27]The PL editor suggests that this verse comes from the oldest Latin version of scripture. It may refer to the sign of dew that God gave Gideon in the morning, in Judg 6.36–40. This interpretation is supported by the reference to dew in the final paragraph of this letter.

holy Sisinnius like an animal, they tied on his neck the hollow ring-ing of an airy witness, which is commonly called a bell, taunting his corpse, reproaching the dead body, accusing Christ of not liberating [him]. And by laughing at the Lord's disciple, they fulfilled the mys-tery of salvation. For what did that ringing or sound useful for the flock that followed [him] mean in itself—[a sound that was] also harmonized with grace, suspended from the neck? [What did it mean], if not that its voice would sound forth the name of Christ, by shouting harshly to the deaf, and it would confirm for all the leader, as of the flock, so also of the people. For he was first to sound the word of a pious voice, first to resonate in the hollow valleys, a leader to untouched pasture still present among the dumb animals or certainly the flocks, one who rings out so that people hear anew, who ruminates on the flourishing law among the peoples.[28]

9   In the designated order,[29] Martyrius fulfilled the prophesy which he was keeping and also earned his name[30] for himself. He revealed the parable of the name, a true revealer in all respects: he smiled at the name that he was being called and piled up merits. His birth name decreed what would happen, both in his beginnings and in his suffering. Why should I reveal the garden's secrets, privy to his punishment? [Why reveal] that he first conferred himself to it, the gate to paradise, which he entered again as a martyr, after contem-plating its pure pleasure and the honorable delights of its spring-time, when he was about to plant the life-giving bloom, which still wrongly clung to the world's thorn, in its flourishing places; [and this] after being guided [to it] by the virgin to whom the garden belonged? Why do you return me again to the mysteries which

[28]Note the pun in *ruminator*, "one who chews [the cud] again," also used of graz-ing animals.

[29]*Ordo*, which refers in this instance primarily to the order of events, may also carry a secondary meaning of "office" or "rank." That is, his martyrdom is directly related to his office as lector. Just as Sisinnius was first in rank and martyrdom, so Martyrius is second in both rank and martyrdom.

[30]L. *martyris* = a "martyr" or "witness," *martyrium* = "martyrdom." His birth name thus foreshadowed his end.

occurred? That virgin gave birth, who always longed to hold her own. It (sc. garden) wanted to send away him whom it received. It chose a worshipper of whom it approved. Now it also held God, summoned by its attitude of well-known love, as Solomon says in the Song of Songs: "My brother went down into his garden" (Song 5.1). He went down and he went down in truth. For he whom the precious will earnestly loved[31] refused to go out too in his time of suffering, as we might express a thing known in our times. In the garden together with the Jews Judas Iscariot arrested the Lord. Let no one debate over such a withdrawal of the disciple: so the Lord and Master is found. He was thought to be the gardener, the one who waters the living, who plants souls. The garden is therefore not a refuge for one in flight but for one who takes refuge; for those who understand, gardens will make them earn paradise.

10   But what was the mystery of death able to confer on Alexander, who while living fulfilled the whole [mystery], if not that his name mocked the vice of his people, so that Anaunia should be thought of as Alexandria, superstitious in individual portents, numerous in demons, such as two-formed Anubis, many-shaped half-human idols, that is, deriders of the law; full of the madness of Isis, the flight of Serapis; in short, the indulgent mother of foreign sins, or rather stepmother? [A city] nourished by the young of vipers, through the offspring of a poisoned people, which cannot be conceived, unless it rejoices in the loss of its father, cannot grow, unless it is born from death, cannot live, unless it kills its mother. As a result, in an inversion of the faith the progeny of the evil offspring, conceived by the loss of God the Father, born through rejection of its head,[32] given birth to by the pierced womb of Mother Church, takes its first life from the death of the saints. But now it grows more fertile from destruction, more lively from death, happier as a result of sorrow.

[31]In reference to the garden of Gethsemane it would make more sense for "precious will" to be the object of Christ's love, but the Latin makes it the subject.

[32]Probably an allusion to the rejection of Christ, the cornerstone, which is part of the rhetoric employed in § 5 above.

For it is clear and fully obvious what is revealed in the scripture, which says: "all were bound by the one sin, so that all might deserve mercy" (cf. Rom 11.32). These are the hundred-fold returns of suffering, by which that population now absolved its own offences. Captivity made them free, gentleness released those who were bound. Then the heavens merged into darkness, the light shuddered with suffering, obscured by the mental blindness of faithlessness, as I believe.

11   Trust your brother's eyes, brother. A kind of shadow of black cloud concealed or connected the whole area; thunderbolts cracked close to the ground; a fearful din thundered over and over; more flashing red fire shone forth; you could say the sky was guilty of blood. Beyond this, after the shadow of a strange night, so to speak, it was not [possible] to conceal the plain truth under a cloud. The day, too, disclosed the horror of the suffering, not only a fugitive, but bereft. For the restoring light of the sixth day of the week[33] had appeared, always friendly to martyrs, next to God. Preserving with reverence a sharing with the Lord's body up to that point,[34] it offered God's servants servitude through its holy nourishing, although envy was jealous of the fate that piety was about to meet. Thus the Lord affirms by his works. Thus he shows himself a companion in all things, so that he may be united in equality and time. I confess, I was a spectator at these mysteries, and a guard over the ashes of the saints. I did not deserve to share in the knowledge to which I could not attain. I saw it, and today I hardly believe myself. The facts exceed in reverence their narration in words. As a consequence, brother, it will be for God to affirm what he chooses and to produce a testimony for the witness. Now, brother, take the gifts of the three young men (sc. the martyrs), or the three young men from the furnace (cf. Dan 3), nearly still walking in the flames of a gasping fire; and if the

[33]I.e., Friday.
[34]Vigilius here invokes a parallel between Christ's crucifixion on Good Friday and the martyrdom of the three.

envious rage of the flame had not left them half-dead, it would have revived the example of history.[35] Thus everything has painted itself with virtually the same honor: the voice, the dew, the number, the furnace. The voice is the harmonious faith; the dew is the rain;[36] the furnace is the fire; the number is the Trinity.

[35]Since the three martyrs were incinerated on a pyre, Vigilius compares them to the three young confessors whom Nebuchanezzar threw into the fiery furnace, but whom God miraculously saved unharmed. Vigilius introduces the parallel here both to stress how recent the martyrs' death was (they are "nearly still walking in the flames") and to pave the way for his trinitarian interpretation of the symbolism.

[36]In the Old Latin and Septuagint account (Dan 3.50) the flames in the middle of the furnace were converted into a breeze with dew on it by an angel. Up to this point in Vigilius' account there has been no mention of rain, but the introduction of it here suggests that rain may have accompanied the dark clouds and stormy weather mentioned at the beginning of § 11, since the parallelism between the furnace and the fire is also literal, rather than theological. With regard to the voice, the reference may be to the song (Dan 3.25ff) which one of the three youths and then all three together sang in the midst of the furnace, in praise of God.

POPULAR PATRISTICS SERIES

ST VLADIMIR'S SEMINARY PRESS

1-800-204-2665 • www.svspress.com